Conservation Law Enforcement

Conservation Law Enforcement

MICHAEL J. SUTTMOELLER

Associate Professor in the Department of Criminology,
Missouri State University

MICHAEL T. ROSSLER

Associate Professor in the Department of Criminal
Justice Sciences, Illinois State University

CAROLINA ACADEMIC PRESS
Durham, North Carolina

Library of Congress Cataloging-in-Publication Data

Names: Suttmoeller, Michael, author.
Title: Conservation law enforcement / by Michael Suttmoeller, Michael
  Rossler.
Description: Durham, North Carolina : Carolina Academic Press, LLC, 2022.
Identifiers: LCCN 2021052137 (print) | LCCN 2021052138 (ebook) | ISBN
  9781531018894 (paperback) | ISBN 9781531018900 (ebook)
Subjects: LCSH: Conservation of natural resources--Vocational guidance. |
  Environmental protection--Vocational guidance. | Conservation of natural
  resources--Law and legislation. | Wildlife conservation--Law and
  legislation.
Classification: LCC S945 .S88 2022 (print) | LCC S945 (ebook) | DDC
  333.72023--dc23/eng/20220104
LC record available at https://lccn.loc.gov/2021052137
LC ebook record available at https://lccn.loc.gov/2021052138

Carolina Academic Press
700 Kent Street
Durham, North Carolina 27701
(919) 489-7486
www.cap-press.com

Printed in the United States of America
2023 Printing

For our families

TABLE OF CONTENTS

ACKNOWLEDGMENTS

The writing of a book requires the support of many people, and I am grateful to everyone that provided support over the last couple years. However first, I would like to not thank COVID-19 for causing countless issues and delays with the writing of this book. Everything would have gone much smoother if you had not arrived, so it is time for you to go. In spite of the challenges of the past couple years, this project did finally get completed and there are several people that were instrumental in this happening. First, I would like to thank my co-author, Mike. Who knew that this book would result from the conversations we had in those basement offices we were banished to in the basement of Baker Hall? Thank you for taking this journey with me — I'm confident I would not have gotten it done without you. Also, please thank Maggie for me for putting up with this. Next, I would like to thank Missouri State University. Even though producing scholarly works is part of my job, Missouri State provided support in several ways throughout this project, and for that I am grateful. Finally, last but certainly not least, I would like to thank my wife Stephanie and my children — Riley and Mason. Thank you. For so many reasons. Thank you, Riley and Mason, for reminding me to not always take everything so seriously and for always being there with a smile, or a magic trick, or to tell me about some new streamer that you were into, and you both are welcome for the "Did you know my dad was writing a book?" joke. Especially thank you to Stephanie for all the support you have given me over the last couple years. I certainly could not have done this without you. Thank you for your patience and support with the amount of time that this project required. Thank you for your patience with the piles of articles and books that accrued in my workspace, that I know drove you crazy. Thank you for being there with words of encouragement when frustrations set in. Thank you for everything.

— **Mike Suttmoeller**

Before the completion of this book, I never thought that I would be capable of writing one. I certainly could not have done it without the support and encouragement of many people. First, I would like to thank my co-author Mike for bringing this to fruition. Without your efforts, encouragement, and pioneering spirit, this book would not have been possible. Second, I would like to thank the conservation departments, departments of natural resources, and officers who took part in our survey research on a variety of topics. While this book draws upon research from many sources, their contributions led to unique findings that put this book on the cutting edge of research on conservation policing in America. Finally, I would like to thank my family. Mom and Dad, thank you for the support and encouragement in both academic and outdoor pursuits that allowed me the opportunity to accomplish a lifelong dream such as this. To my kids, Hazel and Harlan, thank you for giving me the time to write this book, for putting a smile on my face when no one else could, and for keeping me from taking anything too seriously. To my wife Maggie, thank you for all of your love and support, not just in writing this book, but always.

— **Mike Rossler**

Conservation Law
Enforcement

One

INTRODUCTION TO CONSERVATION LAW ENFORCEMENT

Conservation officers are members of the law enforcement community who are primarily assigned to engage in the protection of natural resources. These officers are known by many names, (e.g., game warden, conservation agent, environmental police, fish & wildlife police), and typically have jurisdiction over both environmental violations as well as more traditional law enforcement duties (Eliason, 2007; Falcone, 2004; Shelley & Crow, 2009). While the name by which the law enforcement officers that are responsible for enforcing laws concerning environmental crimes may vary from state to state or country to country, for purposes of this book and the sake of simplicity, we will refer to them as conservation officers throughout the book. While these officers are an often-overlooked segment of the law enforcement community, they are an important part of the larger law enforcement community, not only for their role in the protection of society through the enforcement of laws, but also for their important role in the protection of our natural world and environment.

REASONS FOR THIS BOOK

There are innumerable books written about the many different aspects of traditional police work and numerous books written by former conservation officers that serve as memoirs of their time as conservation officers, but very little attention has been paid to the study of conservation officers, especially from an academic perspective. This book aims to begin to fill this gap and provide an accurate discussion of the various aspects of the important work in which conservation officers participate. Admittedly, this book may not be as exciting as those books that tell stories about being a conservation officer and highlight the most exciting portions of that career. However, this book should provide the reader with a realistic perspective on not only what **conservation law enforcement** is, but also the various aspects of the career that are important to a full understanding of what a career in conservation law enforcement may entail.

This introductory chapter will provide the reader with a concise look into conservation law enforcement and outline the various topics that will be discussed throughout the book.

WHY IS CONSERVATION LAW ENFORCEMENT IMPORTANT?

It is important to study and learn about conservation law enforcement for a variety of reasons. One reason to study and learn about conservation law enforcement is that even though conservation officers have a long history in the United States, they are some of the least well-known or understood members of the law enforcement community. Not only do scholars not agree on which state had the first game warden, but neither do the states—with some such as Trefethen (1975) identifying Maine as having the first game warden, while Falcone (2004) and Bavin (1978) both identified Michigan as having the first salaried game warden. Regardless of which state actually had the first game warden, game wardens have existed in the United States since the mid to late 1800s. By 1912, 41 states had employed some form of game warden (Bavin, 1978). Since that time, the number of conservation officers in the United States has grown to approximately 6,000 officers, and they are represented in all 50 states and the federal government (Patten et al., 2015).

Since the time of the first game wardens, the attitudes of Americans toward the protection of natural resources have changed and with them, the role of conservation officers. Similar to early police officers, early conservation officers were often low-paid political appointees who were used at least in part to harass those with differing political views (Trefethen, 1975). However, conservation agencies began to mature into science-based management agencies, and conservation officers had to mature with them. As part of this maturation process, the practice of hiring political appointees as game wardens ended and higher hiring standards such as written and oral exams became commonplace (Wyoming Game Wardens Association, 2020). As the role of conservation officers evolved through the years, their role within the larger law enforcement and natural resources community evolved as well (Falcone, 2004). While at one time, conservation officers were strictly involved in the enforcement of laws pertaining to fish and game laws, modern conservation officers have begun to fulfill a more traditional police role and address more traditional types of crimes (Falcone, 2004). In addition to this expanded police role, they also participate in other types of activities, such as public relations (Hailey, 1988; Pledger & Hailey, 1981; Tobias, 1998) and educational programming (Falcone, 2004). Despite their long history, the role of conservation officers continues to be one of the least understood in law enforcement, and this book attempts to provide an in-depth discussion of this career to hopefully expand the reader's knowledge about these important law enforcement officers.

Another important reason to study conservation law enforcement is the existing threat that **wildlife crimes** pose to not only the world's natural resources, but also communities and the citizens that live there. Wildlife crimes have ecological, economic, and human costs as well as public health and national security concerns (Moreto & Pires, 2018). Unregulated harvesting of animals and plants may result in severe ecological harm. It may reduce population levels, affect sex ratios, and alter ecosystems. If overharvest or the exploitation of a particular species creates imbalanced sex ratios, it can impact the long-term health of those species, especially if that species is a slow-maturing species. If the species that is exploited is one that is considered to be a "keystone species," it can have a disproportionate impact on the surrounding ecosystem (Moreto & Pires, 2018). The release of invasive species is also a potential ecological impact from wildlife crime. When an exotic animal or plant is introduced into an ecosystem where they do not belong, it can have disastrous effects. While these introductions may occur unintentionally, the exotic pet trade has been identified as a key factor in the introduction of exotic species into ecosystems (Moreto & Pires, 2018). For example, the introduction of Burmese pythons into the Florida Everglades has put the entire Everglades ecosystem at risk (Bilger, 2009). Aside from the overexploitation of animal and plant species, environmental destruction is also an existential threat. Poachers can contribute to environmental destruction through the illegal removal of trees or by cutting down trees to harvest tree-dwelling species. Additionally, the unregulated harvest of forest products has driven some species to extinction, while other practices such as using poison or dynamite to harvest fish has had a detrimental impact on those species (Moreto & Pires, 2018). All these ecological impacts fall under the purview of conservation officers at the local, state, national, and international levels, and they serve as the front line of defense for these animals, plants, and ecosystems.

In addition to ecological costs, there are also economic costs related to wildlife and natural resources crimes. Illegal wildlife markets can negatively impact local communities by removing economic opportunity related to employment and the ability to earn income in developing communities where alternative employment may not be available (Duffy, 2010; Moreto & Pires, 2018). The removal of commodities that the local population could utilize may raise prices for other goods and thereby increase the cost of living for those that are already struggling with earning a living. Finally, the inability of locals to participate in the legal sale of items related to the local flora and fauna that would contribute to the local and national economy can hinder the economic growth of areas that are rich in biodiversity (Moreto & Pires, 2018).

Understandably, when discussing wildlife and natural resources crime, the focus is on the non-human species being affected. However, there are also human costs associated with these crimes (Moreto & Pires, 2018). The first directly relates to conservation officers. Law enforcement work can be dangerous, and the work of conservation officers is no exception. Several factors impact the amount of danger encountered by conservation officers. One important factor that contributes to the danger associated with the work of conservation officers is that they generally work in isolated areas and do not have backup assistance readily available—it is sometimes hours away (Carter, 2006; Eliason, 2006, 2011; Forsyth, 1993), while a traditional law enforcement officer may have backup minutes away (Patten et al., 2014). Not having backup readily available can increase the dangers that conservation officers face from both humans and the environment. Isolated patrol areas may include dangerous terrain (Carter, 2006; Forsyth & Forsyth, 2009), which can put the officer at increased risk of injury as well as potentially harsh weather conditions (Eliason, 2006, 2011; Patten et al., 2014). The other danger conservation officers face is from humans and anglers who are normally armed with knives and firearms (Eliason, 2006, 2011; Forsyth & Forsyth, 2009; Patten et al., 2014). Even though conservation officers face various hazards while working, physical assaults and deaths suffered by conservation officers in the United States are uncommon (Carter, 2006; Eliason, 2006, 2011; Patten et al., 2014). From 1886 to 2010, 253 conservation officers died in the line of duty in the United States. Of those deaths, 149 would be classified as accidental (drowning, freezing, or vehicle accidents), while 104 would be classified as felonious (physical attack or gunfire) (Eliason, 2011; Patten et al., 2014). While encounters with armed hunters and anglers increases the risk of injury or death to conservation officers, most hunters and anglers are not violent criminals and pose little threat to conservation officers. However, that is not the case with all wildlife violators.

In other countries, the human costs inflicted on conservation officers are much greater. For example, in Africa, approximately 1,000 rangers were killed between 2008 and 2018, with 80% killed by poachers or armed militia groups. In Thailand, approximately 40 park rangers were murdered over the course of five years. Further, India, Thailand, Kenya, and the Democratic Republic of Congo have seen increases in the number of park ranger deaths because of conflicts with poachers (Moreto & Pires, 2018).

In addition to the human costs related to conservation officer fatalities, human exploitation also presents a cost related to wildlife crime. Trafficked humans have been found working on deep-sea fishing vessels. These people are not only isolated from the rest of the world, but are also involved in illegal activities, which makes their situation especially perilous. Unregulated fishing also has resulted in the loss of livelihoods and has been linked to an increase in piracy in Somalia (Moreto & Pires, 2018).

Public health concerns are also important when considering the impacts of wildlife crime. The illegal wildlife trade could produce unsanitary or contaminated products that could lead to health problems in those that consume them, including the possible introduction of pathogens that could lead to disease (Karesh, et al., 2005; Moreto & Pires, 2018; Wyler & Sheikh, 2008). Pathogens such as Severe Acute Respiratory Syndrome (SARS), Avian Influenza (H5N1), and Ebola are all examples of pathogens that could be transmitted to humans through the illegal wildlife trade (Moreto & Spires, 2018; Wyler & Shiekh, 2008).

In addition to the environmental, economic, and human costs and the public health concerns associated with the illegal wildlife trade, it also poses a threat to the national security of the United States. At first glance, it may seem that wildlife crimes and the illegal trade in natural resources products would not be related to the national security of the United States. However, it has been recognized as a threat for several reasons. One reason is the link between the illegal wildlife market and trade and transnational criminal and terror groups (Moreto & Spires, 2018; Wyler & Shiekh, 2008, 2013). Organized crime groups in China, Japan, Italy, and Russia are known to be extensively involved in the illegal wildlife trade. For example, groups such as the Wo Shing Wo group, 14K, and the Japanese Yakuza are believed to smuggle elephant ivory, rhino horn, tigers, shark fin, abalone, and whale meat, while the Russian organized crime syndicates are believed to control the trade in caviar (Wyler & Sheikh, 2008). The illicit wildlife trade has also been linked to drug-trafficking enterprises. The routes used to smuggle illegal drugs have also been used to smuggle wildlife, and both legal and illegal shipments of wildlife are used to conceal shipments of illegal drugs. For example, US Customs Service inspectors in Miami discovered 86 pounds of cocaine-filled condoms inside over 200 boa constrictor snakes (Wyler & Sheikh, 2008). In addition to organized crime and drug syndicates, terror groups are also believed to be involved in the illicit wildlife trade. Some insurgent and terror groups have participated in the illegal trade of wildlife for monetary gain in areas with high biodiversity as well as porous borders, weak states, or criminal sympathizers (Wyler & Sheikh, 2008, 2013).

While invasive species impose economic costs, they also can be a threat to national security. Carter and Gore (2013) explained that the intentional release of an invasive species with the intent to harm the environment is an emerging form of bioterrorism. Invasive species can carry disease and other parasites that can have negative impacts on humans and the economy. For example, Striga, a plant parasite, can destroy corn crops, which may in turn harm agricultural commodity markets and bio-fuel production. Barberry plants can spread wheat stem rust, which could result in a decline or demise of wheat production. Additionally, species such as zebra mussels have been identified as a possible species that could be used for bioterrorism. As an example, a person threatened their congressman that if they voted for a bill that would ban Internet gaming, they would release zebra mussels into the lakes within that congressman's district. Prior to the vote, there weren't any zebra mussels in the district, but after the vote, zebra mussels began to appear in the lakes in the congressman's district (Carter & Gore, 2013). Zebra mussels are highly invasive and cause millions or billions of dollars in damage to ecosystems as well as clogging pipes, valves, and drains that impact drinking water, hydroelectric plants, and manufacturing plants (Carter & Gore, 2013; O'Neill, 1993).

As should be apparent from the previous discussion, there are tremendous costs and concerns associated with the illegal harvest and trafficking in wildlife and other natural resources products. Conservation officers at all levels of government are important to begin to address these costs and concerns. To be sure, state-level conservation officers, which are the most common type of conservation officer in the United States, may not be on the front lines in thwarting organized criminal or terrorist organizations that are participating in the illegal wildlife trade, however, there is certainly the possibility that they may encounter those that may be associated with those networks. For example, the Mississippi River has populations of shovelnose sturgeon and paddlefish that are both utilized for caviar, especially since the European and Asian sturgeon population has declined. A conservation officer patrolling the Mississippi River for commercial egg fishermen may encounter a fisherman associated with a criminal syndicate that is trafficking in caviar (Shire, 2013). Even though state-level conservation officers may not be the most common type of conservation officer to encounter the illicit trade in wildlife, conservation officers at other levels of government will.

The US Fish and Wildlife Service has the primary responsibility for monitoring and detecting the illegal trade in endangered species, invasive species, and other statutorily regulated wildlife. Customs and Border Protection is also involved by preventing exotic plants and animals and other agroterrorism and bioterrorism threats from entering the country. They will often collaborate with the Fish and Wildlife Service when suspicious wildlife shipments are found. While they are not technically considered to be conservation officers, Customs and Border Protection agents are important when addressing the illegal trade in wildlife. Other agencies such as the Animal and Plant Health Inspection Service, National Oceanic and Atmospheric Administration, and the Centers for Disease Control are also involved in monitoring the trade in wildlife, fisheries, and other natural resource products (Wyler & Sheikh, 2008). Internationally, organizations such as INTERPOL work to address international wildlife crime through their Environmental Security Unit, which consists of four enforcement teams (fisheries, forestry, pollution, and wildlife). This unit works to address the criminal networks that are involved in environmental crimes (INTERPOL, 2021). The protection of natural resources is a multi-faceted operation that consists of agencies at all levels of government. This book will mainly focus on state-level conservation officers, but discussion of the various entities that participate in conservation law enforcement is also included.

CHAPTER SUMMARIES

The remainder of this book will introduce the reader to various aspects of conservation law enforcement. The following will provide a roadmap for the reader by briefly discussing the topics included in the book.

Chapter Two will cover the history of game laws and conservation law enforcement. The protection of wildlife has a long history in the

United States. This chapter will discuss the origins of both game laws and game wardens dating back to their origins in England. The history in America will begin in the colonies and discuss major advances in the laws that protect wildlife, fisheries, and other natural resources. Important events in history will also be discussed, such as the establishment of national parks, wildlife and natural resources agencies, and the beginning of conservation law enforcement as we know it today. Also included in this discussion will be important people who played key roles in the development of conservation in America, such as Theodore Roosevelt. Finally, the chapter will discuss how conservation officers have changed and evolved over the last 125 years. While this is not a definitive history concerning conservation and conservation law enforcement in the United States, it should provide the reader with the most important events in the history of conservation in the United States and also an understanding how the protectors of the United States' natural resources have evolved.

Chapter Three will discuss the current state of conservation law enforcement. The focus of this chapter will be the various types of conservation officers that exist at the international, federal, state, and local levels. The main focus of the book will be on state-level conservation officers because they are the most numerous and common in the United States. However, there are conservation officers at all levels of government. They may be known by different names, but officers that participate in the protection of natural resources exist at all levels of government. The local level will focus on park rangers that are employed by municipalities. The state level will consist of conservation officers that are employed by state-level departments of conservation or natural resources. The conservation officers discussed at the federal level will consist of those employed by the federal government such as Special Agents employed by the US Fish and Wildlife Service. The international perspective will have two different points of focus. One will be on organizations such as IN-TERPOL that work to address transnational criminal syndicates that traffic wildlife, and the other perspective will focus on conservation officers in other countries such as Kenya or Uganda. While a person's focus is often on their local area, this chapter will expose the reader to the true scope of conservation law enforcement around the world.

Chapter Four will examine conservation law enforcement organizations. Unlike traditional police officers who are housed in law enforcement-specific agencies such as Departments of Public Safety, conservation officers are unique in that they are typically housed in non-law enforcement specific agencies such as Departments of Natural Resources or Departments of Conservation or some similar type of agency. However, this is not the only arrangement for conservation officers. Some conservation officers are also housed in law enforcement-oriented Departments of Public Safety; however, the most common is in a Department of Natural Resources or similar agency (Falcone, 2004). The implications of this type of arrangement will be discussed. In addition to a discussion of the implications for conservation officers being housed in non-law enforcement agencies, a discussion of the characteristics of a bureaucratic organizational structure will also be included, since this is the most typical type of structure for government agencies. It is important to understand this type of structure in order to understand how these agencies operate and the influence it has on conservation officer behavior. The chapter will conclude with a discussion of several different agencies and how they are structured.

Chapter Five will examine the legal aspects of conservation law enforcement. This chapter will take an in-depth look at the important legal frameworks that guide conservation law enforcement. It will include a discussion of the role of international law and treaties in the regulation of natural resources species and products. The most important federal statutes that govern wildlife in the United States, such as the Lacey Act and the Endangered Species Act, will also be discussed at length. In addition to the discussion of federal statutes, a discussion of relevant constitutional issues is also included. Of these constitutional protections, search and seizure laws are an important component. While all law enforcement officers are guided by civil rights protections outlined in the Constitution, some aspects such as search and seizure have particular importance in conservation law enforcement. This topic will be discussed in detail.

Chapter Six will focus on conservation officer hiring requirements and what is involved in being successfully hired. The standards that potential candidates must meet to be eligible for a position as a conservation officer vary between the federal agencies and state agencies.

They also vary between the states. These differences will be discussed. In addition to the differences in the initial hiring requirements, the process through which a potential conservation officer must navigate varies from agency to agency as well. Some aspects, such as a formal interview, are common in all agencies, but other aspects such as physical fitness requirements and testing may vary. The different aspects of these processes will be discussed. Once hired, conservation officers attend a law enforcement academy. While all must attend an academy, the type of academy as well as the coursework included in those academies varies because states have different requirements (Rossler & Suttmoeller, 2018, 2021). The different types of academies as well as curriculum will be discussed. At the conclusion of this chapter, the reader should have a good understanding of the hiring process for potential conservation officers at the state and federal level.

Chapter Seven will focus on conservation law enforcement duties and patrol techniques. A discussion of the general law enforcement duties of conservation officers will be presented as well as a discussion of how the law enforcement role of conservation officers has evolved. In addition, there are various techniques utilized by conservation officers in their law enforcement duties such as community policing, hot spots policing, and problem-oriented policing. These will be discussed within the context of conservation officers. Finally, a discussion of specific law enforcement techniques including patrol strategies, undercover/covert operations, and the utilization of canine units will be presented. At the end of this chapter, the reader should have an understanding of the various ways that conservation officers perform their law enforcement duties.

Chapter Eight will discuss the other aspects of the conservation officer role other than law enforcement. Unlike traditional police agencies that will often have specialized officers that are responsible for public relations or educational programming, conservation officers commonly participate in those types of activities. This chapter will explore the size and scope of the other duties in which conservation officers participate. After finishing this chapter and Chapter Seven, the reader will have a good understanding of the entirety of the role of conservation officers within the larger law enforcement community and their assigned district.

Chapter Nine will provide conclusionary discussion of the conservation law enforcement officer and provide some insights into the future direction of conservation law enforcement as well as challenges that conservation law enforcement agencies and officers may encounter in the future.

DISCUSSION QUESTIONS

1. The illegal wildlife trade has been linked to national security concerns such as transnational criminal and terror groups and also the introduction of exotic and invasive species. The degree to which conservation officers participate in homeland security operations varies state to state. How large of a role should conservation officers have in the homeland security enterprise? Why?

2. The illegal wildlife trade has also been linked to public health concerns such as disease transmission. How large of a role should conservation officers have regarding the prevention of disease transmission from animals to people? Is this role better left to others, such as public health experts? Explain.

Key Terms

Conservation officer: Member of the law enforcement community primarily assigned to engage in the protection of natural resources. These officers may be known by other names such as park rangers, forest rangers, game wardens, conservation agents, fish and wildlife officers, environmental police or fish and game agent.

Conservation law enforcement: The segment of the law enforcement community that primarily consists of conservation officers, park rangers and other officers that specialize in the enforcement of laws that protect natural resources. It also may be known as wildlife law enforcement or natural resources law enforcement.

Wildlife crimes: Acts that are committed in violation of international treaties, national laws and regulations to protect natural resources to include the illegal wildlife market, illegal hunting, poaching for subsistence, hunting violations, illegal killing due to human and wildlife conflicts and politically driven poaching (Moreto & Spires, 2008).

References

Bavin, C. R. (1978). Wildlife law enforcement. In H. P. Brokaw (Ed.), *Wildlife and America: Contributions to an understanding of American wildlife and its conservation* (pp. 350–364). U.S. Government Printing Office.

Bilger, B. (2009). Swamp things: Florida's unwanted predators. *New Yorker*. Retrieved from: https://www.newyorker.com/magazine/2009/04/20/swamp-things.

Carter, J. G., & Gore, M. L. (2013). Conservation officers: A force multiplier for homeland security. *Journal of Applied Security Research, 8*, 285–307.

Carter, T. J. (2006). Police use of discretion: A participant observation of game wardens. *Deviant Behavior, 27*, 591–627.

Duffy, R. (2010). *Nature crime: How we're getting conservation wrong.* Yale University Press.

Eliason, S. L. (2006). A dangerous job? An examination of violence against conservation officers. *The Police Journal, 79*, 359–370.

Eliason, S. L. (2007). From wildlife specialist to police generalist? The scope of nonwildlife violations encountered by conservation officers. *Southwest Journal of Criminal Justice, 42*(2), 120–132.

Eliason, S. L. (2011). Death in the line of duty: Game warden mortality in the United States, 1886–2009. *American Journal of Criminal Justice, 36*(4), 319–326.

Falcone, D. (2004). America's conservation police: Agencies in transition. *Policing: An International Journal of Police Strategies and Management, 27*(1), 56–66.

Forsyth, C. J. (1993). Chasing and catching the "bad guys": The game warden's prey. *Deviant Behavior, 14*, 209–226.

Forsyth, C. J., & Forsyth, Y. A. (2009). Dire and sequestered meetings: The work of game wardens. *American Journal of Criminal Justice, 34*, 213–223.

Hailey, W. F. (1988). Getting the word out—Disseminating information utilizing the print media. *Proceedings of the Southeastern Association of Fish and Wildlife Agencies, USA, 42,* 540–545.

INTERPOL. (2021). *Our response to environmental crime.* https://www.interpol.int/en/Crimes/Environmental-crime/Our-response-to-environmental-crime.

Karesh, W. B., Cook, R. A., Bennett, E. L., & Newcomb, J. (2005). Wildlife trade and global disease emergence. *Emerging Infectious Diseases, 11*(7), 1000–1002.

Moreto, W. D., & Pires, S. F. (2018). *Wildlife crime: An environmental criminology and crime science perspective.* Carolina Academic Press.

O'Neill, C. R. (1993). Control of zebra mussels in residential water systems. *Sea Grant: Coastal Resources Fact Sheet.* https://www.yumpu.com/en/document/read/40481012/control-of-zebra-mussels-in-residential-water-systems.

Patten, R., Caudill, J. W., & Messer, S. (2014). The dirty south: Exploratory research into game warden fatalities in the United States. In A. Nurse (Ed.)., *Critical perspectives on green criminology: An edited collection from the Internet Journal of Criminology* (pp. 29–43). www.internetjournalofcriminology.com.

Patten, R., Crow, M. S., & Shelley, T. O. (2015). What's in a name? The occupational identity of conservation and natural resource oriented law enforcement agencies. *American Journal of Criminal Justice, 40,* 750–764.

Pledger, M., & Hailey, W. F. (1981). Methods of improving public relations. *Proceedings of the Southeastern Association of Fish and Wildlife Agencies, USA, 35,* 727–729.

Rossler, M. T., & Suttmoeller, M. J. (2018). Is all police academy training created equally? Comparing natural resources officer and general police academy training. *Police Journal: Theory, Practice and Principles, 91*(2), 107–122.

Rossler, M. T., & Suttmoeller, M. J. (2021). Conservation officer perceptions of academy training: Resource specific and general policing tasks. *Policing, 15*(2), 980–994.

Shelley, T. O., & Crow, M. S. (2009). The nature and extent of conservation policing: Law enforcement generalists or conservation specialists? *American Journal of Criminal Justice, 34,* 9–27.

Shire, G. (2013, March 14). *Seven men indicted for alleged trafficking of paddlefish "caviar."* US Fish and Wildlife Service. https://www.fws.gov/midwest/news/623.html.

Tobias, M. (1998). *Nature's keepers: On the front lines of the fight to save wildlife in America.* John Wiley & Sons Inc.

Trefethen, J. B. (1975). *An American crusade for wildlife.* Winchester Press.

Wyler, L. S., & Sheikh, P. A. (2008, May 19). *International illegal trade in wildlife: Threat and U.S. policy.* Congressional Research Service. https://www.everycrsreport.com/files/20080519_RL34395_cde8c3750ba147cce630ced60ed6a41b128b68e5.pdf.

Wyler, L. S., & Sheikh, P.A. (2013, July 23). *International illegal trade in wildlife: Threat and U.S. policy.* Congressional Research Service. https://fas.org/sgp/crs/misc/RL34395.pdf.

Wyoming Game Wardens Association. (2020). *History of Wyoming wildlife law enforcement.* https://www.wyominggamewardens.com/history.php.

Two

THE HISTORY OF GAME LAWS AND CONSERVATION LAW ENFORCEMENT

The history of conservation law enforcement and laws regulating the take of animals developed over a period of several centuries and started in Europe. The first evidence of a restriction on hunting appeared in the **Germanic Codes** (Trench, 1965) starting in the sixth century. This early law was not to protect a particular species, but rather to protect crops from damage due to hunting. These laws had punitive sanctions, including being buried alive under a pile of rocks (Stockdale, 1993).

In 1066, William the Conqueror conquered England and assumed control of all the hunting grounds of the Saxon kings. He believed that all wildlife was owned by the king and enacted further restrictions on the Saxon game laws. He also introduced mutilation as a punishment for poaching (Munsche, 1981; Stockdale, 1993; Trench, 1965). William's son Rufus was known for passing a death sentence on those that were found to be poaching on the royal lands (Sigler, 1980). These new restrictions were not readily accepted by the Saxon residents of England, Norman barons, bishops, or abbots. During this time, clergy also participated in poaching, and Henry II (William's son) insisted that clergy should be tried for two offenses—treason and poaching (Stockdale, 1993; Trench, 1965).

Due to the intense resistance to the earlier laws and the resultant problems of enforcing the laws, the **Assize of Woodstock** was passed in 1184. The Assize made a number of concessions to the pressure from the public and the church and stated that poaching offenses should be tried in ecclesiastical courts and mutilation would no longer be used as a form of punishment for poaching offenses (Trench, 1965). The **Forest Charter of Henry III** was passed in 1225. According to this charter, no one would suffer death or mutilation for the crime of poaching (Sigler, 1980). Rather, fines or imprisonment of up to one year were enacted as punishments for poaching. Fines levied were in accordance with a person's means, with the poor often pardoned. However, an allowance was made for nobility who were able to kill deer that were passing through the royal lands. This was supposed to be done in the presence of the king's forester, and if not, they were to sound a horn to alert the forester to the fact that a deer was being taken (Sigler, 1980; Trench, 1965).

In the thirteenth century, a large staff of workers were employed to control forest-grazing (i.e., livestock grazing in the forests), logging, and to enforce poaching game laws in the royal forests. Each forest had a **chief forester**, "riding foresters," "bow bearers," and a large number of other foresters that had multiple other duties (Trench, 1965 p. 262). Additionally, there were verderers, which were usually knights or those of local importance who were responsible for minor magisterial duties within the forest courts. Verderers were normally elected locally, while chief foresters were always appointed by the king, however sometimes the position was inherited. Chief foresters also often had a local castle in addition to being in charge of the forest. Chief foresters had the authority to arrest anyone they found in the forest that had a bow, snare, or hounds. They would then take the suspected poacher to the verderer to provide a surety they would appear in court. They were not allowed to hunt, but patrolled and cared for the deer and received other special privileges (Trench, 1965). These chief foresters, also known as royal foresters (Munsche, 1981) were the main type of gamekeeper in England until the seventeenth century and are the ancestors of today's conservation officers.

In the seventeenth century, royal gamekeepers became more prevalent than royal foresters due to the reduction in the number of royal forests. A royal gamekeeper was a landowner who owned a considerable amount of land and was tasked with protecting the king's game in an area usually between five and ten miles of his county seat. Sometimes they were responsible for a much larger area. For example, some noblemen were responsible for their entire county. Their duties and responsibilities were very similar to the royal foresters in that they could prohibit anyone from taking game within their jurisdiction and could seize the dogs, nets, and snares of those caught attempting to take game without their permission. While there were several similarities between the royal foresters and the royal gamekeepers, the main difference is that the royal foresters could only operate within the confines of the royal forest, while the royal gamekeeper was not restricted to only the royal forests (Munsche, 1981). However, game protection in the seventeenth century was not quite so clear cut. In addition to the remaining royal foresters and the appointed royal gamekeepers, there also were what were known as franchise holders. Franchise holders were granted by royalty since the Middle Ages and granted noblemen the exclusive right to hunt deer or other game within a certain area. The areas that royal gamekeepers were assigned to protect often contained several of these franchises and caused conflict between those with a franchise and those charged with regulating hunting.

Due to conflicts with game keepers and the belief that hunting on one's own land was not the purview of the monarchy, but rather the business of the landowner, the **Game Act of 1671** was passed and became one of the most important pieces of legislation passed in England regarding hunting rights. This act changed the basic property qualification for a sportsman to 100 pounds per year, which was the value of property someone needed to own in order to be allowed to hunt. This basic property requirement now granted several thousand gentlemen with the privilege of taking game. It also no longer restricted the gentlemen to hunting on their own land, but could hunt wherever they chose subject only to the law of trespass, which at the time was considered to be quite weak (Munsche, 1981). No longer was hunting the sole privilege of royalty. By this time in history, colonies in America were being firmly established, and while their roots in England and elsewhere in Europe continued to influence their laws and worldview, they began to develop their own game laws and practices.

HISTORY IN THE UNITED STATES

In early America, wildlife and natural resources were abundant. As many of the early immigrants were from England, they were reluctant to restrict their ability to possess firearms or to participate in hunting. These early American settlers had experienced firsthand the game laws and restrictions on land ownership in England and recognized that this was a freedom that they had previously been denied (Eliason, 2012; Kellert, 1996; Reisner, 1991). Further, these early settlers hunted for subsistence, rather than sport.

Wildlife and natural resources played an important role in the establishment of the early American settlements. Deer, turkeys, and other wild game provided food for the early colonists until they could establish their herds of domestic livestock. In addition, wildlife also provided a source of income in the form of furs, hides, and bird feathers and plumes that could be shipped and sold on the European market (Silver, 1992; Trefethen, 1975). In the 1600s, beaver pelts became an important commodity for sale in Europe because the European beaver had been harvested nearly to extinction. In Canada, the French were taking advantage of the beaver market even before the English settled at Jamestown and Plymouth. John Smith noted that the French had shipped approximately 25,000 furs to Europe in 1607. In addition to the white trappers, Native Americans also trapped beaver in large numbers for trade with the white settlers, which was how white settlers acquired many of their pelts. Because this exploitation of the beaver was unregulated, beaver were trapped nearly to extinction from Maine to the Carolinas by 1650 and from most of the waterways east of Appalachia by 1700 (Trefethen, 1975).

In addition to the fur trade, white settlers also killed turkey, waterfowl, and other birds in large numbers. White settlers would bait an area and then once flocks of birds began feeding in the area, they would shoot and kill as many birds as they could at one time. They also would trap entire flocks of turkeys at one time and track turkeys through the snow, when they are vulnerable. Whatever meat was not immediately needed would then be sold (Trefethen, 1975).

More damaging to the wildlife populations than the large numbers of wild game killed were the habitat changes that were made by the early white settlers. Early colonists depended on the forests for a variety of uses. Obviously, trees were used for the building of homes and for the construction of settlements, forts, protective barricades, furniture, and other household items. However, the vast forests located in America also provided badly needed wood products for England and other European countries. Pine trees were used for masts and spars, while large oak trees were used for ships' knees, beams, keels, and planking. Early on, representatives of the Royal Navy came to America to scout and select trees for use in shipbuilding (Trefethen, 1975). The colonists also wasted large amounts of the wood resources that were present near their settlements. Forests are not the best habitat for grazing animals or for agriculture, so large areas were cleared to make room for early agriculture. Additionally, trees provided cover for hostile groups of Native Americans and also large predators such as wolves and bears. Large areas were cleared to help provide protection for the early settlements. When these areas were cleared, the trees were often cut down and burned, rather than put to other uses. The ash would be used in tanning or as fertilizer, but little other use was made of these trees (Trefethen, 1975).

Even though the trees were cleared to provide some protection from wolves, bears, and other large predators, wolves and bears still preyed upon the livestock of the early settlers. One of the earliest examples of a law related to wildlife, albeit not for their protection, were wolf bounties. The Massachusetts Bay Colony enacted a wolf bounty in 1630. Other colonies such as Virginia followed suit and passed a bounty in 1632 (Kimball & Johnson, 1978; Trefethen, 1975). These bounty laws were replicated in every colony along the east coast of North America, and by other governments as colonial expansion occurred. These laws would pay someone for the taking of a wolf. Sometimes these bounties were paid in cash, such as a shilling or two in Massachusetts or in the form of privileges or goods as in Virginia. These laws persisted for many years, even after wolves were extirpated from eastern America (Trefethen, 1975).

Other wildlife species other than wild turkeys, beaver, and wolves also suffered at the hands of the early colonizers in America. The spawning runs of fish species such as salmon were blocked by dams created for grist mills and sawmills and also to make it easier to transport logs and barges over areas of rapids. Passenger pigeons east of the Appalachians were also harvested heavily by the white settlers because of crop damage caused by the large flocks. While populations west of the Appalachians were still abundant, those populations east of Appalachia were greatly diminished by 1672 (Trefethen, 1975).

The white-tailed deer also suffered from exploitation at the hands of the early settlers. Initially, their habitat was taken over by newly arriving herds of cattle, sheep, and horses, but their hide and meat were also important and used by the early colonists. The meat was eaten and the hides were used for clothing such as gloves, jackets, and pants as well as for greased parchment as a replacement for glass in windows. Antlers were used for handles, chandeliers, clothing racks, and ornaments. The hair was also used for stuffing saddle pads and furniture (Silver, 1992; Trefethen, 1975). Because of these many uses, the deer quickly became scarce around the new white settlements. They were still abundant toward the interior of the country, but that was only until westward expansion brought more white settlers.

The decrease in the deer herd surrounding the colonies sounded an alarm for the early colonial legislators and the town of Portsmouth, Rhode Island, enacted one of the earliest known game laws that was designed to protect an animal, rather than eliminate an animal, as was the case with the wolf. The settlers of Rhode Island enacted a law that made it illegal for anyone to harvest a white-tailed deer between May and November, which protected deer during the time while females were caring for young. It imposed a fine of five pounds. This early ordinance from Portsmouth influenced others to enact similar laws, and most of the colonies had adopted a law similar to this by 1720 (Kimball & Johnson, 1978; Trefethen, 1975). Other types of laws were also enacted in the early colonies; however, some of these laws were enacted to protect livestock and crops, but also benefitted wildlife in the process. South Carolina, for example, enacted a law making it illegal to hunt at night because hunters who shot at a pair of eyes were just as likely to kill a cow or horse as they were a deer. North Carolina also made it illegal to leave deer carcasses in the woods because they would attract wolves, bears, or other vermin (Silver, 1992).

While these laws were on the books, there was little enforcement and few convictions for people taking deer in violation of the law. Prior to 1739, most of the enforcement of these laws was left to local constables or county sheriffs. However, in 1739, the General Court of Massachusetts required every town to appoint two "**deer reeves**" that would enforce the closed season laws. Other colonies soon followed suit, and similar officers were appointed in New Hampshire, Rhode Island, Connecticut, New York, and North Carolina (Bavin, 1978; Trefethen, 1975). While these were not the conservation officers of today, this is one of the earliest examples of a conservation officer in America.

The penalties for being caught illegally killing a deer were steep. In Massachusetts, the fine was ten pounds, which is the equivalent of several hundred dollars today. Half of the fine was given to the deer reeve as a fee for their service. Because the deer reeve benefitted from the apprehension and conviction of people violating this law, there were more convictions than previously when enforcement was left to county sheriffs and constables. Even though there were more convictions, which may have served as a deterrent for some, the long season, no limit on the number of deer that could be taken, and more habitat destruction, resulted in a continued decrease in the number of deer within the colonies. Numbers decreased to such an extent that most colonies had eliminated the position of deer reeve by the time of the American Revolution because there weren't any deer left to protect. Even though the laws were unsuccessful at halting the decline of deer numbers, they did set up a foundation for future laws to protect wildlife (Silver, 1992; Trefethen, 1975).

While many early settlers were carving out an existence on the eastern coast of America, the French were establishing outposts in the area of the St. Lawrence River and the Great Lakes. These outposts were used to exploit the abundant fur resources of America. Around this same time, even though many English settlers were staying east of the Appalachian Mountains, English trappers had moved into Canada and founded the Hudson's Bay Company (Kimball & Johnson, 1978; Trefethen, 1975). Unlike other earlier explorers, such as the Spanish, the French realized that the abundant fur resources of the New World could provide much wealth, rather than gold or other precious metals. After the Seven Years' War, the French gave up their fur trade in Canada to the English. Spain acquired the land in what was to become the Louisiana Purchase from France at the end of the Seven Years' War, but then returned it to France in 1800 (Trefethen, 1975).

After the American Revolution, American settlers began moving westward into Ohio, Kentucky, Tennessee, and other areas west of the Appalachian Mountains. Those lands were still occupied by the French, which made supplying the new settlements difficult because the French controlled the Mississippi Valley. Concerns over supplying these settlers eventually led to the negotiations that provided for the Louisiana Purchase. President Jefferson shortly thereafter enlisted William Clark and Meriwether Lewis to explore the newly acquired territories and provide an American presence in the area. On their journey, Lewis and Clark noted abundant fur and other natural resources. They set out from St. Louis, which was the most significant northernmost settlement in the new territory. St. Louis's position at the confluence of the Missouri and Mississippi Rivers allowed it to become an important fur trading outpost. However, the War of 1812 again slowed westward expansion (Trefethen, 1975).

Once the War of 1812 ended in 1814, settlers once again headed west. The type of exploitation that occurred earlier east of the Appalachian Mountains once again occurred, only this time at a much greater rate. Populations in the new territories were increasing at a much faster rate than when the original colonies were settled. Settlers once again burned and cleared large expanses of land for pastures, farm sites, and agricultural fields. The eastern elk and woodland bison soon disappeared to herds of livestock. A few beaver remained until around 1850 (Trefethen, 1975).

Further west, the abundant fur resources and fur trade had created a new type of American settler—the mountain man. These men, mostly in their 20s, lived a solitary existence and were often freelancing trappers, selling their furs to whomever they chose. Outside of the freelancers, there were also three main trapping companies operating that employed mountain men to trap for them. They were the Missouri Fur Company, French Fur Company, and a third run by Andrew

Henry and William Ashley, two former mountain men, the Rocky Mountain Fur Company. This was the company that employed famous mountain men Jim Bridger and Jedediah Smith. Henry and Ashley offered mountain men a wage of 50% of their profits from the sale of their furs, instead of a set wage. This encouraged these trappers to catch as many animals as they could because the more they caught, the more money they made (Trefethen, 1975).

While the Hudson's Bay Company and the French before them had taken a conservative approach to trapping in an attempt to allow for sustainable populations of beaver, the Americans did not operate under those same guidelines. Because they were losing out to the unrestricted Americans, the Hudson's Bay Company changed strategies and encouraged their trappers to catch as many animals as possible. Because of the large amount of ground that the trappers from the three companies and the free lancers could cover, by 1830 most of the beaver in America was gone. Fortunately, around that same time, beaver pelts were no longer prized by English hat makers because they had found a cheaper alternative with South American nutria. When the market collapsed, most mountain men ceased trapping. This collapse saved the remaining beaver from extinction (Trefethen, 1975).

In addition to animals who were prized for their fur, other animals were also under threat due to the value of their meat. Settlers that were not part of a town or village would generally rely on wildlife resources for their food and other items that they needed. They would harvest what they needed for their family. However, as towns and villages grew, there was a need for wild game to feed those that were living in these towns and villages. In order to supply these settlements with the meat they needed, **market hunters** would harvest large quantities of game and sell it to butcher shops or the inns. Generally speaking, the market hunters took game with few to no restrictions. The only limits would be based on their equipment or ability to harvest game (Trefethen, 1975).

The technological advancements of the nineteenth century made market hunters even more efficient. The invention of percussion cap firearms to replace flintlock firearms was a major advancement for market hunters. Not only were firearms now more reliable, but the use of percussion caps now allowed for firearms to have multiple barrels.

Another technological development that greatly aided the market hunters was the railway system. The railroad allowed market hunters to ship quantities of game to the city markets, whereas before they had to operate close to their markets. Eventually the railroad started to include dining cars for passengers and wild game was often on the menu. In fact, supplying the railroad with wild game was so profitable that some market hunters only worked to supply the railroad. Because of the activities of market hunters, the population numbers of numerous species began to dwindle, including the passenger pigeon (Posewitz, 1999), heath hen, and pinnated grouse (Trefethen, 1975).

Due to a lack of regulations or laws governing the taking of game, it was very difficult to tell the difference between a market hunter and a **recreational hunter**. While market hunters hunted for profit, the recreational hunter, if they harvested too much game, could sell that game. However, after the War of 1812, this distinction began to become clearer. The growth of cities and towns in the northern part of America not only created a whole host of new environmental problems, such as water and air pollution, they also spawned the American sport hunter. The average working man was too busy working 10–12-hour days for six days a week to have time for sport hunting. The more affluent class of factory owners or professionals were some of the first who had the time and the money for recreational sport hunting. With the growth of this new kind of hunter in America, conflicts with the market hunters were inevitable (Trefethen, 1975).

Market hunters were used to being able to operate with impunity; however, they now had to compete with recreational hunters for game. In order to combat these market hunters, sportsmen and sportsmen groups began to purchase the prime hunting ground and then attempt to keep the market hunters from accessing it. The Carroll's Island Club, located near Baltimore and founded in 1832, is the first known example of a sportsmen's club. Some clubs were solely to provide hunting opportunities for their members, but others such as the New York Sportsmen's Club, which was founded in 1844, were formed to work for the protection and preservation of wildlife (Trefethen, 1975).

Hunting clubs began to become involved in the protection of game through legal influence as well. In New York state in the 1840s, the responsibility for wildlife conservation was left to the counties, rather than the state. The New York Sportsmen's Club were able to get a game law passed in Orange and Rockland Counties that provided for closed seasons for woodcock, ruffed grouse, quail, and deer hunting, as well as trout fishing. At the time of this law, there weren't any conservation officers, and the county sheriffs and constables were generally not interested in enforcing game laws. Because of the lack of enforcement, members of the New York Sportsmen's Club began to sue poachers, hotels, and dealers for the possession or sale of illegally killed game. The ability to sue game law violators was a remedy that hearkened back to the colonial days of the deer reeves. Many of the club members were attorneys, so this was an effective method of "enforcement" for them. Even though the game laws they advocated for were only enacted in a few counties, by suing commercial businesses in New York City, the club was able to address market hunting and poaching issues in areas outside that three-county area. The successes of the New York Sportsmen's Club became well known, and similar clubs began to organize in other cities. By the time of the outbreak of the Civil War, most major cities in the eastern United States had at least one sportsmen's club that was working for stronger game laws and bans on poaching (Trefethen, 1975).

Around this same time and into the later years of the nineteenth century, concerns about the preservation of natural areas began to become more important. The first of these areas was the area that is now known as Yellowstone National Park. A group of explorers decided that areas such as Yellowstone should be preserved for everyone. The **Yellowstone Protection Act** was passed through Congress and signed by President Grant in 1872 that created Yellowstone National Park. While the passage of the Yellowstone Protection Act in 1872 created Yellowstone National Park and allowed the Secretary of the Interior to create regulations governing the new park, it did not provide a mechanism for enforcement of those regulations. As a result, market hunters, vandals, loggers, and others operated within the park boundaries with near impunity. The park superintendents could do very little to stop the poachers, market hunters, and vandals. In 1883 an act was passed that allowed for troops to be sent to the park to provide for its protection, and the commanding officer would be named the park superintendent (Trefethen, 1975).

Captain Moses Harris, a Civil War Medal of Honor awardee, was sent with the First Calvary to Yellowstone to restore law and order. Even though the troops were more successful at keeping poachers and others at bay, there still were issues related to enforcement and prosecution of those found in violation within the park's boundaries. When Harris was replaced in 1889, he became a member of the Boone and Crockett Club, which had been founded by Theodore Roosevelt in 1887, after spending an extended period of time out West and witnessing the exploitation and wasteful killing of wild game (Trefethen, 1975).

The Boone and Crockett Club was founded by Roosevelt and his personally selected cadre of some of the nation's leading explorers, military leaders, scientists, political leaders, and writers. All the men who formed the core of the Boone and Crockett Club were avid hunters who had spent time out West, including time at Yellowstone National Park. Some of the early members of the Boone and Crockett Club included Senator Henry Cabot Lodge and General William Tecumseh Sherman. The members of the Boone and Crockett Club, along with influential politicians such as Senator Vest from Missouri, worked toward legislation to protect Yellowstone Park. After several attempts at legislation, some high-profile events including the murder of one of Superintendent Anderson's scouts, and other poaching incidences reported for the first time in the national press, increased public interest in the park. This interest increased pressure on Congress to do something about the situation at Yellowstone. Finally, in 1894, the Lacey Bill was signed into law by President Cleveland. This law was much more comprehensive and provided everything that was needed for enforcement within the park boundaries. The Yosemite National Park Act of 1890 was passed and created Yosemite National Park. Kings Canyon and Sequoia National Park also came into being in 1890 (Trefethen, 1975).

At the same time that the first national parks were being created, the United States was also setting aside forest reserves for the purpose of protecting large expanses of the forests in America. The first forest reserves were created in 1891. Once these reserves were created it was made illegal to harvest timber or run livestock on the forest reserves. However, as happened previously, the acts that created these reserves did not provide for an enforcement mechanism, so even though there were laws governing the new forest reserves, there was no enforcement, so the settlers and others around these reserves continued to use them however they saw fit. In addition to settlers using the reserves as they saw fit, there was also much opposition to the forest reserves because the Western settlers believed that their lives were being controlled by people from the eastern United States who did not understand their way of life (Trefethen, 1975).

After their initial creation as strictly a preservationist reserve, due to the widespread opposition to the reserves, the ban on all use was lifted and some use of the forest reserves resources were allowed. By allowing some use, the forest reserves as a program was protected and maintained. Then, in 1905, a bill was passed that transferred the forest reserves to the Department of Agriculture and allowed for the creation of the US Forest Service. This transfer placed 86 million acres of forest land under the purview of the Department of Agriculture (Trefethen, 1975).

In addition to the establishment of national parks and national forest reserves, the late nineteenth century also saw an increase in public interest in game management. Prior to this time, some game laws had been attempted in some places such as the closed deer season regulations in most of the eastern states. Some such as New York attempted closed seasons on animals such as the heath hen as well. These early attempts at laws regulating the taking of game were largely ineffective due to rural communities not enforcing the law because they did not agree with the law and believed it was being forced on them by those in the towns and metropolitan areas. Also, there was little enforcement because enforcement was generally left up to the local constables and sheriffs, neither of which regularly patrolled areas where hunting would be taking place. There weren't any game wardens or conservation officers. About the only enforcement that took place were the civil suits brought by the New York Sportsmen's Club (Trefethen, 1975).

At the same time, interest in nature and wildlife was increasing in America in large part due to the availability of books, magazines, and other written articles. Regular citizens could now read about the natural world by reading the works of Thoreau, Audubon, and others. This new interest in wildlife led to enactment of new laws such as those protecting songbirds in Vermont in 1851. By 1864, eleven other states had adopted similar laws. However, the concept of a central authority to manage fish and wildlife resources did not really gain any momentum until after the Civil War (Trefethen, 1975).

One of the earliest forms of central authority was the United States Fishery Commission, which was established by Congress in 1871 in order to manage and reinvigorate the country's fisheries, which had been exploited much like all other natural resources. The establishment of the commission motivated most of the states to also create a version of a fisheries commission by 1880. The US Fishery Commission launched a campaign of propagation and stocking. They were met with some successes, such as black bass introduction, but also created some problems, such as the stocking of carp. While carp were a popular game fish in Europe, they competed with native fish and other wildlife and were not positively received in the United States. However, carp became established across the country, and still are today. Similar methods were also used by some to try and propagate and transplant game birds. California did not have much success with a wild turkey propagation program, but a ring-necked pheasant program was more successful in establishing the pheasant in large areas of the country. However, this was also a non-native species, having originated in China. It was so successful in Oregon that they were able to hold a pheasant hunting season (Trefethen, 1975).

As public interest in wildlife and fisheries continued to expand, a need was realized for more game laws and the enforcement of game laws. Deer reeves were the first attempt at providing for the enforcement of a game law, and the soldiers that patrolled Yellowstone National Park also had "conservation officer"-type duties (Falcone, 2004; Trefethen, 1975). Trefethen (1975) identified Maine as being the first state to have salaried game wardens, while Falcone (2004) and Bavin (1978) both identified Michigan as having the first salaried game warden. Additionally, Bavin (1978) stated that Minnesota and Wisconsin also appointed game wardens in 1887. Regardless, Maine appointed one game warden in 1852 for each of the seven counties to enforce deer and moose hunting regulations, and they were paid between $25 and

$75 a year. In 1873, Maine also established a harvest limit or bag limit on deer, limiting hunters to three deer per year. This is most likely the first bag limit established in history. In 1880, it also placed its enforcement officers under the state fish commission. This essentially created one of the first fish and game commissions (Trefethen, 1975). By 1912, 41 states had some form of game wardens (Bavin, 1978).

The concept of bag limits was not limited only to big game, although Michigan had imposed a five deer limit as well. Other states began to consider bag limits on other species, with Iowa creating the first bag limit for an upland game species by limiting the harvest of prairie chickens to 25 per day. Bag limits were beginning to be considered by many of the states for a variety of different game species, but they were not universally adopted for many years. During this time, states were also beginning to consider regulating methods of taking game. Wisconsin outlawed using dogs to hunt deer in 1876, and Michigan outlawed the use of traps, snares, and pitfalls for the taking of deer, as well as prohibited shooting deer while in the water in 1881. The open seasons on big game were also being reconsidered during this time, and many were reduced from an average of six-month long seasons to approximately two months in the last decade of the nineteenth century (Trefethen, 1975).

Even though more states were interested in enacting hunting regulations, their implementation was difficult. One of the issues holding back the regulation of hunting and fishing was that often county or local governments could either veto regulations or could exempt their residents from state-level hunting restrictions. In addition, local and county governments would also often create a competing hunting regulation that could be in direct opposition to the state-level regulation. They could also enact laws prohibiting hunters from outside that county or local jurisdiction from hunting within their area (Trefethen, 1975).

In 1879, the New York Association for the Protection of Game, which was an expansion of the earlier New York Sportsman's Club, was headed by Robert Roosevelt, Theodore Roosevelt's uncle. They campaigned for a more universal and accepted set of game laws. They were able to get the Act for the Preservation of Moose and Wild Deer, Birds,

Fish and Other Game passed. This act created a uniform state-wide game and fish code and also removed the ability of county and local jurisdictions to make their own game laws. Additionally, it made the possession of game during closed season an offense. However, even though this was a state-wide code, enforcement powers were relegated to local authorities. This was an important step forward for the protection of game and fish (Trefethen, 1975).

In 1894, further reforms were needed to address issues related to the deer season in New York, but that legislation was not supported in the legislature. However, at the same time, a bill was passed that allowed for the appointment of the Fisheries, Game and Forest Commission. This is one of the first examples of an agency of this type in the United States (Trefethen, 1975). Even though these legislative efforts were unsuccessful, proponents did not stop attempting to address issues such as hunting deer with dogs. In 1897, the New York legislature passed a law that prohibited the use of dogs and jacklights for hunting deer for five years. By the time the five years had expired, most hunters had grown accustomed to not participating in those types of activities, and those methods were outlawed permanently. This law provided a template for other states, and many other states soon followed suit with similar laws outlawing these types of provisions (Trefethen, 1975).

In addition to New York creating a fish and game commission, during the latter part of the nineteenth century other states were also creating some form of fish and game agencies. The Massachusetts Commission of Fisheries and Game predated New York's and was created in 1865. New Hampshire expanded the Fisheries Commission to also include responsibilities for wildlife and renamed the agency the Commission on Fisheries and Game in 1880 (Trefethen, 1975). South Dakota (Trefethen, 1975) and Michigan created theirs in 1887 and Missouri in 1905 (Falcone, 2004; Keefe, 1987). These new agencies were very small and often operated at the political whim of whomever was in power in those states, as these agencies were financed with appropriations from state legislatures.

Discontent with the current political fish and game agency and the realization that political interference was an impediment to scientific wildlife management and enforcement led a group of sportsmen and concerned citizens to introduce an amendment to the Constitution of Missouri to create a non-political fish and game department. The amendment passed, and the Missouri Department of Conservation was created on July 1, 1937. The new non-political agency was to be led by a four-person commission who were appointed by the governor. They chose to pursue a constitutional amendment because if the department had been created by legislation, it could have easily been overturned at a later legislative session or otherwise usurped. Further, the new non-political department was allowed to spend all monies raised from the sales of licenses and other sources and did not have an appropriation from the state legislature (Keefe, 1987). After the department was created, all the original employees were retained on a temporary basis. The forty politically appointed game wardens that were employed by the department at the time had to apply to keep their jobs when the department hired its first class of conservation officers. Of the forty original game wardens, only fourteen were retained (Keefe, 1987).

Another issue facing early fish and game agencies was a lack of funding. In order to supplement the meager state appropriations, in 1895, North Dakota passed a law requiring all hunters to purchase a license from the state. Many other states followed North Dakota's lead, such as Missouri in 1905 (Keefe, 1987), and now purchasing licenses is commonplace in America (Blevins & Edwards, 2009). Other states have explored other means for increasing their funding. For example, in Missouri, in 1976, a Missouri constitutional amendment was passed that provided for a 1/8 of 1% sales tax that is earmarked for the Missouri Department of Conservation (Keefe, 1987).

While states were beginning to organize individual game and fish departments, albeit rudimentary, in the late 1800s, other than the establishment of forest reserves and the four national parks, the federal government was not very active regarding fish and game conservation. There was progress toward a national focus on conservation, but there wasn't a cohesive movement or centralized authority that was spearheading the effort. Aside from the Yellowstone Protection Act, the Lacey Game and Wild Birds Preservation and Disposition Act of 1900, also known as the Lacey Act, was the first legislation passed by the federal government that directly related to wildlife conservation (Trefethen, 1975). This act required that anyone transporting wild game across state lines must clearly label the packages so that law enforcement could determine the contents. It also reinforced states' laws by making the interstate shipment of wild birds and mammals that are taken in violation of state laws a federal offense and regulated the importation of foreign species (Dunlap, 1988; Freyfogle & Goble, 2009; Trefethen, 1975).

However, several obstacles presented themselves in the implementation of the Lacey Act. First, there wasn't a clear mechanism for the federal enforcement of this act. Customs officials could certainly enforce the sections of the Lacey Act that dealt with importation, but when passed there wasn't a clear mechanism for the enforcement of the other provisions (Dunlap, 1988; Trefethen, 1975). Another obstacle that presented itself was that at that time, state game laws were still in their infancy. Most states did not have strong, cohesive, state-wide wildlife codes, with many states still having county and local ordinances that regulated hunting and fishing. States did, however, recognize the benefits of the Lacey Act, and many moved to create stronger, clearer, and more cohesive state-wide hunting and fishing laws (Trefethen, 1975). Toward this end, the National Association of Game Wardens and Commissioners was founded at a meeting of the heads of the state fish and game departments in Yellowstone National Park in 1902. The purpose of the meeting was to work on the development of state and national conservation programs and also to discuss cooperating on interstate problems. This organization was important in the development of the wildlife conservation movement (Trefethen, 1975).

One of the main motivators of the Lacey Act was to address the issue of the plume and feather market. Large numbers of birds were being killed for their feathers for the fashion market (Dunlap, 1988; Trefethen, 1975). Another nationwide problem was the killing of large numbers of birds for the meat market. Not only were waterfowl and other common game birds being killed in large numbers for their meat, songbirds such as robins and other birds were also being killed and sold for their meat. Adding to the difficulty was that any state regulations that attempted to regulate the taking of waterfowl could be ineffective because as waterfowl migrated, they may be protected in one state, but not protected in another, which made trying to protect them futile (Freyfogle & Goble, 2009; Trefethen, 1975). On August 16, 1916, the Convention Between the United States and Great Britain for the Protection of Migratory Birds was formally signed for Canada, and then on December 7, 1916, President Woodrow Wilson signed the legislation for the United States. However, the treaty had to be ratified by Congress. The Senate passed the Treaty on July 30, 1917, and the House of Representatives approved it on June 6, 1918. The Migratory Bird Treaty Act of 1918 provided for the protection of migratory birds everywhere in North America north of Mexico (Bean, 1978; Dunlap, 1988; Freyfogle & Goble, 2009; Trefethen, 1975).

The treaty was met by quite a bit of opposition, mostly from market hunters and the owners of large duck hunting clubs in the Midwest and especially Missouri. A legal challenge to the treaty was made by the Attorney General of Missouri at the time, Frank McAllister, after he was arrested by a federal game warden. The case reached the United States Supreme Court, and it ruled in favor of the treaty, which made it indisputably the law of the land (Bean, 1978; Trefethen, 1975). The treaty prohibited the sale of game birds, the shooting of birds in the spring or at night and any birds classified as plume birds or song and insectivorous species were given full legal protection. It also closed seasons on many birds and placed bag limits and methods restrictions on the taking of migratory birds. Finally, it allowed the states to make regulations regarding migratory birds, but they had to be the same or more restrictive than the federal laws. This also allowed for state and federal game warden cooperation. A state officer could choose either to charge a violator in state court, or could refer the charges to a federal officer and have the violations filed in federal court (Bean, 1978; Dunlap, 1988; Trefethen, 1975).

One of the next important pieces of legislation that impacts not only wildlife management, but also conservation law enforcement, was the Migratory Bird Hunting Stamp Act. It became law in 1934. This act required all migratory bird hunters to purchase a federal stamp, the proceeds of which would be earmarked for the purchase, development, and management of waterfowl refuges (Dunlap, 1988; Trefethen, 1975). This stamp is also commonly known as a "duck stamp" and has become a collector's item for hunters, as well as a permit.

One of the most important pieces of legislation for wildlife in the United States was passed in 1937. This law did not directly manage or protect a particular species, but the Pittman-Robertson Federal Aid in Wildlife Restoration Act provided funds in the form of an excise tax on firearms and ammunition (Bean, 1978; Dunlap, 1988; Trefethen, 1975). These funds were to be used for wildlife land acquisition, development, and research. Possibly the most important provision of this act was that for states to be eligible for these funds, they had to pass a bill that prohibited the diversion of the funds from hunting and fishing license sales from the fish and wildlife agency. This was important, as it was fairly common practice for legislatures to take the funds from the license sales and use them for items other than fish and wildlife management or protection (Dunlap, 1988; Trefethen, 1975). In 1950, a companion law to Pittman-Robertson, the Federal Aid in Sport Fish Restoration Act, was passed. This act provided federal funds for state-level fish management programs through a federal excise tax on fishing equipment (US Fish and Wildlife Service [USFWS], 2013).

One of the next important federal statutes to come into place was the Bald and Golden Eagle Protection Act. It was enacted in 1940 and then expanded in 1962 to include golden eagles (Freyfogle & Goble, 2009; Trefethen, 1975). This act was part of a larger movement at the time that was reforming the previous system of bounties and predator control. Prior to this act there was a national movement to reform the accepted thinking regarding the role of predators in the ecosystem and their role in the management of prey species. Wolves, mountain lions, hawks, owls, and other predators were increasingly being given protection, rather than being the subject of bounty laws (Trefethen, 1975).

The 1960s and 1970s were important decades in the management of the nation's natural resources. Three very important pieces of legislation were passed by Congress in the 1960s and 1970s. The first of these is the Marine Mammal Protection Act, passed in 1972 (Dunlap, 1988; Trefethen, 1975). This act sought to preserve the marine ecosystem and covered all marine mammals, rather than specific animals as had been covered in previous acts. Additionally, this act did not focus on the maximum sustainable harvest for one particular species, but focused instead on optimum sustainable populations (Bean, 1978; Dunlap, 1988). This act defined "take" very broadly and established a series of regulations concerning the commercialization of marine species and products (Dunlap, 1988; Trefethen, 1975). It is also important because it foreshadowed two seminal pieces of legislation that would pass through Congress the following year.

In 1973, two very important pieces of conservation legislation were passed by Congress: the Convention on International Trade in Endangered Species of Wild Fauna and Flora (CITES) and the Endangered Species Act (Dunlap, 1988; Freyfogle & Goble, 2009; Trefethen, 1975). The Endangered Species Act of 1973 was the third iteration of endangered species legislation. The first was passed in 1966, the second in 1969, and the third in 1973 (Environmental Law Institute [ELI], 1977). Each iteration of the act attempted to rectify deficiencies in the earlier versions. This act requires all federal agencies to work for the conservation and protection of endangered species. It provided for the Secretary of the Interior to list species, but private citizens could also petition to have species listed (Dunlap, 1988; ELI, 1977). It also created two groups of protected species: endangered and threatened species. In addition, states may enter into cooperative agreements with the federal government for the protection of endangered species and be eligible for federal funding to assist in those endeavors (ELI, 1977).

In 1973 the United States also entered into CITES. CITES also focused on endangered species, but it only focused on the trade in flora and fauna. It provided for a mechanism to classify species differently based on the immediacy of the threat to their existence. It required all shipments to have import and export paperwork, and all signatories agreed to appoint a national scientific authority to oversee population statuses and have the authority to oversee the regulations (Dunlap, 1988; ELI, 1977). There are currently 183 signatories to the convention (CITES, 2020).

Since the time of the adoption of the Endangered Species Act, several additional important pieces of legislation have been enacted in the United States. These acts are collectively known as the Multinational Species Conservation Acts. Each of these acts works to protect a particular species, and most are directly related to the Endangered Species Act or CITES. The African Elephant Conservation Act of 1988 was the first. It was followed by the Rhinoceros and Tiger Conservation Act of 1994, the Asian Elephant Conservation Act of 1997, the Great Ape Conservation Act of 2000, and the Marine Turtle Conservation Act of 2004 (USFWS, 2020).

CITES and the Endangered Species Act are also related to the Wild Bird Conservation Act (WBCA) that was enacted in 1992. This act ensures that exotic bird species are not harmed by international trade. With a few exceptions, most of the bird species listed in the WBCA are also listed under CITES (USFWS, 2020).

Early Game Wardens

Most fish and game agencies concentrated on law enforcement rather than game management in the early years (Trefethen, 1975). While today there are strict guidelines for who can apply for the job as a conservation officer, those restrictions did not exist during the time of the first game wardens. Pay was very low, so the early game wardens came from a variety of social backgrounds and were somewhat of a mixed lot. Because there weren't any set standards for this type of job and very little experience with managing those doing these jobs, agencies searched for candidates who were physically strong and had some outdoor skills. Secondarily, they searched for intelligent and tactful candidates. Very few potential game wardens had any experience in policing or court procedures. Some states abided by the thinking that in order to catch a poacher, it would take a poacher, so they would hire former poachers or market hunters as game wardens (Trefethen, 1975). This thought process was also commonplace in early policing and described by Bittner (1970) as having to determine how much of the dragon is needed in the dragon slayer.

In addition, many early game wardens were political appointees and were used to harass citizens of opposing views or, if they happened to arrest someone with strong political relationships, could be fired (Trefethen, 1975). In Missouri, early game wardens were political appointees that were full-time wardens, but there were also special deputy wardens that were political cronies that were hired on a temporary basis and paid $4 a day when they were "needed." Additionally, honorary law enforcement commissions were given out as well as "courtesy cards" that identified the owner as a "friend of conservation and of this Department" (Keefe, 1987 p. 216). These types of activities certainly impacted the ability of a politically appointed game warden to conduct their duties.

Conservation officers today are often the public face of their department (McGarrell et al., 2009). However, these early officers were essentially tough enforcers, who did very little to promote their respective agencies. However, there were some young, more idealistic, principled officers who held a more future-oriented view of their responsibilities. As minimal entry job requirements increased, most of the enforcer types were eliminated in favor of the more principled officers (Trefethen, 1975).

Most of the early natural resource agencies were small and focused on law enforcement. Because they were small, the number of conservation officers was also small in the beginning. For example, in New York, eight "Game Protectors" were appointed in 1880 and were responsible for patrolling the entire state (New York Department of Environmental Conservation [NYDEC], 2005). Until 1925, a law existed in New Hampshire that limited the number of conservation officers to ten (Walsh, 2020). The conservation officers of today are often spread somewhat thin and have large amounts of ground to cover (Tobias, 1998), but they are not spread as thin as these early officers.

During these early years of conservation law enforcement, officers experienced little public support (NYDEC, 2005; Trefethen, 1975). Many hunters and anglers were used to hunting and fishing by any means and taking game in whatever amount they chose, and the early conservation officers were interrupting them (Mehn, 2020; Richardson, 2011). Over time, some of these negative attitudes toward conservation officers have abated; however, similar to traditional police officers, there will always be those with negative attitudes toward law enforcement officers. Officers were also not paid well in the early days. Officers in Georgia were paid a salary of three dollars per day, but were also assigned a percentage of the fines resulting from successful prosecutions of their cases (Richardson, 2011). In the 1930s and 1940s, officers began to wear an official uniform for the first time (Wyoming Game Wardens Association [WGWA], 2020). Also, as was seen in the transition to the professional model in traditional policing (Walker, 1984), the time of the political appointees had come to an end, and state agencies were beginning to require higher hiring standards, such as written and oral exams (WGWA, 2020).

World War II presented a special challenge for conservation officers. Some officers were sent overseas to fight in the war. Others remained at home and participated in a variety of duties, such as assisting other law enforcement agencies or the FBI with investigations. Many were auxiliary firemen and police and helped patrol power lines, dams, canal locks, and bridges. The return of the veterans from World War II brought with it an increased interest in outdoor recreation, and a subsequent increase in hunters and anglers. Because of the increase in outdoor recreational activities, state departments responded by increasing their conservation officer forces (Mehn, 2020; NYDEC, 2005; Walsh, 2020). For example, by 1950, New York state had 160 uniformed conservation officers. Budgets continued to increase throughout the 1950s, and state wildlife agencies were able to acquire new equipment for conservation officers, such as boats, handheld radios, motorcycles, and airplanes (NYDEC, 2005).

Prior to officers driving cars or trucks, officers had to patrol by foot, horse, bicycle, train, or trolley (Martiak, 2006; Mehn, 2020). Once cars became commonplace, many game wardens were required to utilize their own personal vehicles for patrolling, and states began supplying patrol vehicles in the 1950s. In New York, the first patrol vehicles were tan four-door 1958 Fords (NYDEC, 2005). Officers in Montana and New Hampshire were also issued a state-owned vehicle around this time (Mehn, 2020; Walsh, 2020). Many conservation officers today customarily drive four-wheel-drive vehicles. In the 1960s, it become commonplace to have two-way radios installed in patrol cars.

As more duties and equipment were added to a conservation officer's duties, it required an increase in training. The first conservation officers did not have much, if any training. In the 1960s and 1970s, there was an increased focus on officer training, and New York State established an academy for conservation officers. In addition to advances in training and equipment, conservation officers also began utilizing canine units in the 1970s to assist in apprehending violators, but also to assist in locating lost people. New York acquired its first canine in 1978 (NYDEC, 2005).

Also, in the 1960s and 1970s were calls for law enforcement agencies to actively recruit and hire minorities. While many states did not hire their first female game warden until the 1970s, the first recorded instance of a female game warden is in Michigan. Huldah Neal was appointed in 1897. Even though Michigan clearly had hired the first female game warden, there would not be another one in Michigan until 1977 (Michigan Department of Natural Resources, 2018). The Missouri Department of Conservation hired their first female conservation officer in 1975 (Keefe, 1987) and Colorado in 1974 (Gerhardt, 2019). Oklahoma, on the other hand, did not hire a female conservation officer until 1990 (Gerhardt, 2019), and Kansas hired their first female conservation officer in 2014. Even though more and more women are being hired into conservation law enforcement, only about 22% of all conservation officers are female (Schmitt, 2017).

Early conservation officers were exclusively protectors of fish and game. As society evolved and citizens realized more discretionary time to recreate in the outdoors, more pressure was placed on conservation agencies to accommodate these outdoor enthusiasts. As more and more people began to recreate in the outdoors, conservation officers were required to begin to fulfill more of a traditional police role and address more traditional types of crimes (Falcone, 2004). As these responsibilities have expanded, conservation officers have also been called upon to provide security at Olympic games (NYDEC, 2005; Richardson, 2011), respond to terror attacks such as the attacks on 9/11 (NYDEC, 2005), and to assist after natural disasters such as Hurricane Katrina (Richardson, 2011).

US Forest Service

After the Civil War, there began to be interest in the federal government acquiring forest lands to preserve and manage them. Several different federal laws were passed to this end. However, the **Organic Act of 1897**, while it provided for the care and management of the new federal forest reserves and an organization to manage the reserves, also provided for the first forest rangers. Bill Kreutzer was the first ranger and was appointed in 1898. The main duty of these early rangers was to fight forest fires in the summer, and they were known for their toughness, which was a similar attribute sought by early state wildlife agencies (Trefethen, 1975).

For the next seven years until the forming of the US Forest Service in 1905, forest rangers were appointed by U.S. Senators and the Department of the Interior's General Land Office. Because these early rangers were political appointees, many were simply incompetent, while some participated in corruption. Once the Forest Service was officially established on July 1, 1905, rangers could no longer be political appointees. They now were subject to comprehensive field and written civil service exams, in order to produce qualified rangers that had at least some knowledge of forestry (Williams, 2005). Needless to say, most of the politically appointed rangers quit once they were transferred to the new Forest Service. The written test contained questions related to ranching and livestock, forest conditions, lumbering, surveying, mapping, and cabin construction. The field examination required the applicants to demonstrate horsemanship, orienteering, and marksmanship with a rifle and pistol. Applicants had to provide their own equipment and horses. They were paid $60 per month (Williams, 2005).

These early rangers were issued what was known as a "Use Book," which was updated yearly and contained all the federal laws and regulations used by the rangers (Williams, 2005, p. 18). Comparatively, a book that contained all the laws a Forest Service ranger would need today would contain more than 1,000 pages. These early rangers participated in a variety of activities while on duty, such as mapping the national forests, fighting wildfires, administering grazing permits, protecting the forests from poachers, and arresting trespassing loggers and ranchers and others who might try to exploit the resource. Prior to 1910, sites for remote ranger outposts were established to provide for on-site management of the new national forests. Then, between 1910 and 1920, the number of remote ranger stations was expanded. Fire suppression continued to be one of the main responsibilities of the Forest Service. Shortly after World War I, the Forest Service installed an extensive network of field telephones to make communication between the fire lookout towers and the ranger stations more efficient. In addition, two-way radios were invented during World War I and were put to use by the Forest Service rangers (Williams, 2005). Very little changed for rangers for several decades. One change was that more and more applicants began to have college degrees in forestry, as colleges and universities were beginning to have degree programs in forestry.

National Park Service

Similar to the Forest Service, the legacy of law enforcement with the National Park Service (NPS) began prior to the creation of the actual organization that is known today as the NPS. Harry Yount became the first national park ranger when he was appointed as "game keeper" of Yellowstone, which was prior to the assignment of soldiers to Yellowstone for security (Albright, 1985). His duties were to enforce game laws and protect the park's geological features. Yount resigned in 1881, and then in 1886, soldiers were sent to Yellowstone to protect the park. In the late 1890s the national parks located in California began to hire temporary forest rangers to replace the troops that had been sent to the Philippines to fight. Their jobs were to prevent poaching, keep sheep from grazing in the park, and prevent and fight fires. After the troops returned from the Philippines, some of these temporary rangers were hired as full-time rangers (Albright, 1985).

Prior to 1915, each park had distinct rules and regulations for their park rangers. In 1914, the national park rangers were beginning to be organized and become more uniform. This formalization was accelerated in 1915, when Stephen Mather (the first director of the NPS) distributed the regulations to every national park. These regulations outlined the ranger uniform and required the rangers to write monthly reports describing their work activities. Because the park rangers at this time were still quite unorganized, the new regulations created much confusion, but then in 1917, the National Park Service (NPS) was created, and the rangers were subsumed under the new agency. Stephen Mather enacted entrance exams and wanted rangers to meet civil service requirements and to be educated, with a college education being preferred (Albright, 1985). In 1918, the army officially left Yellowstone Park and left the park in the hands of the first contingent of park rangers, which consisted of 23 men (Manns, 1980). In 1926, President Coolidge issued an executive order that ended the appointment of rangers without passing an examination. He also directed the Civil Service Commission to design and develop park ranger qualifications and a written examination. At this time, the job was open to anyone aged 21–45 that had one year's experience in outdoor work (Albright, 1985). Beginning in 1927, park rangers officially came under the Civil

Service (Manns, 1980). The first patrol vehicles were introduced in 1936, and rangers have benefited from other technological advancements throughout history.

The number of rangers assigned to Yellowstone and other national parks has fluctuated over time. For example, at Yellowstone, there were 42 full-time rangers in 1942, but then the number of rangers decreased during World War II. The number of rangers assigned to Yellowstone has varied, but is in proportion to the number of visitors (Manns, 1980). The national parks are also not immune from societal changes. As crime rose in the United States in the 1960s and 1970s, the amount of crime also rose in the parks and led to the increased professionalization of the ranger force. In addition, snowmobiling gained in popularity during the 1970s and transformed Yellowstone from a seasonal park to an all year-round park and added snowmobile patrol to the duties of the park ranger. The 1970s also saw the NPS hire the first full-time female park ranger in 1976 (Manns, 1980).

US Fish and Wildlife Service

While there were officers that enforced poaching laws prior to the enactment of the Lacey Act in 1900, such as Yellowstone rangers (Albright, 1985), the official origins of federal fish and wildlife law enforcement begins with the Lacey Act. (USFWS, 2018). However, it was not enforced by the US Fish and Wildlife Service, but rather by its predecessor, the Division of Biological Survey, which was located in the US Department of Agriculture (USFWS, 2018; Trefethen, 1975). One of the main catalysts for the Lacey Act was the plume trade. At the time of the enactment of the Lacey Act, the American Ornithologist's Union hired their own version of warden to enforce the provisions regarding plume hunters. One of the first of these wardens, and also one of the first wardens to be killed in the line of duty, was Guy Bradley (McIver, 2003).

In 1903, President Roosevelt established the first wildlife refuge at Pelican Island National Bird Reservation (USFWS, 2018; Trefethen, 1975). The American Ornithologist's Union agreed to pay Paul Kroegel, the warden assigned to the new refuge. In 1905, the Division of Biological Survey was renamed the Bureau of Biological Survey and replaced the Division of Economic Ornithology and Mammalogy. This new bureau was now responsible for the new refuges and other areas. In 1934, wildlife law enforcement was given its own division within the Bureau of Biological Survey when the Division of Game Management was created. Then, in 1940, the Fish and Wildlife Service was officially created by combining the Bureau of Fisheries and the Bureau of Biological Survey. In 1956, the Fish and Wildlife Service was reorganized once again and became the United States Fish and Wildlife Service and contained the Bureau of Sport Fisheries and Wildlife and the Bureau of Commercial Fisheries. In 1989, the National Fish and Wildlife Forensics Laboratory was established in Ashland, Oregon. This lab was created to assist with law enforcement investigations (USFWS, 2018).

CONCLUSION

The history of game laws and conservation law enforcement is rich and closely linked with the founding and settling of the United States. The early settlers were influenced by their previous experiences in the English system, but put a unique American viewpoint on fish and wildlife management and game law enforcement. From the near extinction of many species of wildlife to the burgeoning populations today of many game animals, the history of laws and enforcement have played an important role in the current status of conservation in America today.

DISCUSSION QUESTIONS

1. Discuss and explain the impact and influence of the English heritage of game laws on the modern system of conservation law enforcement and game laws in America. Is the American system rooted in England? Is it separate? How much influence is there? Explain.

2. Conduct an online search for the conservation or natural resources agency for the state in which you live and examine the history section of the division that houses the conservation officers. What

types of information are contained in that section? Now compare it to the history section of the larger natural resources or conservation agency that houses the conservation officers. How does the information contained in the agency compare to that of the law enforcement division? How much focus is placed on the law enforcement history of the larger agency?

Key Terms

Assize of Woodstock: Passed in 1184 and stated poaching offenses would be tried in ecclesiastical courts and mutilation would be no longer used as punishment for poaching.

Chief forester: The main type of gamekeeper in England until the 17th century.

Deer reeve: An early official appointed in Massachusetts that enforced closed season laws.

Forest Charter of Henry III: Death and mutilation were removed as punishments for poaching and were replaced with fines and imprisonment.

Game Act of 1671: Important piece of legislation that changed the property qualification for a someone to hunt to 100 pounds per year.

Germanic Codes: Early law from the 6th century to protect crops from damage due to hunting that had punitive sanctions such as being buried alive.

Market hunters: A person who harvests wild animals with the intention of selling their meat, hides, plumage, or products derived from these items, and is primarily focused on these harvests to make or supplement their living. Market hunting has largely been outlawed in the United States.

Organic Act of 1897: Provided for the care and management of newly created federal forest reserves as well as the first forest rangers.

Recreational hunters: People who participate in hunting as a form of recreation, rather than as an occupation such as market hunters.

Yellowstone Protection Act: Legislation that created the first national park—Yellowstone National Park.

References

Albright, H. M. (1985). *The birth of the National Park Service: The founding years, 1913–1933*. Howe Brothers.

Bavin, C. R. (1978). Wildlife law enforcement. In H. P. Brokaw (Ed.), *Wildlife and America: Contributions to an understanding of American wildlife and its conservation* (pp. 350–364). U.S. Government Printing Office.

Bean, M. J. (1978). Federal wildlife law. In H. P. Brokaw (Ed.), *Wildlife and America: Contributions to an understanding of American wildlife and its conservation* (pp. 279–289). U.S. Government Printing Office.

Bittner, E. (1970). *The functions of the police in modern society: A review of background factors, current practices, and possible role models*. National Institute of Mental Health Center for Studies of Crime and Delinquency.

Blevins, K. R., & Edwards, T. D. (2009). Wildlife crime. In J. M. Miller (Ed.), *21st century criminology: A reference handbook. Volume 1* (pp. 557–563). Sage.

Convention on International Trade in Endangered Species of Wild Fauna and Flora (CITES). (2020). List of parties to the convention. https://www.cites.org/eng/disc/parties/index.php.

Dunlap, T. R. (1988). *Saving America's wildlife*. Princeton University Press.

Eliason, S. (2012). From the king's deer to a capitalist commodity: A social historical analysis of the poaching law. *International Journal of Comparative and Applied Criminal Justice, 36*(2), 133–148.

Environmental Law Institute (ELI). (1977). *The evolution of national wildlife law*. U.S. Government Printing Office.

Falcone, D. (2004). America's conservation police: Agencies in transition. *Policing: An International Journal of Police Strategies and Management, 27*(1), 56–66.

Freyfogle, E. T., & Goble, D. D. (2009). *Wildlife law: A primer*. Island Press.

Gerhardt, G. (2019). Female game wardens praised. *Tulsa World*. https://tulsaworld.com/archive/female-game-wardens-praised/article_f1ebed19-234b-50d4-9ffe-bd9b6843d36e.html.

Keefe, J. F. (1987). *The first 50 years*. Missouri Department of Conservation.

Kellert, S. R. (1996). *The value of life.* Island Press.

Kimball, T. L., & Johnson, R. E. (1978). The richness of American wildlife. In H. P. Brokaw (Ed.), *Wildlife and America: Contributions to an understanding of American wildlife and its conservation* (pp. 3–17). U.S. Government Printing Office.

Manns, T. R. (1980). *History of the park ranger in Yellowstone National Park.* National Park Service. http://www.npshistory.com/publications/yell/ranger-history.pdf.

Martiak, S. (2006). *New Jersey's wildlife law enforcement—A history.* New Jersey Department of Environmental Protection. https://www.state.nj.us/dep/fgw/artlawhist06.htm.

McGarrell, E. F., Suttmoeller, M., & Gibbs, C. (2009). Great lakes fisheries enforcement. In W. W. Taylor, A. J. Lynch, & N. J. Leonard (Eds.), *Great lakes fisheries policy and management* (pp. 455–472). Michigan State University Press.

McIver, S. B. (2003). *Death in the Everglades: The murder of Guy Bradley, America's first martyr to environmentalism.* The University Press of Florida.

Mehn, M. (2020). *A look back—and ahead.* Montana Fish, Wildlife and Parks. http://fwp.mt.gov/enforcement/wardens/history/.

Michigan Department of Natural Resources. (2018). First female conservation officer celebrated during Women's History Month. *Outdoor News.* https://www.outdoornews.com/2018/02/28/first-female-conservation-officer-celebrated-womens-history-month/.

Munsche, P. B. (1981). The gamekeeper and English rural society, 1660–1830. *Journal of British Studies, 20*(2), 82–105.

New York Department of Environmental Conservation (NYDEC). (2005). *Standing watch—125 years of conservation law enforcement in New York State.* https://www.dec.ny.gov/regulations/2744.html.

Posewitz, J. (1999). *Inherit the hunt: A journey into the heart of American hunting.* Falcon.

Reisner, M. (1991). *Game wars: The undercover pursuit of wildlife poachers.* Viking.

Richardson, A. (2011). *100 years of Georgia game wardens.* https://www.gon.com/hunting/100-years-of-georgia-game-wardens.

Schmitt, K. A. (2017). These women are changing the face of the outdoors. *USA Today.* https://www.usatoday.com

/story/sports/2017/08/01/jennifer-drake-angie-reisch-cheryl-bowden/528032001/.

Sigler, W. F. (1980). The role of wildlife law enforcement. In W. F. Sigler (Ed.), *Wildlife law enforcement* (3rd ed., pp. 1–27). William C. Brown Publishers.

Silver, T. (1992). Outlaw gunners and hunting law in the English colonial south. *Transactions of the North American Wildlife and Natural Resources Conference, USA, 57,* 706–710.

Stockdale, M. (1993). English and American wildlife law: Lessons from the past. *Proceedings of the Southeastern Association of Fish and Wildlife Agencies, USA, 47,* 732–739.

Tobias, M. (1998). *Nature's keepers: On the front lines of the fight to save wildlife in America.* John Wiley & Sons Inc.

Trefethen, J. B. (1975). *An American crusade for wildlife.* Winchester Press.

Trench, C. C. (1965). Game preserves and poachers. *History Today, 15,* 259–268.

United States Fish and Wildlife Service (USFWS). (2013). Federal Aid in Sport Fish Restoration Act. https://www.fws.gov/laws/lawsdigest/FASPORT.html.

United States Fish and Wildlife Service (USFWS). (2018). USFWS History: A timeline for fish and wildlife conservation. https://training.fws.gov/history/USFWS-history.html.

United States Fish and Wildlife Service (USFWS). (2020). U.S. conservation laws. https://www.fws.gov/international/laws-treaties-agreements/us-conservation-laws/.

Walker, S. (1984). "Broken windows" and fractured history: The use and misuse of history in recent police patrol analysis. *Justice Quarterly, 1*(1), 75–90.

Walsh, D. (2020). *History of the law enforcement division.* New Hampshire Fish and Game. https://www.wildlife.state.nh.us/law-enforcement/history.html.

Warren, L. S. (1992). Poachers, conservationists, and ecosystems: Local struggles over American wildlife. *Transactions of the North American Wildlife and Natural Resources Conference, USA, 57,* 711–716.

Williams, G. W. (2005). *The USDA Forest Service—The first century.* US Department of Agriculture.

Wyoming Game Wardens Association (WGWA). (2020). *History of Wyoming wildlife law enforcement.* https://www.wyominggamewardens.com/history.php.

Three

THE CURRENT STATE OF CONSERVATION LAW ENFORCEMENT

Conservation Law Enforcement occurs at many levels, from international and transnational fusion center- and task force-type operations to extremely localized park rangers within an individual city. These law enforcement organizations also exist at varying levels in between, including the national, state, and county levels. Of course, the roles and responsibilities of conservation law enforcement agencies often differ, and a great deal of this diversity is a product of the geopolitical strata in which the organization operates. The following chapter will detail the current state of entities responsible for thwarting ecological harms, beginning with the international scene, and progressing stepwise into more locally operated agencies.

INTERNATIONAL LEVEL

Wildlife crime is an international issue, and therefore is addressed at an international level. While individual agencies, such as the United Nations and INTERPOL, operate at the international level, other countries outside of the United States in Asia, Africa, and Latin America have national, state, and localized agencies that address issues related to wildlife crime. The United Nations was founded in 1945 and is comprised of 193 member states (countries). The United Nations was founded as a body where countries from around the world can meet to discuss common problems and find solutions that benefit people across the world (United Nations, 2021). One of the global issues addressed by the United Nations is wildlife and forest crime through its Office on Drugs and Crime. The United Nations Office on Drugs and Crime (UNODC) focuses on illicit drugs and transnational organized crime. They are involved in wildlife crime due to organized crime groups participating in the trafficking of wildlife and natural resources products (CITES, 2021b). One way that wildlife and forest crime are addressed by the UNODC is through the Global Programme for Combating Wildlife and Forest Crime. While this office does not directly conduct law enforcement operations, they work to link regional efforts throughout the world and enhance capacity-building and wildlife law enforcement networks at the regional and sub-regional levels. They attempt to accomplish this through providing technical assistance in the form of legislative assistance, training, and providing equipment (UNODC, 2021a). This **technical assistance** is provided in support of the six thematic areas of the Global Programme: strengthening national legal frameworks; reducing supply and demand through alternative livelihoods; strengthening international cooperation among law enforcement agencies; strengthening national law enforcement, prosecutorial, and judiciary capacity; data gathering, analysis and reporting; and raising awareness and civil society empowerment (UNODC, 2021b).

The UNODC is also involved in thwarting international wildlife crime through the International Consortium on Combating Wildlife Crime (ICCWC). The ICCWC is also not a law enforcement agency but is comprised of five inter-governmental agencies that are working to provide coordinated support to national wildlife law enforcement agencies and to regional and sub-regional networks that directly combat wildlife crime. In addition to the UNODC, it is comprised of the Convention on International Trade in Endangered Species of Wild Fauna and Flora Secretariat (CITES), the International Criminal Police Organization (INTERPOL), the World Bank, and the World Customs Organization (WCO) (CITES, 2021a). While this may seem like an interesting group of agencies that are working together to address natural resources crime, each agency brings specific technical and programming expertise. CITES is involved because it is an international agreement between governments to ensure the international trade in wildlife and plants does not have a deleterious effect on their survival. It regulates the trade in over 37,000 species of animals and plants. INTERPOL is the world's largest international criminal police organization and provides support for any organization that is combatting international crime (INTERPOL will be discussed at length later in this chapter). The World Bank provides financial and technical assistance to developing countries around the world. They provide technical assistance related to money laundering and support investments to protect the environment and natural resources and promote rural economies. The WCO focuses exclusively on matters related to customs. They are responsible for developing global customs standards, simplifying and harmonizing customs procedures, facilitating international trade, protecting trade supply chains, and enhancing customs and compliance activities, as well as anti-counterfeiting and piracy initiatives, public-private partnerships, promoting integrity, and sustaining global customs capacity-building programs (CITES, 2021b).

In addition to the expertise each of them contributes to the consortium, they also have databases and secure communications networks that can be utilized by law enforcement agencies. These capabilities allow for information and intelligence to be disseminated to agencies quickly to support their law enforcement investigations. Additionally, the ICCWC members also assist in the facilitation and coordination of multi-national law enforcement operations that target the illegal trade and trafficking of natural resources both regionally and globally (CITES, 2021a). The ICCWC partners also produce a variety of different training opportunities, tool kits, and publications that can assist law enforcement agencies across the world to assess the extent of the wildlife trade issues in their respective country, address already known problems, and develop expertise in any number of issues related to transnational wildlife crime. They also produce the World Wildlife Crime reports that focus on the illicit trafficking of specific species of wildlife and plants and coordinate global meetings of national agencies responsible for wildlife crime to enhance collaboration and coordination between those agencies (CITES, 2021a).

As evidence of these efforts to provide support and assistance to national wildlife enforcement agencies, the ICCWC has participated in and coordinated several large-scale enforcement efforts such as Operation Thunderball in 2019 and Operation Thunderstorm in 2018. Operation Thunderball resulted in the identification of approximately 600 suspects in 109 countries. It also netted the seizure of 23 live primates, 30 big cats and numerous parts, 440 pieces of elephant tusks and an additional 545 kilograms of ivory, five rhinoceros horns, more than 4,300 birds, approximately 1,500 live reptiles and approximately 10,000 live turtles and tortoises, 7,700 other wildlife parts, 2,500 cubic meters of timber (74 truckloads), approximately 2,600 plants, and approximately 10,000 marine wildlife items, including coral, seahorses, dolphins, and sharks (INTERPOL, 2019).

Operation Thunderstorm occurred in 2018 and involved law enforcement officers in 92 countries and the identification of approximately 1,400 suspects. It resulted in the seizure of 43 metric tons (1 metric ton = approximately 2,200 pounds) of wild meat, 1.3 metric tons of elephant ivory, 27,000 reptiles, approximately 4,000 birds, several metric tons of wood and timber, 48 live primates, 14 big cats, the carcasses of 7 bears, and 8 metric tons of pangolin scales (CITES, 2021c).

International and Transnational Conservation Law Enforcement Agencies

Perhaps the best-known law enforcement agency that spans the geopolitical boundaries of nation-states is INTERPOL (INTERPOL, 2021b). INTERPOL is a politically neutral intergovernmental organization that provides intelligence information such as data on criminal offenders and offenses to law enforcement organizations within its 194 member countries and associated governmental entities. Through these mechanisms, INTERPOL is generally not out making individual arrests, but rather providing technical and operational support to police agencies operating within respective member nations.

Most commonly, INTERPOL is focused on combatting international issues such as terrorism, cybercrime, and organized crime. Given the challenges of any single individual nation-state in combatting these globalized crimes, INTERPOL can assist in data management and data sharing through its command and coordination centers. This provides for a conduit of information sharing within and between police agencies who are responsible for addressing the criminal activity. In addition to these responsibilities, INTERPOL also offers support in the areas of fugitive investigation, forensic analysis, criminal analysis, and capacity building and training (INTERPOL, 2021b).

Given their focus on assisting with criminal enterprises and crimes that extend beyond national borders, INTERPOL also addresses environmental crime with a similar approach to the more commonly known issues such as terrorism and cybercrime. Specifically, INTERPOL targets fisheries, forestry, pollution, and wildlife crimes by offering support to law enforcement. Frequently, this may take the form of investigation assistance when crimes or criminals are international in nature, as well as support in coordinating operations, and data sharing and analysis of criminal networks to dismantle their criminal organizations and operations (INTERPOL, 2021a).

The overarching group within INTERPOL that addresses environmental crimes is termed the Environmental Compliance and Enforcement Committee (ECEC). This group is comprised of executives within member countries, and this board is responsible for determining which environmental issues are trending or increasing, what harms or enforcement-related issues should take precedence, as well as serving as a generalized clearinghouse for police in member nations to share effective strategies in combatting environmental harms and crimes (INTERPOL, 2021a).

Within the ECEC, there are four working groups that target specific international criminal issues related to fishing (i.e., Fisheries Crime Working Group [FCWG]), forestry (i.e., Forestry Crime Working Group [FoCWG]), pollution (i.e., Pollution Crime Working Group [PCWG]), and wildlife (i.e., Wildlife Crime Working Group [WCWG]). Within these working groups, INTERPOL uses several strategies in order to fight crime, including task forces, often termed National Environmental Security Task Forces (or NEST), case meetings, investigative support teams, training, notices, and analytical support (INTERPOL, 2021a).

INTERPOL has become a preeminent organization in the ferreting out of illegal environmental activities, particularly as globalization increases, and the criminal enterprises that operate across borders become more complex. Illegal fishing is infinitely more complex than simply the captains of vessels and their respective crews operating in violation of fishing laws for personal economic gain. INTERPOL has identified that what they label **illegal, unreported, and unregulated (IUU) fishing** is often also associated with money laundering, labor exploitation, human trafficking, corruption, and forgery. These activities also bring in a host of characters outside of fishers, including politicians, lawyers, and accountants, as well as business owners and other executives (INTERPOL, 2021a).

Through their website, INTERPOL has claimed a number of successes as a result of their activities to combat IUU fishing. For example, INTERPOL maintains that their efforts have increased the awareness that policing organizations around the world have with respect to the existence and nature of fishing that occurs outside of regulatory requirements (INTERPOL, 2021a). INTERPOL has also provided enhanced operational capacity and intelligence through their "notices," which alert enforcement officials in affected countries of suspicious vessels and other associated illegal activities. Additionally, INTERPOL's FCWG has unraveled links between IUU fishing activities and other criminal offenses such as fraud, corruption, and tax evasion.

In addition to combatting IUU fishing, INTERPOL also addresses illegal timber harvesting, pollution, and wildlife crime. Much like with fishing, it is not simply the act of cutting trees that are not to be cut by individual timber harvesters that makes combatting timber crime so challenging. Illegal timber harvesting is also associated with a host of related offenses, including criminal, corrupt, and fraudulent behaviors that span the supply chain. At the outset, illegal activity may precede the actual harvest at the stage where loggers are seeking permits. For example, corrupt officials may be bribed to issue problematic logging permits or violate bid ethics, inspectors or enforcement may be bought off to ignore illegal harvests, transportation documents may be falsified, export or checkpoint inspectors may be bribed, and sawmills can mix legally and illegally sourced materials to hide illegal activities (INTER-POL, 2021a).

Again, INTERPOL cannot directly engage in enforcement activities, but rather provides support in the form of identifying behaviors of repeat offenders, trafficking routes, intelligence, and data sharing across borders, as well as training for law enforcement in Latin America, Asia, and Africa. Some of the operations of INTERPOL in these areas include providing strategic advice to officials in South America (e.g., Peru, Colombia, Brazil), West Africa, and Central America, as well as training enforcement officers in these areas. Across three operations (Amazonas II, Log, and Putumayo), officers seized approximately $168 million worth of illegal timber, as well as making 349 arrests (INTERPOL, 2021a).

INTERPOL also addresses environmental harms via its PCWG, which seeks to reduce the impact of illegal contamination on global health and wellness. Pollution is an area where INTERPOL is particularly well suited to assist in addressing the harms caused, as global inequality has created a vast market for acceptance of waste transfer from wealthier to more impoverished nation states, as well as to populations with less political efficacy within nation states (Gibbs et al., 2011; Pellow, 2007; White, 2008). Generally, wealthier nations have more stringent environmental protection laws.

Africa

Even though this book is primarily focused on conservation law enforcement in the United States, wildlife crime and trafficking are international problems. Because of the international nature of wildlife crime already discussed in this chapter, it is important to examine how conservation law enforcement is organized in other countries as well. This section will focus on responses to environmental threats in several countries found on the continent of Africa.

Africa is a continent that is rich in biodiversity and contains many of the animals and plants that are exploited by traffickers. Elephants, rhinoceros, and big cats are only a few of the animals that are native to Africa that are exploited in the illegal wildlife trade. Individual countries in Africa have law enforcement agencies that attempt to combat the exploitation of natural resources, but there is also an international focus on Africa as a whole due to the prevalence of African species in the illegal wildlife trade market (Horn of Africa Wildlife Enforcement Network [HAWEN], 2021). There is not space in this book to discuss the conservation law enforcement landscape in every country in Africa, so this section focuses specifically on areas of high concern in the international sphere, namely Kenya, Uganda, and South Africa. We also provide a less detailed discussion of the various cooperative agreements across the African continent.

Kenya

The **Kenya Wildlife Service** (KWS) is the main agency that is responsible for the protection of wildlife resources in Kenya. The KWS is responsible for the protection of wildlife both within and outside of the boundaries of protected areas. Approximately, eight percent of Kenya is designated as a protected area, such as a national park or a national reserve. Currently, there are twenty-three terrestrial national parks, twenty-eight terrestrial national reserves, four marine national parks, six marine national reserves, and four national sanctuaries. In addition to these parks and reserves, the KWS also maintains approximately 100 field stations and outposts outside of the protected areas. Within the parks, only tourism and research are allowed, while in reserves other activities such as fishing or firewood collecting are allowed (KWS, 2021a).

The Security Division is the department within the KWS that is charged with the protection of natural resources. There are four departments within the Security Division that contribute to the protection of natural resources, but the two main departments that deal directly with wildlife law enforcement are the Wildlife Protection Department and the Intelligence Department. The Wildlife Protection Department is the department that houses the line-level ranger units that are responsible for the daily law enforcement duties. They are responsible for not only the protection of the wildlife and its habitat, but also the security of visitors within the protected areas and other tourist activities that occur within the jurisdiction of the KWS. They conduct foot, vehicle, and aircraft patrols. Additionally, the Wildlife Protection Department also employs a canine unit that assists with wildlife enforcement. They also operate specialized units that are responsible for rapid deployment to emerging threats (KWS, 2021b).

The Intelligence Department is responsible for collecting and analyzing security-related information on wildlife, tourists, and other KWS resources. They surveil organized crime groups and other groups that participate in the illegal harvest and trafficking in wildlife. They also carry out investigations of wildlife crimes and illegal trade in wildlife and wildlife products and parts (KWS, 2021b).

Areas outside of the KWS are typically managed and protected by the specific county government overseeing the land (KWS, 2021a). Despite the county governments holding jurisdiction over these areas, most county governments work closely with the KWS, which helps to establish a county wildlife conservation committee. In 2019, the government of Kenya overhauled the locally operated Community Wildlife Conservation and Compensation Committees (CWCCC) through the Wildlife Conservation and Management Act after determining that the structure was not viable and the organizations were not meeting their prescribed functions (Laikipia Forum, 2019; *The Kenya Gazette*, 2019). Post-2019, the focus of managing natural resources shifted to the county level. The county boards are chaired by the county commissioner and have four representatives, one each from wildlife, agriculture, livestock, and medical backgrounds. Additionally, four at-large positions are filled by community members. Thus, these nine-person committees are then tasked with approving compensation structures and mitigating human-wildlife conflict. However, the funding structures that allow these boards to achieve their goals are unclear (Laikipia Forum, 2019; *The Kenya Gazette*, 2019).

One highly notable exception to the dominance of the KWS and associated County Wildlife Conservation Committees is the oversight of the Kenyan portions of the Serengeti-Mara Ecosystem bordering the Serengeti National Park of Tanzania. This ecosystem in the Kenyan rift valley is managed by two groups. The eastern portion is managed as the Maasai Mara National Reserve (MMNR) in Narok County, Kenya. The administration of this area is conducted by the Narok County Government. The MMNR is an area of global importance, as it represents a quarter of all wildlife in Kenya and serves as a migration corridor for animals such as wildebeests, gazelles, and zebras in and out of the Serengeti (Western et al., 2009). The western portion of the Kenyan-held area in this ecosystem became a National Game Reserve in 1948, which regulated hunting activity. In 1961, this area was brought under the authority of the Narok government. Today, this area of land, frequently referred to as the Mara Triangle, is managed by the Mara Conservancy, which is a non-profit organization (Allen et al., 2019; Watson, 2014). The Mara Conservancy operates contractually under the direction of the Narok County government, while the MMNR is operated directly by county staff (Watson, 2014).

Uganda

Uganda is an important country in Africa related to the illegal transportation and smuggling of wildlife. It has been recognized as a "hub" for traffickers, and the government has taken steps to attempt curbing the illegal flow of wildlife products through Uganda (Cakaj & Lezhnev, 2017). In addition to organized crime syndicates engaged in the smuggling of illegal wildlife, impoverished individuals may also illegally harvest animals for personal consumption or the bushmeat trade, making issues around justice somewhat unclear. Uganda is rich in biodiversity, and the Uganda Wildlife Authority (UWA) manages ten national parks, twelve wildlife reserves, five community wildlife management areas, and thirteen wildlife sanctuaries. Tourism is important, and activities such as savanna safaris, boat tours, forest hikes, mountain climbing, fishing, birdwatching, and wildlife research activities are all allowed within the parks (UWA, 2021). Uganda has both law enforcement rangers and an intelligence unit that works to combat the illegal trafficking in wildlife.

The main role of law enforcement rangers is to patrol the various protected areas and protect the natural resources within the park. They accomplish this through different types of patrols such as marine, aerial, and foot patrols. The most common method of patrol for these rangers is foot patrol. The type and duration of foot patrols may vary, as rangers may participate in routine day patrols, extended patrols, ambush patrols, emergency response, and trans-boundary patrols (Moreto & Matusiak, 2017). Routine day patrols are patrols that last one day and focus on a specific area. Extended patrols are similar to day patrols, but they are longer in duration. Ambush patrols occur when the rangers receive information of possible poaching activity, and they wait for the poachers in a particular location. Emergency patrols are used for situations that require an immediate response, and trans-boundary patrols include patrolling in conjunction with other agencies in other countries. Depending on the type and duration of the patrol, ranger activities could range from actively patrolling to conducting an investigation or passively observing an area (Moreto & Matusiak, 2017). In addition to law enforcement duties, law enforcement rangers may also conduct tourism tours, engage the local community in educational activities, and investigate nuisance wildlife issues near the park.

Uganda also has an investigative unit that participates in wildlife law enforcement. This division was established in 2013 and is responsible for gathering intelligence and conducting investigations. The investigative unit gathers security intelligence, operational intelligence, and criminal intelligence, and conducts reconnaissance. Large-scale investigations such as trafficking investigations would be conducted by the investigative unit (UWA, 2013).

Much like the Mara Triangle in Kenya, wildlife law enforcement in Uganda also benefits from public-private partnerships with non-governmental organizations (NGOs). One NGO that assists in conservation efforts from a law enforcement angle in Uganda is the Wildlife Conservation Society (WCS). The WCS has assisted the UWA in Uganda as early as 1957, when the organization bought an aircraft to assist in surveillance of the national parks. In 2000, the WCS established an official office in Uganda, which allowed the WCS to assist in information sharing across national borders in Africa. This assisted in the apprehension of poachers who were able to escape across borders into areas such as Virunga Park in the Democratic Republic of Congo (DRC) (WCS Uganda, 2021).

WCS has also added capacity to law enforcement and conservation efforts through the establishment of several databases. The WCS is currently developing a database focused on the identification of offenders, their areas of operation, and modus operandi. Additionally, the WCS has provided technical assistance such as evaluation of patrol methods and information technology to identify the movement of contraband such as ivory. Beyond law enforcement assistance, the WCS has also worked to develop databases that allow for the reporting of animal sightings in addition to monitoring the patterns of illegal wildlife poaching and trafficking (WCS Uganda, 2021).

Lusaka Agreement Task Force

The **Lusaka Agreement Task Force** was formed as part of the intergovernmental treaty the Lusaka Agreement on Cooperative Enforcement Operations Directed at Illegal Trade in Wild Fauna and Flora in Africa. The Lusaka Agreement was adopted in 1994 and was ratified in 1996. The Republic of Congo, Democratic Republic of the Congo , Kenya, Liberia, Tanzania, Uganda, Zambia, and the Kingdom of Lesotho are parties to the agreement and the Republics of South Africa, Ethiopia, and the Kingdom of Swaziland are signatories. The task force itself came into existence in 1999. The main purpose of the Task Force is to coordinate cooperation among the countries in investigations of the illegal trade in fauna and flora (Lusaka Agreement, 2020).

Horn of Africa Wildlife Enforcement Network

The Intergovernmental Authority on Development (IGAD) in Eastern Africa recognized that wildlife trade and trafficking in the Horn of Africa region was a significant problem and created the Horn of Africa Wildlife Enforcement Network (HAWEN) to coordinate wildlife trafficking law enforcement, provide a regional platform for information sharing, promote uniform enforcement standards and coordinate capacity building, training, and public outreach. Additionally, this network will coordinate with other wildlife enforcement networks and other organizations including the ICCWC. It will also assist in the implementation of the African Strategy on Combating Illegal Exploitation and Illegal Trade in Wild Fauna and Flora in Africa (IGAD, 2017). Members of HAWEN include Djibouti, Ethiopia, South Sudan, Eritrea, Kenya, Sudan, Somalia, and Uganda (HAWEN, 2021). Information sharing is an important component of wildlife enforcement networks, including HAWEN. The Trade in Wildlife Information Exchange (TWIX) is one platform that assists with facilitating information sharing among countries.

Trade in Wildlife Information Exchange (TWIX)

TWIX is maintained by a non-governmental organization known as TRAFFIC (a wildlife trade monitoring network) and is a centralized web-based platform that is designed to allow for information exchange and promote coordination and cooperation between law enforcement agencies that are responsible for combatting the illegal wildlife trade and implementing CITES. There are two main parts to TWIX—a website and a mailing list. The website maintains records of national, regional, and international wildlife seizures and various other resources such as training materials and a mailing list that allows law enforcement officials to communicate, collaborate, seek assistance, and alert others to enforcement actions. Officials eligible to participate in TWIX are those in customs, CITES, wildlife and forestry services, police, prosecutors, criminal justice departments, and international organizations such as INTERPOL and the World Customs Organization. (TRAFFIC, 2021). There are currently three TWIX networks in Africa.

The first is AFRICA-TWIX. It is implemented in seven central African countries—Cameroon, Congo, Gabon, Democratic Republic of the Congo, Central African Republic, Chad, and Rwanda. AFRICA-TWIX was utilized in investigations that resulted in the recovery of four tons of pangolin scales that were seized in Hong Kong, but originated in Cameroon, 7.3 tons of pangolin scales that were also seized in Hong Kong that originated in Nigeria, and 207.7 kilograms of ivory that were seized in Cameroon that were destined for Nigeria. It resulted in forty-two suspects from Nigeria, Togo, Cameroon, and Gabon being arrested. These are just a few examples of investigations that utilized AFRICA-TWIX (TRAFFIC, 2019).

SADC-TWIX was the second TWIX network to be established in Africa. It consists of 450 officials from twelve south African countries—Angola, Botswana, Eswatini, Lesotho, Madagascar, Malawi, Mauritius, Mozambique, Namibia, South Africa, Zambia, and Zimbabwe. Even though this network has only been in existence since late 2019 and early 2020, it has already resulted in collaborative investigations between customs agencies in Mauritius and Madagascar, officers in Namibia and Zambia, and another between Zimbabwean and Mozambican authorities (TRAFFIC, 2020).

The third TWIX network in Africa is Eastern Africa-TWIX, which consists of Kenya, Tanzania, and Uganda. This network is currently being established. Once this network is established, it is hoped that more nations that are part of HAWEN will become members of this network and expand its effectiveness and reach (TRAFFIC, 2021).

Asia

Asia and especially Southeast Asia are at the epicenter of the legal and illegal wildlife trade. Southeast Asia is not only a source of wildlife for the legal and illegal wildlife trade, but it is also a destination for wildlife and wildlife parts both legal and illegal. There are many reasons for the demand for wildlife in Southeast Asia, not the least of all that native species have been driven to extinction from over harvest and are being replaced by similar species from other parts of the world. There are numerous issues hindering enforcement efforts, such as corruption and a lack of coordination. These problems persist even though the ten countries in Southeast Asia, Brunei Darussalam, Cambodia, Indonesia, Lao PDR, Malaysia, Myanmar, Philippines, Singapore, Thailand, and Vietnam, are all members of CITES and the **Association of Southeast Asian Nations (ASEAN)** (Krishnasamy & Zacagli, 2020).

ASEAN Wildlife Enforcement Network

ASEAN has attempted to support the enforcement of CITES regulations and facilitate coordination and cooperation among member states through the creation of the ASEAN Wildlife Enforcement Network (ASEAN-WEN). ASEAN-WEN created an integrated network among law enforcement agencies and membership was open to CITES authorities, customs officials, police, prosecutors, specialized wildlife law enforcement agencies and any other related law enforcement agencies. This network allows for information sharing and coordination at both national and regional levels to combat the illegal trade in wildlife as well as to more effectively enforce CITES regulations throughout Southeast Asia. In addition to promoting coordination and information sharing among member nations, ASEAN-WEN will also participate in educational activities such as producing publications and other materials to raise awareness of wildlife crime and also produce training materials for law enforcement officers (ASEAN, 2021; CITES, 2014a).

South Asia Wildlife Enforcement Network

Another collaborative network established in Asia is the South Asia Wildlife Enforcement Network (SAWEN). SAWEN is a regional wildlife law enforcement network that is comprised of officials from eight countries—Afghanistan, Bangladesh, Bhutan, India, the Maldives,

Nepal, Pakistan, and Sri Lanka. This network has similar goals to other wildlife enforcement networks. It aims to promote cooperation and information sharing among member states. In addition, one of the goals of SAWEN is to promote the harmonization and standardization of policies and laws related to wildlife law enforcement in member countries and promote collaboration with regional and international agencies (SAWEN, 2021).

China

While not a part of a wildlife law enforcement network, China is important relative to the illegal wildlife trade. China represents one of, if not the, largest market for the importation of illegal wildlife parts, including bear gall bladders, turtles, birds, and pangolin scales. In addition to creating a market for both legal and illegal wildlife parts, China also serves as a source of illegal wildlife and parts (Krishnasamy & Zavagli, 2020). In an effort to combat the illegal wildlife trade in China, several ministries within the Chinese government, along with CITES, formed the National Inter-Agencies CITES Enforcement Coordination Group (NICECG). NICECG was established to increase interagency cooperation, coordination, and information sharing related to the enforcement of CITES regulations within China (TRAFFIC, 2011). It includes the Department of Wildlife Conservation and Nature Reserves Management; the Forest Public Bureau; Public Security Department under Ministry of Public Security; Bureau of Fisheries and Fisheries Law Enforcement under Ministry of Agriculture; Department of Customs Control and Inspection: Anti-smuggling Bureau under General Administration of Customs; Department of Supervision on Animal and Plant Quarantine under the General Administration of Quality Supervision, Inspection and Quarantine; the Headquarters of the China Coast Guard; and Department of Market Supervision and Inspection under State Post Bureau (CITES, 2016).

These wildlife enforcement networks have had some successes, as exemplified by Operation COBRA II. COBRA II involved officers from 28 countries and resulted in the seizure of 36 rhino horns, over 3 tons of elephant ivory, over 10,000 turtles, over 1,000 skins from protected species, over 10,000 European eels, and more than 200 tons of rosewood logs. This operation was conducted by members of the

Lusaka Agreement Task Force and NICECG, as well as officials from the United States, South Africa, ASEAN-WEN, and SAWEN. In addition to the large number of seizures, over 400 people were arrested. This operation was expansive and was made possible due to the information sharing and coordination in place within and between the various wildlife enforcement networks (CITES, 2014b).

UNITED STATES

Federal Level

Conservation law enforcement at the federal level in the United States is conducted by numerous federal agencies. The commonly known agencies usually include the United States Fish and Wildlife Service (USFWS), National Park Service (NPS), and the United States Forest Service (USFS). However, numerous other agencies also participate in conservation law enforcement, such as the Bureau of Land Management (BLM), National Oceanic and Atmospheric Administration (NOAA), and the United States Coast Guard (USCG).

Far and away, the most well-known agency at the federal level that participates in conservation law enforcement is the USFWS. The Office of Law Enforcement is the division within the USFWS that houses conservation law enforcement officers. The overall duties of the Office of Law Enforcement include investigating wildlife crimes, regulating wildlife trade, educating the American public about wildlife laws and their importance, and partnering with international, state, and tribal agencies to enforce regulations concerning wildlife. They participate in activities such as investigating international wildlife smuggling rings, preventing the unlawful commercial exploitation of protected species, enforcing federal migratory bird hunting regulations, inspecting wildlife shipments, and distributing information and educational materials (USFWS, 2013a).

There are two main types of conservation law enforcement officers that are employed by the USFWS Office of Law Enforcement, namely special agents and wildlife inspectors. At full strength, there are 261 special agents and 140 wildlife inspectors employed by the USFWS. In addition to these law enforcement officers, the Office of Law Enforcement also oversees the **Clark R. Bavin National Fish and Wildlife**

Forensics Laboratory, the National Wildlife Property Repository, and the National Eagle Repository (USFWS, 2013a).

USFWS special agents are the face of conservation law enforcement at the federal level in the United States. They are plainclothes criminal investigators who are responsible for enforcing federal wildlife laws throughout the United States, as well as protecting threatened and endangered species, migratory birds, marine mammals, and other vulnerable plants and animals throughout the world. Because they are responsible for enforcing federal wildlife laws throughout the United States, special agents are stationed throughout the country from the most urban to the most rural settings. Special agents are assigned to locations such as New York City, Los Angeles, or Miami, and there may even be multiple special agents stationed in these urban environments. In other locations, such as less populous regions, a single special agent may be responsible for an entire state (USFWS, 2013b).

Special agents investigate a wide variety of crimes ranging from international wildlife smuggling to the illegal hunting of migratory game birds. For example, agents may be tasked with investigating the killing of endangered species or other protected wildlife. Additionally, special agents also have the capacity to support species reintroduction programs and prosecute those participating in habitat destruction or contamination, investigate chemical spills and poisonings that kill wildlife, and work with industries and companies to reduce potential hazards to wildlife. Some of their work requires the use of covert tactics to infiltrate wildlife trafficking rings, illegal guiding operations, and other types of criminal organizations and groups. Some of these covert operations are simple buying transactions, not unlike the drug buys that are ubiquitously used by conventional police. Alternatively, other investigations span multiple years and require the establishment of false identities and businesses to gain the confidence of the targets of the investigation (USFWS, 2013b).

In addition to working individually, special agents also collaborate with other federal, state, tribal, or foreign law enforcement agencies. They commonly work with the US Customs and Border Protection or Department of Homeland Security on wildlife smuggling cases, or with the Environmental Protection Agency on oil or chemical spills or pesticides. They assist state-level agencies with the enforcement of regulations concerning migratory game birds such as mourning doves or waterfowl as well as with cases that involve the exploitation of wildlife across state lines. Their work with tribal authorities occurs when wildlife crimes span both federal and tribal laws and regulations (USFWS, 2013b).

One example of the type of covert investigations in which special agents participate is Operation Renegade. Operation Renegade focused on the illegal smuggling of parrots, macaws, and eggs into the United States. It uncovered a smuggling operation that involved Africa, South America, New Zealand, Australia, Mexico, Los Angeles, Chicago, and New York (US Department of Justice [USDOJ], 2020; Tobias, 1998). One part of the investigation focused on a smuggling ring that was bringing cockatoo eggs into the United States from Australia. The eggs were collected from the wild in Australia and then smuggled into the United States. The offspring from these eggs were then sold in the United States under the guise that they had been legally raised by breeders in captivity. More than 800 eggs worth more than $1.5 million dollars were smuggled during the time of the operation. The main person responsible was sentenced to five years in prison (USDOJ, 2020).

The other prong of the investigation centered on the illegal trade of parrots between Mexico, Central and South America, and the United States. The parrot trade is highly regulated not only because of the negative repercussions it can have on the native population numbers of parrots, but also because of the possibility of disease transmission, most notably Newcastle Disease (USDOJ, 2020; Tobias, 1998). An elaborate smuggling scheme was created whereby a supplier in Argentina would sell to another person in Paraguay, who then would ship them to Mexico. Once in Mexico, they would be shipped to Chicago. Upon arriving in Chicago, the illegally imported birds were co-mingled by one of the conspirators with birds that were legally imported, at the quarantine station. However, Chicago was not the only place that received smuggled birds. Birds were also being imported into San Diego, Los Angeles, and Miami. During the investigation, the importer in Chicago quit the bird business and was no longer involved in the scheme. However, other conspirators were soon found, and the smuggling continued. In addition to the hundreds of birds that were smuggled into the United States, other animals, such as golden lion tamarins, white-faced marmosets, and wooly spider monkeys were also smuggled into the United States. In the end, multiple arrests were made, and the ringleader pled guilty to a broad felony charge of the conspiracy to commit wildlife smuggling and filing a false tax return. Another conspirator also pled guilty to filing a false tax return. It seems that those involved in this smuggling ring did not properly report their income to the Internal Revenue Service (Tobias, 1998).

Other times, special agents will assist state-level agencies in their investigations. In Missouri, a state-level conservation agent enlisted the help of special agents to assist with his investigation into possible poaching activity. The suspected poacher was a real estate agent who specialized in hunting properties, so two special agents (a male and female pretending to be married) assumed the role of interested real estate buyers. Over the course of two days, the agents were able to gather enough evidence to apply for search warrants. The suspect and his son had poached 287 deer, 300 wild turkeys, and other wildlife in Missouri in addition to four bighorn sheep, 19 pronghorn antelope, four elk, squirrels, prairie dogs, and other wildlife in Wyoming, Montana, and Alaska. Two of the bighorn sheep were killed in Glacier National Park and at least one elk was killed in Yellowstone National Park (Tobias, 1998). Some of these animals had been brought across state lines, which is a violation, and had been transported across federal property, such as that owned or administered by the National Park Service. In the end, the father paid tens of thousands of dollars in fines and spent 21 months in a federal prison for the felony charges and 12 months for the misdemeanor charges to run concurrently with the felony confinement. The son was found guilty of four misdemeanor counts and spent six months in confinement and was ordered to undergo psychological evaluation and treatment (Tobias, 1998).

In addition to special agents, the USFWS also has wildlife inspectors that perform conservation law enforcement duties. Wildlife inspectors are import/export control officers that specialize in the illegal wildlife trade. Their job is to inspect shipments containing wildlife or wildlife products that are entering the United States through established ports, airports, and border crossings. By law, most wildlife shipments must enter the country through one of eighteen specific ports. The ports include Anchorage (AK), Atlanta (GA), Baltimore (MD), Boston (MA), Chicago (IL), Dallas/Fort Worth (TX), Honolulu (HI), Houston (TX), Los Angeles (CA), Louisville (KY), Memphis (TN), Miami (FL), New Orleans (LA), New York (NY), Newark (NJ), Portland (OR), San Francisco (CA), and Seattle (WA). In addition to these designated ports of entry, wildlife inspectors are also assigned to the Mexican and Canadian borders and other ports that are designated to receive specific types of wildlife (USFWS, 2019).

Notably, the United States is one of the largest markets in the world for not only live wildlife, but also items manufactured from wildlife parts, such as boots and jewelry, as well as other, less processed, items such as hunting trophies, furs, and shells. Wildlife inspectors must understand and enforce federal and international laws, treaties, and regulations that govern the commercial trade in wildlife. As they check shipments, inspectors must identify thousands of different species of plants and animals, not only alive, but also those which have been manufactured into a variety of different products. In addition to commercial shipments, wildlife inspectors must also be aware of possible wildlife souvenirs that passengers may either knowingly or unknowingly bring back into the United States from abroad. They work closely with special agents as well as other federal agencies that regulate international trade (USFWS, 2019).

In addition to special agents and wildlife inspectors, the USFWS also employs another type of conservation officer that is responsible for national refuges, called federal wildlife officers. Federal wildlife officers are responsible for law enforcement duties on the approximately 560 National Wildlife Refuges and 38 wetland management areas that encompass approximately 850 million acres. They occupy more of what would be considered a traditional role of conservation officer than special agents or wildlife inspectors. Federal wildlife officers enforce hunting and fishing regulations on federal refuges in addition to providing traditional police responses to crimes on the refuge. They also provide educational programming to refuge visitors, assist refuge biologists with population surveys, conduct search and rescue operations, and partner with state conservation officers on law enforcement operations (USFWS, 2018).

National Park Service

The NPS is another federal agency that employs officers that participate in natural resources law enforcement. There are two main types of officers within the NPS, park rangers and special agents. The NPS is an interesting agency in that not all park rangers are law enforcement officers. Park rangers in the NPS can carry out a wide variety of roles, including interpretation and education. However, this discussion will focus on NPS rangers who have law enforcement responsibilities in US national parks. There are approximately 1,300 full-time law enforcement park rangers stationed throughout the national park system. The NPS also employs seasonal park rangers that carry out law enforcement duties. These seasonal officers are typically hired during the summer months. In addition to the 1,300 park rangers, there are also approximately 33 special agents employed by the NPS (DeSantis, 2020).

Park rangers are responsible for all law enforcement within the boundaries of the national park. They are responsible for patrolling the park grounds for violations of federal laws, regulations, and policies. Depending on the park to which they are assigned, this may include extremely rugged and backcountry areas. Rangers are known for participating in community-oriented policing and investigating traditional legal violations such as assault, in addition to natural resources violations such as poaching. They are also responsible for responding to any emergencies within the park, which could include medical emergencies, search and rescue missions, or fire suppression. Rangers assist other park staff by participating in resource management efforts such as population surveys, performing routine maintenance work such as vehicle maintenance or brush removal, and also conducting educational programming and other outreach for park visitors. If the investigations are complex, or will require an extended amount of time, they will refer those investigations to the Investigative Service unit (NPS, 2015; USAJOBS, 2021).

The NPS also employs special agents that serve as criminal investigators. These special agents conduct criminal investigations into a wide variety of crimes that occur within the national parks, including crimes of violence, property crimes, fraud, embezzlement, major resource violations, and drug cultivation. These investigations can be conducted overtly or covertly (NPS, 2019).

U.S. Forest Service

The USFS is another federal agency that employs natural resources law enforcement officers. Their main job is to enforce federal laws and regulations that govern the National Forest System and resources, under the US Department of Agriculture (USDA). There are two types of law enforcement officers that work for the USFS—uniformed law enforcement officers and special agents. The uniformed law enforcement officers are responsible for the day-to-day law enforcement duties within the national forest system (USFS, 2021), which encompasses 193 million acres (USDA, 2021).

Because of the vastness of the national forest system, USFS law enforcement officers are responsible for a wide range of enforcement responsibilities. In areas that have sites of archeological importance, officers are responsible for protecting those resources from collectors or treasure hunters. Investigating timber theft is also an important aspect of their job. As identified in their name, most of the area that is patrolled by USFS law enforcement officers is forested, so investigating timber theft is an important aspect of their job. The enforcement of fish and wildlife regulations are also an important part of their duties. The lands owned by the USFS are public areas that are generally open to hunting and fishing. In addition to these duties, they also conduct vehicle accident investigations, enforce traffic laws on forest service roads, investigate wildfires, investigate controlled substance distribution and manufacture, and provide emergency medical aid when needed. In addition, they assist USFS special agents with investigations and work closely with other federal, state, and local law enforcement officials on a variety of law enforcement concerns including search and rescue missions (USFS, 2021).

In addition to regular uniformed law enforcement officers, the USFS also employs special agents. Special agents are generally plainclothes officers who conduct investigations that are too complex for a regular uniformed officer to conduct efficiently. They work collaboratively with other federal, state, local, and tribal law enforcement agencies on investigations such as those that involve drug trafficking or domestic terrorism. Other types of investigations could include illegal guiding and outfitting on national forest property, theft of government property, timber theft, wildfire origins, manufacture and distribution of controlled substances, and assaults on federal employees or volunteers. While some of these investigations may be conducted overtly, some may require undercover and surveillance operations. There are fewer investigators than uniformed law enforcement officers, with one investigator being assigned to each of the nine geographic units (USFS, 2021).

Bureau of Land Management

The BLM also has law enforcement officers that participate in natural resources protection. The BLM is responsible for the management of approximately 245 million acres of public land and 700 million acres of subsurface minerals and employs approximately 200 uniformed law enforcement officers, known as law enforcement rangers, and 70 special agents, who serve as criminal investigators. The areas managed by the BLM are generally located in the Western United States and Alaska and encompass a wide variety of landscapes, including grasslands, forests, mountains, arctic tundra, and desert. While the responsibility of the BLM rangers is the enforcement of federal laws on those areas, the types of violations and activities within which they participate will vary considerably depending on the areas to which they are assigned. For example, the officers assigned to the desert in the southwestern portion of the United States will deal with very different activities than would someone stationed in Alaska. Regardless of where the ranger is stationed, they are responsible for the protection of the timber, forage, and energy and mineral resources as well as recreation areas, wild horse and burro populations, fish and wildlife habitat, wilderness areas, national monuments, and archeological and paleontological sites. Like other federal officers, BLM rangers and special agents work closely with other federal, state, and local law enforcement agencies to investigate crimes such as wildland arson, mineral resource theft, hazardous material dumping, archeological and paleontological theft, and illegal marijuana cultivation (BLM, 2021).

Special agents are typically plainclothes officers that conduct investigations into criminal violations that occur on BLM managed lands that are too complex for a regular BLM ranger to conduct (DeSantis, 2020). For example, a BLM special agent partnered with a special agent from the Internal Revenue Service to conduct a multi-year investigation into a drug ring that resulted in the seizure of 53 pounds of methamphetamine, 26 kilograms of cocaine, 20,000 marijuana plants that were growing on BLM lands, two kilograms of heroin, and a kilogram of fentanyl. Additionally, $300,000, ten vehicles, and 40 firearms were seized. The investigation resulted in 26 people being convicted for crimes such as drug trafficking, money laundering, and firearms offenses (BLM, 2019).

National Oceanic and Atmospheric Administration

Another federal agency that has officers who participate in natural resources protection is the NOAA. The Office of Law Enforcement within NOAA consists of enforcement officers and special agents and is responsible for conserving and protecting the United States' marine resources and marine habitat. NOAA's jurisdiction includes ocean waters between three and 200 miles offshore and adjacent to all U.S. states and territories, which includes 3.36 million square miles of open ocean, more than 95,000 miles of coastline, 14 national marine sanctuaries and five marine national monuments (NOAA, 2021).

NOAA officers conduct patrols both on and off the water, electronically monitor vessels, conduct criminal and civil investigations, and partner with state, tribal, and federal entities and NGOs. NOAA officers also conduct outreach to industry and aid in getting various stakeholders to remain compliant with federal regulations. They enforce more than 40 laws that protect marine life and habitat as well as international treaty requirements. Examples of specific laws they enforce include the Magnuson-Stevens Fishery Conservation and Management Act, the Marine Mammal Protection Act, the Endangered Species Act, and the Lacey Act (NOAA, 2021).

To assist them in their law enforcement duties, NOAA officers utilize the Vessels Monitoring System (VMS) to monitor for compliance, track violators, and collect evidence. The VMS employs a satellite surveillance system that tracks and monitors the location and movements of commercial fishing vessels. It monitors approximately 4,000 vehicles and operates 24 hours a day, seven days a week. Vessels are required to carry an onboard transceiver unit that sends location data once per hour unless it is approaching an environmentally sensitive area. The signals increase in frequency as the vessel approaches those areas (NOAA, 2021).

Domestic and international partnerships are important to assist NOAA enforcement officers in their mission to protect marine resources. Domestic partnerships are managed through the Cooperative Enforcement Program. Partnerships with state and U.S. territorial marine conservation officers are managed through Cooperative Enforcement Agreements, which allow those officers to enforce federal laws and regulations. Joint Enforcement Agreements are also included in this program, and they include a formal operations plan that transfers funding to state and territorial agencies to perform law enforcement services that support federal regulations. These partnerships provide for a greater officer presence, increased officer visibility, and increased interactions with commercial fishermen (NOAA, 2021).

NOAA also forges international partnerships. The United States imports approximately 90% of the seafood that is consumed domestically, so NOAA must work with international partners to maintain regulatory compliance. As part of this enforcement, NOAA enforces international laws, treaties, and agreements. In addition to providing technical expertise and training to other countries, international agreements are important for the regulation of IUU fishing. IUU fishing is very difficult to combat without the help of international partners. The Office of Law Enforcement partners with INTERPOL in their Fisheries Crime Working Group. In addition to information sharing within this group, NOAA also actively participates in coordinated operations with other countries through this group. They also partner with Canada and Mexico. Because these are neighboring countries, NOAA officers will conduct joint enforcement operations with officers from these countries. They also have agreements with the European Union and Russia to share information and combat IUU fishing and the trafficking in those products (NOAA, 2021).

United States Coast Guard

While not traditionally thought of as a conservation law enforcement agency, the USCG participates in natural resources protection through its enforcement of laws and regulations related to IUU fishing, often in partnership with NOAA. They achieve this through three efforts: promoting targeted, effective, intelligence-driven enforcement operations, countering predatory and irresponsible state behavior, and expanding multilateral fisheries enforcement cooperation. The first effort is important because those participating in IUU activities have shown they are able to readily adapt to enforcement efforts and are becoming more technologically sophisticated. As a member of the intelligence community, the USCG is well suited to the accomplishment of this first effort. They have the capability to collect intelligence, analyze it, and disseminate it. This information sharing is important to other agencies that also participate in combatting IUU fishing. Predatory and irresponsible nations are those that attempt to manipulate fisheries markets through their aggressive economic policies, create instability around the globe, and expand their own power at the expense of other nations. The USCG promotes partnerships with nations at risk from these nations and confronts these nations and their corrupt and illegal operations. Sometimes these types of operations involve more than fishing to include the illegal trade in weapons and drugs or human trafficking. The final effort is to expand multilateral fisheries enforcement cooperation. The United States is party to international agreements for the management of transboundary and migratory fish populations. The USCG is the main agency that enforces and monitors compliance with these agreements. They work alongside other nations to ensure adherence to these agreements (USCG, 2020). While the mission of the USCG certainly is much broader than simply fisheries enforcement, they play an important role (often in conjunction with NOAA) in the enforcement of fisheries regulations on the oceans. This partnership with NOAA is exemplified by joint operations between the USCG and NOAA, where multiple fishermen were cited with Lacey Act violations for fishing in Bahamian waters without the proper permits and then transporting the fish back into waters under the jurisdiction of the United States (*Homeland Security Today*, 2021).

State-Level Agencies in the US

While there are many law enforcement officers employed throughout the world, and at the federal level in the United States, most fish and wildlife law enforcement in the United States is done by state-level conservation officers (Falcone, 2004). In the United States, the development of both criminal law and management of fish and wildlife has operated at the state level of government. In fact, while the federal government has control of vast areas of land through conservation agencies such as the NPS, USFS, and BLM, states retain ownership of wildlife on those lands within their borders. The state-level employ of conservation law enforcement is expansive, with Patten and colleagues (2015) estimating that there are as many as 6,000 sworn officers in the US, and that all 50 states have some type of conservation law enforcement agency. Due to extensive coverage of state conservation officers elsewhere in this book, as well as several other research contributions (Falcone, 2004; Tobias, 1998), we choose to focus on other state-level entities engaging in natural resources protection.

Park Rangers

Similar to the capacities of law enforcement working for the NPS, many states also employ **park rangers** to assist in the protection and public enjoyment of natural resources. In states such as Michigan, park rangers occupy some of the most expansive roles in the law enforcement community. Given the quite limited size of most state parks, rangers get tasked with handling many different issues. For example, rangers may be tasked with search and rescue of lost or injured hikers, grooming hiking and skiing trails, cleaning vault toilets, picking up litter, repairing plumbing, writing tickets for illegal activities (such as noncompliance with permits), or even making arrests (Gwizdz, n.d.). Some state parks employ no park rangers, while others may employ several. Staffing is usually dependent upon the size and service demands placed upon each individual park (Gwizdz, n.d.).

In perhaps the most extensive and highly trained park ranger organization operating at a state level, the Missouri State Park Rangers are fully commissioned, state-certified police officers, and have full police authority on any lands that are under the auspices of the Missouri DNR (Missouri Department of Natural Resources, 2021). Missouri State Park Rangers are full-time employees, contrary to many other states who employ rangers as part-time or seasonal workers. Rangers attend a certified training academy and operate as the police agency for all state parks.

City/County-Level Agencies

In addition to state-level protection of natural resources, local governments may also establish local law enforcement entities that specifically engage in the protection of natural resources. Generally, the formation of a specific law enforcement agency focused on natural resource protection at the local level is confined to large municipalities with important natural features, such as expansive parks. Naturally, in the United States, localities such as the City of New York come to mind. In total, the city operates over 29,000 acres of greenspace, in addition to 14 miles of beaches, as well as stadiums, ice rinks, and golf courses. The City of New York does in fact have a dedicated Parks Enforcement Patrol (PEP), and all PEP officers are New York State-certified peace officers. These officers have authority to make arrests and issue summonses (NYC Parks, 2021). PEP officers have a mandate for outreach, seeking to educate the public on proper use of city park property, such as playgrounds, beaches, marinas, recreation centers, and other common-use property managed by the parks. Additionally, the Parks Enforcement Patrol maintains order by controlling crowds associated with special events (e.g., concerts, parades), preventing and responding to illegal dumping, and assisting with medical concerns. Furthermore, the PEP take responsibility for directing at-risk persons (e.g., the unhoused) using the park to social services (e.g., homeless shelters, permanent housing) that may be of assistance (Local 983, 2021). To meet these demands, the PEP maintains harbor patrols, a mounted unit, and a search and rescue team.

PEP officers are not the only certified law enforcement employees to work in NYC Parks. The city also has a group of employees titled as urban park rangers (UPRs). The UPR job title encompasses both the PEP, as well as those titled specifically as Urban Park Rangers (Local 983, 2021). UPRs primarily focus on outreach, seeking to get New Yorkers to connect to the environment. They seek to educate residents about outdoor recreation opportunities, history, flora, fauna, and even astronomy. UPRs host school field trips, family events, camping programs, and summer camps and even operate the city nature centers. They also assist injured wild animals, particularly raptors and other birds of prey, to appropriate wildlife rehabilitation centers. Much like their PEP counterparts, PEP patrol the parks in marked police vehicles and are New York State-certified peace officers, and New York City

Special Patrolmen. Unlike PEP officers, UPR are primarily outreach focused, and the law enforcement aspects of their job are generally secondary. In total, the numbers of UPR and PEP officers have been as high as 450 officers in the 1990s, but continuous budget cuts have reduced the number of officers drastically (Local 983, 2021).

In addition to the sworn PEP and UPR officers, the New York City Urban Park Service also enlists the help of both city security workers and local volunteers. Along with PEP officers, the city employs a Parks Security Service (PSS), which is comprised of seasonal security guards who work in the protection of the parks. Unlike PEP officers, PSS employees are not certified police officers, but rather public employees who help protect the parks while learning the skills necessary for employment in private security (NYC Parks, 2021).

Beyond these paid public security employees, the PEP also maintains a volunteer contingent of mounted auxiliary officers. Auxiliary mounted patrol officers wear uniforms and use horses maintained by the parks to deter or observe and report illegal or unsafe actions to the PEP, police, fire, or other emergency services. In order to qualify, volunteers must pass a riding and grooming evaluation, as well as an in-field evaluation, and then pass a six-week academy that meets three hours per week. Mounted Auxiliary officers are required to volunteer a minimum of 48 hours annually, as well as purchasing a ticket to the Parks Gala, selling tickets to the Gala, donating auction prizes, and volunteering at the event (NYC Parks, 2021).

In other cities, rangers ensure compliance with park rules and regulations but are not certified police officers, and do not carry arrest authority. For example, Denver, Colorado, park rangers have authority to issue citations for violations of park rules (City of Denver, 2021). They also assist fire departments and the police when emergency responses are necessary. Outside of this, their function is quite aligned with New York's PEP. Other cities have struggled with how much authority to give their rangers, with opponents arguing that arrests and firearms are not compatible with local outdoor recreation, while proponents of keeping arrest authority argue that local police are often understaffed and not able to effectively make arrests in situations where rangers are better equipped to address the issues (Manzano, 2000).

CONCLUSION

As detailed in this chapter, responsibilities for protection of natural resources and prevention of harm to the environment run the gamut and are highly specialized to the uses of the landscape by the local inhabitants. International organizations, which operate at the most expansive geopolitical level, generally seek to prevent harm to resources held in the common interest, such as open ocean fisheries and pollution of water and air. Additionally, environmental law enforcement at the international level focuses on crimes that cross borders, such as the poaching of migratory species and trafficking of wildlife. Furthermore, these organizations also focus on protection of locations and species that are recognized as having global significance, such as the parks and preserves of Africa (many of the protected preserves and parks that international organizations take an interest in are recognized as world heritage sites). International organizations, particularly those supported by donations and tourism, also have a penchant for focusing on protection of charismatic megafauna. It is also apparent that international organizations step in when a nation is struggling with the capacity to protect its own valuable natural resources.

National organizations take on some of these responsibilities as well. Certainly, organizations at the federal level in the United States focus on protection of federal public lands, nationally significant species, as well as ensuring that the US upholds its responsibility as a member state of CITES. This is certainly evident as the mission of other national environmental protection agencies throughout the world, such as those present in much of Africa and Asia.

Unsurprisingly, the majority of conservation law enforcement activity in the United States takes place at the state level. Most criminal statutes in the US are at the state level, and most fish and wildlife are managed by state agencies. Given this reality, large portions of this book focus on state conservation law enforcement in great detail. It is sufficient to say that states are the primary conservation law enforcement presence in the United States.

Finally, local governments also engage in protection of natural resources, but the avenues they choose are far more outreach and educationally focused, as opposed to law enforcement focused. Even in localities where city or county park police have arrest authority, ensuring compliance with rules and laws is primarily conceptualized as an educational endeavor as opposed to a legalistic approach. In this essence, park police may really be the quintessential community policing officers that are so elusive in nearly every other law enforcement organization. Park rangers have an extremely broad role (e.g., educational outreach, park programming, maintenance of park facilities, first aid, addressing litter) compared to international organizations, which are often singularly focused (i.e., reduction of poaching). This process tracks along with the role conception and geopolitics found in conventional police organizations. Overall, conservation law enforcement occurs at virtually every level of government, and the roles of these organizations are strongly coupled to the demands placed upon them.

DISCUSSION QUESTIONS

1. Natural resources law enforcement at the federal level in the United States involves multiple agencies within separate organizations. Is this the most efficient arrangement for natural resources law enforcement? If not, how could it be organized more efficiently? If so, why is this the best arrangement?

2. There is an important international component to combatting the illegal trade and trafficking in wildlife and other natural resources. Multiple agencies are involved as well as task forces that are spread throughout the world. Is this the best way to address the illegal trade and trafficking of wildlife and natural resources? If not, what would be a better arrangement? Is so, why is the best method for addressing the illegal trade and trafficking in wildlife and natural resources?

Key Terms

ASEAN: An association of Southeast Asian nations that seeks to initiate economic growth, promote peace, share training and research resources, and maintain international cooperation.

Clark R. Bavin National Fish and Wildlife Forensics Laboratory: Forensic crime lab operated by the USFWS that identifies animals and animal parts, determines animal cause of death, assist in determinations of illegal activities, and utilizes physical evidence to link suspects, victims, and crime scenes.

IUU fishing: Fishing activity that violates the laws and regulations of a government entity, that is not reported to the relevant authorities, or that occurs in areas that are unregulated and are inconsistent with international law.

Kenya Wildlife Service (KWS): A state corporation operating with the goal to provide management and conservation of wildlife in Kenya.

Lusaka Agreement Task Force: An inter-governmental organization focused on creating cooperation among member states to investigate illegal trade in flora and fauna.

Park ranger: Person who is entrusted with the protection of the environment within a park, as well as outreach, education, programming, and mitigation of human-wildlife conflict within a park. These individuals may or may not be sworn officers with arrest authority.

Technical assistance: Help provided to an organization that does not directly involve doing the labor of the organization. Examples might include policy briefs and analysis, needs assessments, outcome evaluations, training, or organizational development.

References

Allen, L., Holland, K. K., Holland, H., Tomé, S., Nabaala, M., Seno, S., & Nampushi, J. (2019). Expanding staff voice in protected area management effectiveness assessments within Kenya's Maasai Mara National Reserve. *Environmental Management*, *63*, 46–59.

Association of Southeast Asian Nations (ASEAN). (2021). The ASEAN Wildlife Enforcement Network (ASEAN-WEN). https://environment.asean.org/the-asean-wildlife-enforcement-network-asean-wen/.

Bureau of Land Management (BLM). (2019, April 3). *BLM-California special agent recognized for investigative excellence.* https://

www.blm.gov/blog/2019-04-03/blm-california-special-agent-recognized-investigative-excellence.

Bureau of Land Management (BLM). (2021). Law enforcement. https://www.blm.gov/programs/public-safety-and-fire/law-enforcement.

Cakaj, L., & Lezhnev, S. (2017). *Deadly profits: Illegal wildlife trafficking through Uganda and South Sudan.* The Enough Project. https://enoughproject.org/wp-content/uploads/2017/07/DeadlyProfits_July2017_Enough_final_web-1.pdf.

City of Denver. (2021). Park rangers. https://www.denvergov.org/Government/Agencies-Departments-Offices/Parks-Recreation/Parks/Park-Rangers.

Convention on International Trade in Endangered Species of Wild Fauna and Flora (CITES). (2014a). *ASEAN launches the ASEAN Wildlife Law Enforcement Network (ASEAN-WEN).* https://cites.org/eng/news/sundry/2005/ASEAN-WEN.shtml.

Convention on International Trade in Endangered Species of Wild Fauna and Flora (CITES). (2014b). *African, Asian and North American law enforcement officers team up to apprehend wildlife criminals.* https://cites.org/sites/default/files/eng/news/sundry/2014/operation_cobra_ii_pr.pdf.

Convention on International Trade in Endangered Species of Wild Fauna and Flora (CITES). (2016). National Inter-agency CITES Enforcement Coordination Group of People's Republic of China (NICECG). https://cites.org/sites/default/files/eng/prog/iccwc/WENs/NICECG-info_sheet_Sept16.pdf.

Convention on International Trade in Endangered Species of Wild Fauna and Flora (CITES). (2021a). The International Consortium on Combating Wildlife Crime. https://cites.org/eng/prog/iccwc_new.php.

Convention on International Trade in Endangered Species of Wild Fauna and Flora (CITES). (2021b). ICCWC partners. https://cites.org/eng/prog/iccwc/partners.php.

Convention on International Trade in Endangered Species of Wild Fauna and Flora (CITES). (2021c). *Month-long transcontinental operation hit wildlife criminals hard.* https://cites.org/eng/news/month-long-trans-continental-operation-hit-wildlife-criminals-hard_20062018.

DeSantis, M. K. (2020). *Department of the Interior (DOI) law enforcement programs.* Congressional Research Service (CRS). https://crsreports.congress.gov/product/pdf/IF/IF11709/2.

Falcone, D. (2004). America's conservation police: Agencies in transition. *Policing: An International Journal of Police Strategies and Management, 27*(1), 56–66.

Gibbs, C., McGarrell, E. F., Axelrod, M., & Rivers III, L. (2011) Conservation criminology and the global trade in electronic waste: Applying a multi-disciplinary research framework. *International Journal of Comparative and Applied Criminal Justice, 35*(4), 269–291. http://www.doi.org/10.1080/01924036.2011.625229.

Gwizdz, B. (n.d.). State park rangers wear many hats. https://content.govdelivery.com/accounts/MIDNR/bulletins/1e2684e.

Homeland Security Today. (2021, June 23). Coast Guard, NOAA enforce Lacey Act off Florida coast. https://www.hstoday.us/subject-matter-areas/maritime-security/coast-guard-noaa-enforce-lacey-act-off-florida-coast/.

Horn of Africa Wildlife Enforcement Network (HAWEN). (2021). About Hawen. https://www.hawen.org/index.php.

Intergovernmental Authority on Development (IGAD). (2017, November 21). *IGAD member countries establish the Horn of Africa Wildlife Enforcement Network (HAWEN).* https://igad.int/divisions/agriculture-and-environment/1700-igad-member-countries-establish-the-horn-of-africa-wildlife-law-enforcement-network-hawen.

International Criminal Police Organization (INTERPOL). (2019). *Wildlife trafficking: Organized crime hit hard by joint INTERPOL-WCO global enforcement operation.* https://www.interpol.int/en/News-and-Events/News/2019/Wildlife-trafficking-organized-crime-hit-hard-by-joint-INTERPOL-WCO-global-enforcement-operation.

International Criminal Police Organization (INTERPOL). (2021a). Environmental crime. https://www.interpol.int/en/Crimes/Environmental-crime.

International Criminal Police Organization (INTERPOL). (2021b). Who we are. https://www.interpol.int/en.

The Kenya Gazette. (2019, August 16). Gazette Notice No. 7262, The Wildlife (Conservation and Management) Act (no. 47 of 2013) Community Wildlife Conservation Committees. https://gallery.mailchimp.com/d53d01de8887e62f430469897/files/6c302ed8-75aa-4701-bc33-085e88519b66/Amendment_to_County_CWCCC_Vol.CXXI_No_.pdf.

Kenya Wildlife Service (KWS). (2021a). Overview. http://www.kws.go.ke/content/overview-0.

Kenya Wildlife Service (KWS). (2021b). Wildlife security. http://www.kws.go.ke/content/wildlife-security.

Krishnasamy, K., & Zavagli, M. (2020). *Southeast Asia at the heart of wildlife trade.* TRAFFIC. https://www.traffic.org/site/assets/files/12648/sea-traps-february-2020.pdf.

Laikipia Forum. (2019). Kenya government overhauls the county wildlife conservation and compensation committees. https://laikipia.org/2019/09/10/kenya-government-overhauls-the-county-wildlife-conservation-and-compensation-committees/.

Local 983. (2021). Urban park rangers. https://local983.com/index.php/local-983-titles/urban-park-rangers.

Lusaka Agreement on Cooperative Enforcement Operations Directed at Illegal Trade in Wild Fauna and Flora in Africa. (2020). About us. https://lusakaagreement.org/about-us/.

Manzano, R. J. (2000, May 22). City may limit park rangers' authority to make arrests. *Los Angeles Times.* https://www.latimes.com/archives/la-xpm-2000-may-22-me-32796-story.html.

Missouri Department of Natural Resources. (2021). State park rangers. https://mostateparks.com/rangers.

Moreto, W. & Matusiak, M. C. (2017). "We fight against wrong doers": Law enforcement rangers' roles, responsibilities, and patrol operations in Uganda. *Deviant Behavior, 38*(4), 426–447.

National Oceanic and Atmospheric Administration (NOAA). (2021b). Enforcement. https://www.fisheries.noaa.gov/topic/enforcement.

National Park Service (NPS). (2015). Coronado National Memorial. https://www.nps.gov/coro/getinvolved/workwithus.htm.

National Park Service (NPS). (2019). Investigative services. https://www.nps.gov/orgs/1563/index.htm.

NYC Parks. (2021). Parks Enforcement Patrol. https://www.nycgovparks
.org/about/urban-park-service/park-enforcement-patrol.

Patten, R., Crow, M. S., & Shelley, T. O. (2015). What's in a name?
The occupational identity of conservation and natural resource
oriented law enforcement agencies. *American Journal of Criminal
Justice, 40,* 750–764.

Pellow, D. N. (2007). *Resisting global toxics: Transnational movements
for environmental justice.* MIT Press.

South Asia Wildlife Enforcement Network (SAWEN). (2021). Establishment of SAWEN. https://www.sawen.org/.

Tobias, M. (1998). *Nature's keepers: On the front lines of the fight to
save wildlife in America.* John Wiley & Sons, Inc.

TRAFFIC. (2011, December 21). *China kicks off new era of inter-agency
co-operation on wildlife law enforcement.* https://www.traffic.org/news
/china-kicks-off-new-era-of-inter-agency-co-operation-on-wildlife-
law-enforcement/.

TRAFFIC. (2019). *TWIX: Trade in Wildlife Information Exchange:
Promoting information sharing and co-operation to reduce illegal
wildlife trade in central Africa.* https://www.traffic.org/site/assets
/files/3792/africa-twix-leaflet-2019-en-web.pdf.

TRAFFIC. (2020). *TWIX: Trade in Wildlife Information Exchange: A
tool to facilitate the exchange of information on illegal wildlife trade
between law enforcement agencies of the Southern African Development Community.* https://www.traffic.org/site/assets/files/3792
/sadc-twix-leaflet-oct2020.pdf.

TRAFFIC. (2021). *TWIX: Trade in Wildlife Information Exchange:
Promoting information sharing and co-operation to reduce illegal
wildlife trade in eastern Africa.* https://www.traffic.org/site/assets
/files/3792/east-twix-leaflet-vweb.pdf.

Uganda Wildlife Authority (UWA). (2013). UWA gets first ever intelligence unit. https://www.ugandawildlife.org/queen-elizabeth
-national-park/uwa-gets-first-ever-intelligence-unit.

Uganda Wildlife Authority (UWA). (2021). Uganda Wildlife Authority home. https://www.ugandawildlife.org/.

United Nations. (2021). About us. https://www.un.org/en/about-us.

United Nations Office on Drugs and Crime (UNODC). (2021a). Global programme. https://www.unodc.org/unodc/en/wildlife-and-forest-crime/global-programme.html.

United Nations Office on Drugs and Crime (UNODC). (2021b). Global Programme thematic areas. https://www.unodc.org/unodc/en/wildlife-and-forest-crime/objective-and-thematic-areas.html.

United States Coast Guard (USCG). (2020). *Illegal, unreported and unregulated fishing strategic outlook.* https://www.uscg.mil/iuufishing/.

United States Department of Agriculture (USDA). (2021). Meet the Forest Service. https://www.fs.usda.gov/about-agency/meet-forest-service.

United States Department of Justice (USDOJ). (2020). Operation Renegade. https://www.justice.gov/enrd/operation-renegade.

United States Fish and Wildlife Service (USFWS). (2013a). About service law enforcement. https://www.fws.gov/le/about-le.html.

United States Fish and Wildlife Service (USFWS). (2013b). About service special agents. https://www.fws.gov/le/special-agents.html.

United State Fish and Wildlife Service (USFWS). (2018). Refuge law enforcement. https://www.fws.gov/refuges/lawenforcement/index.php.

United States Fish and Wildlife Service (USFWS). (2019). About service wildlife inspectors. https://www.fws.gov/Le/wildlife-inspectors.html.

United States Forest Service (USFS). (2021). USDA Forest Service law enforcement and investigations. https://www.usajobs.gov/GetJob/ViewDetails/596265100.

USAJOBS. (2021) Park ranger. https://www.usajobs.gov/GetJob/ViewDetails/596265100.

Watson, D. (2014). *Masai Mara: The Mara Triangle official guide.* Photoprint, Scotland.

Western, D., Russell S. C., & Cuthill, I. (2009). The status of wildlife in protected areas compared to non-protected areas of Kenya. *PLoS ONE, 4*(7).

White, R. (2008). *Crimes against nature: Environmental criminology and ecological justice.* Willan.

Wildlife Conservation Society (WCS) Uganda. (2021). Initiatives: Law Enforcement. https://uganda.wcs.org/initiatives/law-enforcement.aspx.

Four

CONSERVATION LAW ENFORCEMENT ORGANIZATIONS

In the United States, conservation law enforcement occurs at every level of government: federal, state, and local. Unlike at the turn of the century when private organizations would hire game wardens (McIver, 2003), conservation law enforcement officers are employed by government agencies, regardless of which level of government they represent. There are federal-level special agents, park rangers, and forest rangers; state-level conservation officers and park rangers; and local-level park rangers (Sparling, 2014). This chapter will examine the types of conservation or natural resources organizations that are involved in conservation law enforcement as well as some of the non-governmental organizations they interact with. The chapter will begin with a discussion of the types of organizational structures that are prevalent in natural resources or conservation government agencies and then will discuss the specific agencies themselves, such as the US Fish and Wildlife Service.

STATE-LEVEL CONSERVATION ORGANIZATIONS

Conservation law enforcement officer agencies are not generally independent law enforcement organizations. Rather, they are typically housed within larger state-level departments of conservation or departments of natural resources. Within these larger parent organizations are included a wide variety of different divisions of which one is conservation law en-

91

forcement (Falcone, 2004). Less commonly, state-level conservation officers are located within larger departments of public safety, such as in Oregon, where conservation officers are located in the Division of Fish and Wildlife within the Oregon State Police (Oregon State Police, 2020). Most of the following discussion in this chapter will focus on the natural resources and conservation agencies, but much of what will be discussed can also be applied to departments of public safety or state police agencies.

One of the unique, but fairly common aspects of the structural organization of natural resources agencies is the inclusion of a **commission** in the **organizational hierarchy**. Approximately 55% of natural resources agencies have some type of commission within their hierarchy. Generally, commissioners are appointed by the governor (Sparling, 2014). The Management Assistance Team (2010) in conjunction with the Association of Fish and Wildlife Agencies (AFWA) reported that 67% of the states have commissions that are appointed by the governor. Even though they are appointed, ideally, they should have some experience in natural resources or business experience, but political patronage appointees also occur (Sparling, 2014). Of those agencies that have a commission, approximately, 75% of them have only one commission, while some have up to four different commissions. Approximately 60% of the commissions are comprised of six to ten members, some have up to sixteen members (Management Assistance Team, 2010; Sparling, 2014), while others such as Missouri have four (Keefe, 1987). The role of a commissioner is almost always a voluntary, unpaid position. If any compensation is provided, it is almost always limited to travel costs (Management Assistance Team, 2010; Sparling, 2014).

Even though having a commission within the hierarchy is fairly common, the responsibilities of those commissions and commissioners varies between agencies. Some of the commissions have a very specific advisory function, such as endangered species or land zoning, but these are not the most common types of commissions that are present in natural resources agencies. Of those agencies that have a commission with broader advisory responsibilities, approximately 75% of them fill a mainly advisory role. They are responsible for establishing policy, representing various sections of the state, and hiring or appointing the director or chief executive. Under this arrangement, the daily decision making and administration for the organization is delegated to the director or chief executive officer. The remaining 25% of commissions fill a more supervisory role, rather than an advisory role. These commissions are more similar to a board of directors, where the chairperson of the commission and the commission fill both an advisory role and the role of the director (Sparling, 2014).

For those agencies where the commission does not fill the role of an advisory council and the director, they are headed by a chief executive officer. The exact title of these types of positions will vary from agency to agency. Director is a common title for this executive position, but other names such as commissioner (even when the agency is not run by someone from the commission) or executive director are also common. The function of this position is to oversee the functions of the agency, and their responsibilities are similar to those of executive directors of businesses or the director of other types of state agencies. Generally, these positions are administrative positions and are not directly involved in the management of natural resources (Sparling, 2014).

Commissions and directors are located at the top of the organizational structure for these agencies. State-level natural resources agencies consist of a structure that contains various bureaus or divisions located within the larger parent organization. The law enforcement division is one of these divisions that is located within the hierarchy underneath the commission and the director. Other divisions may consist of fisheries management, wildlife management, boating, parks, and forestry (Sparling, 2014). Larger organizations may include even more divisions, such as an education division. This differentiation is one of the hallmark characteristics of a bureaucracy.

The organizational structure is how an organization not only divides up the work of the organization, but also how it coordinates the work (Maguire, 2003; Scott, 1992). Organizational structures may be mechanistic or organic. Mechanistic organizations are generally referred to as bureaucratic, formal, or hierarchical systems, while organic structures are characterized by more flexible and informal systems (Stojkovic et al., 2015). Because government agencies, such as departments of natural resources or conservation, are government agencies, they adhere to a bureaucratic structure (Wilson, 1989).

A **bureaucratic structure** is an example of a formal organizational structure that creates a hierarchy or chain of command that coordinates the organization's activities, outlines formal roles and responsibilities, divides the work of the organization, and requires an adherence to the rules of the organization (Bolman & Deal, 2003). This type of structure may be applied to not only the overall natural resources agency, but also to the law enforcement divisions where the conservation officers are housed. The hierarchy of a state-level natural resources agency commonly begins with the governor. Under the governor is the commission, followed by the director. Under the director are the various different divisions such as wildlife, fisheries, parks, or law enforcement. Each of these divisions has a director or division administrator. Then, within each of these divisions is a hierarchy that delineates the chain of command or how the labor is distributed within each of the divisions (Sparling, 2014). For example, the Law Enforcement Division in Virginia had a chief, assistant chief, warden supervisors, assistant supervisors, area patrol leaders and the line-level wardens (Palmer & Bryant, 1985). These types of structures are commonly represented by a pyramidal diagram (Giblin, 2014), with the chief executive officer or director at the very top of the pyramid. The shape of the pyramid represents the number of employees at each level. As the pyramid becomes wider, that represents more divisions and more employees (Giblin, 2014). Street-level conservation officers would be located at the bottom of the pyramid. Directly above them would be their immediate supervisor, and this type of arrangement would continue throughout the pyramid. See Figure 4.1 for an example of a state-level natural resources organizational structure.

The pyramid shape represents the hierarchy for the organization or division within the organization. Hierarchies may also be characterized by vertical and horizontal complexity (Giblin, 2014; Stojkovic et al., 2015). **Vertical complexity** is directly related to how tall the hierarchy is, which means the number of layers within the hierarchy. The taller the organization, the more vertically complex the organization. The vertical structures of organizations separate those that are responsible for policy formulation from those that actually enact the policy by carrying out the business of the organization. In a criminal justice organization, which would be similar to the law enforcement division, the vertical complexity is characterized by the rank structure and chain of command (Giblin, 2014). Returning to the Virginia example, the Law Enforcement Division would have six levels in the hierarchy

4.1. Example of Natural Resources Agency Organizational Structure

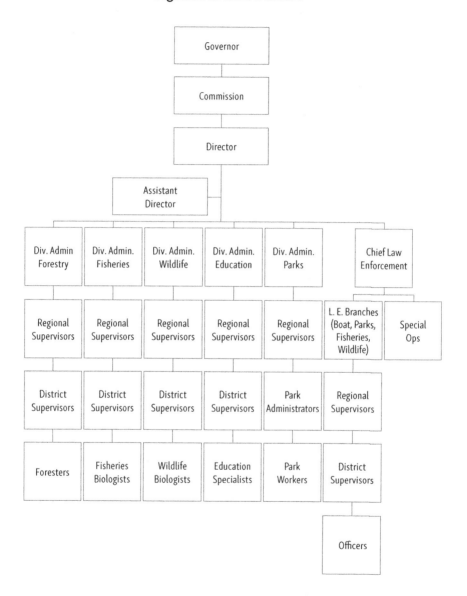

within the division, and the line-level wardens would be the rank of employees that are located at the bottom of the pyramid and are directly responsible for carrying out the work of the organization. By having more layers in the hierarchy, it decreases the span of control for supervisors. The span of control is the number of employees any given supervisor is responsible for supervising. As layers are added to the hierarchy, supervisors are responsible for fewer subordinates. These extra layers not only decrease the span of control, but they also provide more opportunities for advancement (Giblin, 2014).

Horizontal complexity is also a characteristic of bureaucratic organizations, and is related to how wide the organization is. It is characterized by the number of subunits within the division or the number of divisions within the overall hierarchy of the natural resources agency and consists of both occupational differentiation and functional differentiation (Giblin, 2014). Occupational differentiation is also known as role specialization. It is when the work of the organization is differentiated and divided into smaller parts with individuals being assigned only to be responsible for their part. This results in specialization within the organization. Specialists are often grouped into distinct units, divisions, or departments within the organization (Giblin, 2014). Within a natural resources law enforcement division, the line-level conservation officers would be considered law enforcement generalists, but specialists within that division could be represented by special operations/covert units (White, 1995) and canine units (Criscoe, 1999). This is very similar to how occupational differentiation would be exhibited in a traditional police agency. The line-level patrol officers would be considered to be generalists, while those in specific areas with specific responsibilities would be considered specialists (Giblin, 2014).

Functional differentiation is also a characteristic of horizontal complexity. Functional differentiation occurs when those with specialized skills are put into groups or divisions. These divisions are based and created on specific job functions (Giblin, 2014). Functional differentiation may occur in a natural resources agency both at the agency level and also within the law enforcement division. At the agency level, there are separate divisions for specific specialties. For example, the forestry specialists are in the forestry division, while the wildlife specialists are in the wildlife division. Within the law enforcement division, conservation officers are separated by specific job function. For example, if there is a separate division for the special operations/covert unit, that would be an example of functional differentiation.

Spatial complexity is also important when examining an organizations structure. Spatial complexity is defined by how an organization is organized across a geographic area. Many different types of organizations have branch offices, such as banks, or a police agency that has districts, precincts, and beats that are spread over a particular geographic area. Being a more spatially complex organization may help it to more readily address local issues and increase their accessibility to the public, but it will also most likely increase communication issues as well as create issues with coordinating the work of the organization (Giblin, 2014).

For state-level natural resources agencies, commonly a main headquarters is maintained in the state capital. However, there is no way for all the work that needs to be conducted across the state to originate in the main headquarters, so they have offices throughout the state. For example, in Missouri, there are eight regional offices that are spread across the state of Missouri. The employees from the different divisions that work in that particular region of the state are headquartered in the regional office, rather than the main office in the state capital. Conservation officers are normally even more spatially distributed. Instead of all the conservation officers in a particular region having their headquarters in the regional office, they will regularly be assigned to a particular county within the state and be headquartered in that particular county, rather than in the regional office (Missouri Department of Conservation, 2020). By assigning officers to each county, those officers may more readily address the concerns of their particular district, than if they were located in a regional office, or the main headquarters. However, because of the large amount of spatial complexity related to the assigning of conservation officers, coordination and communication with regional offices or the main headquarters can become complicated.

Formalization is another key characteristic of a bureaucratic organization (Blau & Scott, 2003; Giblin, 2014). In a bureaucratic organization, the activities of the organization are governed by rules and regulations that identify appropriate activities and practices. These formal rules and procedures are intended to ensure that all employees are completing the tasks of the organization utilizing the most appropriate and efficient methods and also provides for continuity within the organization regardless of personnel turnover (Blau & Scott, 2003; Giblin, 2014). Law enforcement agencies are known to have very formalized procedures. Traditional law enforcement agencies generally have policies that cover topics such as use of force, handling the mentally ill, citizen complaints, domestic disturbances (Maguire, 2003), and pursuits (Kenney & Alpert, 1997). Some police agencies are known to have policy manuals that are several inches thick (Maguire, 2003). Even though police agencies attempt to codify appropriate behavior, it is impossible to create policy for every possible scenario that a law enforcement officer may encounter in the course of their duties (Giblin, 2014). Officers will at times have to use their professional judgment or discretion to develop solutions to a particular situation they are required to solve.

Bureaucratic organizations are also characterized by a selection and advancement process that is based on merit. Job descriptions are formalized, and workers are hired for specific positions. Once hired the most technically qualified will then be promoted into supervisory positions based on a system that promotes the most highly qualified employees. These procedures are designed to ensure that the most qualified employees are hired into the organization and then promoted into supervisory positions. Employees in this system are believed to view positions within the organization as a career and will invest in their organization without fear of unwarranted termination (Giblin, 2014; Perrow, 1986; Scott & Davis, 2007).

Finally, bureaucratic organizations are characterized by impersonal relations. In a true bureaucracy, the organization is operated without consideration for personal needs or preferences and without any emotional attachment. Rules, regulations, and procedures are what guide a bureaucratic organization and are what are used to influence organizational decision making (Blau & Scott, 2003; Giblin, 2014). Friendships and personal relationships between employees cannot be allowed to interfere with the business of the organization.

Bureaucratic organizations were originally designed to operate in a closed system, which means that they were not designed to have to interact with or take into account their environments or other outside influences. However, this is not reality. Organizations must interact with their environments and function as more of an open system (Giblin, 2014; Katz & Kahn, 1978). An organization's environment can be defined as any phenomenon, event, group, or individual that is external to the organization and impacts that organization. An organization's environment contains multiple components: technological, legal, economic, demographic, cultural, ecological, and political (Smith, 2010; Stojkovic et al., 2015).

Technological advancements have had an important impact on all organizations and have also had an important impact on criminal justice agencies. Historically, technological advancements such as the automobile had an important impact on law enforcement officers. For example, the automobile made it much easier for the police to patrol their beat and respond to calls. However, it also made criminals much more mobile, and they were no longer more or less confined to a limited geographic area. Additionally, cars became an object that thieves wanted to steal as well (Stojkovic et al., 2015). Similarly, the automobile would have impacted conservation officers. The use of automobiles for patrol (NYDEC, 2005) would have made the conservation officer much more efficient when patrolling, but it also made poachers more mobile as well. In more modern times, the advancement of computer technology and the Internet has changed some aspects of both traditional police organizations, as well as conservation law enforcement. A report by TRAFFIC (2019) identified that wildlife crime and trafficking online was an important international problem and suggested that law enforcement agencies should increase their presence on various online platforms as well as create wildlife cybercrime divisions. The advent of the Internet and other computer technologies has created new types of crimes and created new challenges for both traditional and conservation law enforcement officers.

The law or legal aspects of the environment will also influence conservation law enforcement agencies. The law or legal aspects of the conservation law enforcement environment are generally represented by legislation and court decisions. Legislation and court decisions provide the basis for the rules and authority that guide the criminal justice system. Conservation law enforcement agencies are subject to state and federal statutes that guide their behavior. Arrest procedures, certification procedures, and search and seizure are all clarified in legislation and provide the framework for law enforcement officers.

Additionally, they are influenced by what is classified as a crime. Federal and state statutes identify which types of behaviors are classified as crimes (Stojkovic et al., 2015). In addition to state and federal statutes that define crimes, other legislation such as the Civil Rights Act of 1964 will also impact conservation law enforcement agencies. This act opened the door for more participation by women and minorities as members of the criminal justice community. It also required policies and procedures to be created within the criminal justice system and within agencies to ensure that no one's civil rights were violated, or else the agency would be subjected to civil legislation (Stojkovic et al., 2015).

Economic conditions also influence criminal justice organizations. The resources available to public bureaucracies or organizations are impacted by the overall economic health of the external environment. Even though government agencies are not producing a product or conducting a service that those in the community would pay for directly, they are impacted by the external economic environment because the budgets of government agencies are generally comprised of tax monies. When the economy is good, there are more tax revenues available, and when economic conditions are less than ideal, there is less tax revenue, which results in budgetary shortfalls (Stojkovic et al., 2015). If economic conditions are such that people may not be purchasing hunting or fishing licenses, then that particular conservation agency would experience a loss of revenue (Blevins & Edwards, 2009). Other sources, such as from the Pittman-Robertson Act or the Federal Aid in Sport Fish Restoration Act, can be impacted by whether or not people are willing to purchase the items taxed under these Acts (Bean, 1978; Dunlap, 1988; Trefethen, 1975; US Fish and Wildlife Service, 2013).

In addition, economic conditions may also influence hiring practices within these organizations. Conservation law enforcement agencies compete with other organizations for employees. When unemployment rates are high, agencies have a much bigger pool of candidates from which to choose, however they may not have the money necessary to hire new officers or may be limited in how many they may hire. Conversely, in times of economic prosperity when unemployment is low, conservation law enforcement agencies may be able to fill all of their available positions, but may have a much smaller pool of potential candidates from which to choose (Stojkovic et al., 2015).

Demographic conditions also impact an organization through its environment. The composition of the people of an area will impact the organizations in that area. Characteristics such as age, sex, race, ethnicity, and population size will all influence the constraints or influences the community will exercise over the organizations in that community. For example, areas that have a large percentage of residents who are under the age of 25 will most likely have a higher crime rate than communities who do not have a large percentage of their residents under the age of 25 (Giblin, 2014). Other aspects may also influence an organization, especially a conservation law enforcement organization.

Locally, aspects such as urban sprawl, the closing of a manufacturing plant, or the opening of a manufacturing plant in a nearby town could all impact the demographics of an area. If urban sprawl creeps into a formally rural area, it will bring with it more housing and more residents that may be from communities that have different value systems than the formally rural community. This may impact conservation law enforcement officers because there may now be less area for hunting or fishing, which can lead to problems such as hunter trespass or hunter/landowner conflicts. Additionally, the new residents may not subscribe to the same belief system regarding hunting and fishing and that may cause conflicts as well. If a local manufacturing plant closes, it may lead to residents moving to other communities to find work. This may lead to decreased tax revenue in an area or an age class of residents disappearing from the local community, which may lead to a decrease in services or other detrimental effects. If a new manufacturing plant were to open, it might lead to an increase in population for the local community and result in changing demographics depending on who chooses to move into the area to work at the new plant. These are just a couple of examples of events that may impact the demographics of an area. Any changes to the demographics in an area will impact the local organizations, the services they provide, and their calls for service.

Cultural conditions may also impact how an organization interacts with its environment. Cultural conditions can impact conservation law enforcement agencies at several levels—local, state, and federal. A society's culture is the collective norms, values, symbols, behaviors, and expectations of members of that society. Norms are codified into laws, and the validity and legitimacy of organizations are intertwined with society's culture. Overall, American culture is quite heterogeneous, however some areas are very homogenous. If an area is homogenous, then society's culture in that area is most likely stable and would make routine demands on the local organizations and the conservation law enforcement agency. However, in heterogeneous portions of society, society's culture would also be heterogeneous and less stable than a homogenous area and would create unique and changing demands on the local criminal justice agencies, including the conservation law enforcement agency (Stojkovic et al., 2015).

Ecological conditions also will influence the behavior of an organization through its environment. Ecological conditions are characteristics of the environment such as climate, geographic location, and the type of local economy—whether it is industrial, agrarian, or service based (Giblin, 2014). For a state-wide agency such as a department of natural resources, the ecological conditions may vary widely depending on the region of the state, and the ecological conditions of the local community will impact conservation law enforcement officers. For example, Missouri has six distinct geographic regions: Glaciated Plains, Osage Plains, Ozark, Ozark Border, Mississippi lowlands, and Big Rivers (Thom & Wilson, 1983). Each of these regions of Missouri are distinct geographically (Thom & Wilson, 1983) and will impact the types of activities in which conservation officers participate and also may impact the types of calls for service they receive. Missouri is also unique in its geographic position within the United States, so the overall geographic location of Missouri will impact the types of activities and calls for service that conservation officers receive, as well as the various geographic regions within the state. For example, an officer that works in the Mississippi Lowlands region in the extreme southern part of Missouri may encounter different local issues related to conservation than an officer in the Glaciated Plains region in the northern section of the state.

The final environmental characteristic that may impact an organization is political conditions. Generally, an organization can be impacted by political pressure both directly through constituents and also indirectly through government action. For government agencies, they can be impacted politically by legislators through budgetary considerations, mandated change, or by replacing top administrators. Legislators may enact legislation that impacts an organization. Court rulings may also influence an organization. Court rulings are supposed to occur in a non-partisan fashion, but that is rarely that case (Giblin, 2014).

Natural resources agencies are somewhat unique among government agencies regarding budgets. Commonly, a significant portion of their budget is the result of hunting and fishing license sales (Blevins & Edwards, 2009) with a smaller percentage coming from acts such as Pittman-Robertson and the Sport Fish Restoration Act (Bean, 1978; Dunlap, 1988; Trefethen, 1975; US Fish and Wildlife Service, 2013). Some agencies receive operating funds from the state legislature, while other agencies, such as Missouri's, receive no general revenue funds, but rather are supported by a sales tax that was enacted by an amendment to the Missouri Constitution (Keefe, 1987). Even though Missouri's agency would appear to be free from political influence due to its budgetary independence, legislators could still threaten to attempt to enact legislation that would take away its funding in an effort to influence it. Threats such as these are indirect ways that legislators may enact informal political pressures on an organization (Giblin, 2014).

Political pressure may also be enacted by outside interest groups. This pressure may be exerted directly by the outside interest group, rather than through official government channels (Giblin, 2014). Even though these groups may tend to operate outside of official government channels, they also may petition and lobby legislators to pass legislation. The type of non-governmental organizations (NGOs) that may attempt to apply pressure on a natural resources agency varies and will promote the interests of their particular group. They will attempt to achieve their objectives through public campaigning to bring attention to the particular issue, carrying out their own research to prove their case, lobbying legislators for legislative change, or by influencing public opinion in their favor to pressure law makers or agency administrators to enact the proposed changes (Nurse, 2013).

If normal channels do not accomplish their goals, some NGOs may resort to lawsuits and other legal remedies in order to accomplish their objectives. For example, the Animal Legal Defense Fund and the Humane Society of the United States filed suit in an attempt to stop the Missouri Department of Conservation from enacting an otter trapping season. The court found that MDC was able to enact this season, but not before going to court (Krause, 2012). Examples of other types of NGOs that may interact with conservation organizations are the National Wild Turkey Federation (NWTF), Pheasants Forever, Rocky Mountain Elk Foundation, People for the Ethical Treatment of Animals (PETA), the National Audubon Society, the Sierra Club, the Nature Conservancy, the National Wildlife Federation, and many other different national, state, and local wildlife, fisheries, or outdoor recreation-oriented groups. The news media is another example of an outside group that may place pressure on a natural resources agency in order to influence them (Giblin, 2014).

In addition to the various components of an organization's environment and the various NGOs that may interact with and attempt to influence an organization are the citizens that comprise the largest group of stakeholders for the organization. As a government agency, natural resources agencies and conservation law enforcement officers are responsible to the citizens within their jurisdiction. Even though government bureaucracies were initially created as closed systems that were not supposed to be influenced by outside factors, government agencies must interact with the citizens in the communities that they serve (Giblin, 2014).

State-level departments of natural resources and conservation utilize a variety of different methods to engage the public. One of the most common ways of engaging with the public is through the use of meetings. The types and frequency of meetings may vary. One of the most common ways is the commission or governing board meeting. These meetings are open to the public and provide direct feedback to the commissioners from the public. Other types of regular public meetings are also used by natural resources agencies to engage their constituents (Lord & Cheng, 2006). The Missouri Department of Conservation utilizes public meetings and also public comment periods. Some of these meetings are held in person, but others are held virtually, where stakeholders may submit their comments electronically, rather than in a public meeting. They use these meetings and forums as opportunities for the public to comment on current and proposed hunting and fishing regulations, management plans for various wildlife species, and management plans for public use areas owned and managed by the department (MDC, 2020). Some other methods that natural resources agencies use to engage the public are advisory boards, task forces with citizen members, open houses, surveys, and agency websites (Lord & Cheng, 2006).

In addition to methods such as meetings, agencies will also use other methods of outreach to their constituents. Some agencies have volunteer programs that allow members of the community to volunteer in a variety of ways, including helping at a nature center, becoming a member of a stream team that cares for a particular stretch of stream, or teaching hunter education courses (MDC, 2020). Other opportunities, such as becoming a volunteer campsite host, conservation educator, or someone that assists the agency in conducting wildlife population surveys, are also available in several states (Iowa Department of Natural Resources, 2020).

Another way that agencies engage with the public is through citizen reporting programs that alert authorities to poaching violations (Nelson & Verbyla, 1984). The most common of these programs is Operation Game Thief that began in New Mexico in 1977, and was modeled after the crime-stoppers program utilized by the Albuquerque Police Department at the time (New Mexico Department of Game and Fish [NMDGF], 2020). Currently, 49 of the 50 states have adopted Operation Game Thief or a very similar program (Colorado Department of Parks and Wildlife [CDPW], 2020). The Operation Game Thief program allows citizens to report poaching violations and request a reward if they choose. The individual states have somewhat different avenues for someone to report a poaching incident, but the most common is a toll-free number that can be called any time. Some states also have online reporting forms (NMDGF, 2020) or an email address that can be used to report violations (CDPW, 2020). Regardless of how someone chooses to report a violation, they may choose to remain anonymous. Those reporting incidents may request a reward if the information leads to an arrest or summons. A citizen review board reviews all requests for rewards and decides on the appropriate amount of reward that may be given. The reward systems are funded through donations from various interested clubs, organizations, and individuals (CDPW, 2020; NMDGF, 2020).

Conservation law enforcement officers also interact with and engage with the public through the course of their duties. Conservation officers engage with the public in a variety of ways, aside from their interactions during enforcement contacts. One of the most common ways that enforcement officers interact with the public is through hunter education classes. States require that anyone born after a specific date (varies by state) must pass a hunter education course in order to purchase a hunting license. Some of these courses were taught by the officers exclusively, while others were taught by some combination of the officer and volunteer instructors. Conservation law enforcement officers also participate in a variety of conservation education programs such as Project Wild, Becoming an Outdoor Woman, youth hunting clinics, state and regional fairs, boat shows, hunting expos, and aquatic education (Pepper, 2003). Each of these types of outreach programs engages a specific set of stakeholders for not only the conservation law enforcement officer, but also the larger natural resources agency.

FEDERAL AGENCIES

The first half of this chapter has focused on state-level conservation law enforcement agencies and their larger parent organizations, departments of natural resources or conservation. Several federal agencies also have conservation officers as part of their bureaucracy. The main four agencies with conservation law enforcement responsibilities are the United States Fish and Wildlife Service (USFWS), United States Park Service (USPS), the Bureau of Land Management (BLM), and the United States Forest Service (USFS). Similar to the state-level organizations, the law enforcement officers of these agencies are housed within a larger non-law enforcement agency. However, within the federal government, there is an additional layer of organization that is not present at the state level. Each of these four agencies are housed within a larger federal agency. The USFWS, USPS, and the BLM are all housed within the United States Department of the Interior (USDOI), and the USFS is housed within the United States Department of Agriculture (USDA).

Department of the Interior

The DOI was created in 1849. It is the main federal agency that is responsible for the management of natural resources other than agriculture, oceans, and the forests. When it was first created, the DOI had many more responsibilities other than natural resource protection. It was responsible for the United States capital's water system, the District of Columbia jail, management of hospitals and universities, public parks, colonization of freed slaves from Haiti, and the exploration of the West, among others. Over time, most of the responsibilities other than natural resource protection were assigned to other agencies or departments until the primary responsibility of the DOI became natural resource protection (Sparling, 2014).

The DOI employs approximately 70,000 people who are spread out across 2,400 locations in the United States, Puerto Rico, and other territories (USDOI, 2020a; Sparling, 2014) and had an annual budget of approximately 12 billion dollars in fiscal year 2020 (Bernhardt, 2019). Obviously, there are not 70,000 law enforcement officers within the DOI. The DOI employs biologists, meteorologists, climate experts, social scientists, geologists, hydrologists, and many other various types of employees in addition to law enforcement officers (Sparling, 2014).

Like other government departments or agencies, the DOI adheres to a decentralized hierarchical bureaucratic structure. The DOI is led by a secretary and with a deputy secretary and assistant secretaries directly underneath the secretary in the hierarchy. The secretary and the deputy secretary of the DOI are appointed by the president and require the approval of the United States Senate. The Assistant Secretary of the Interior for Fish, Wildlife and Parks and all of the directors of the different agencies within the DOI are also appointed by the president (Sparling, 2014). The DOI currently houses ten federal agencies. They are the Bureau of Indian Affairs, Bureau of Indian Education, Bureau of Land Management, Bureau of Ocean Energy Management, Bureau of Reclamation, Bureau of Safety and Environmental Enforcement, National Park Service, Office of Surface Mining, US Fish and Wildlife Service, and the US Geological Survey (USDOI, 2020b). In addition to the ten bureaus or departments that are part of the DOI, there are also various support offices within the department, such as the solicitor and inspector general and an assistant secretary for policy, management, and budget. Each of the bureaus and departments within the DOI also have support offices within them. While specific organizational charts or structures may shift with budget or administrative priorities (Sparling, 2014), the DOI is a hierarchical bureaucratic agency and most likely will remain that way for the foreseeable future because it is a government agency, and that is how government agencies are structured and function (Wilson, 1989).

US Fish and Wildlife Service

The USFWS is the primary federal agency tasked with fish and wildlife management in the United States. The department has undergone quite a few changes since its earliest iteration in 1871 as the Commission on Fish and Fisheries. It was modified into its current form in 1993 (Sparling, 2014). It currently employs approximately 8,000 people (USFWS, 2020a) and is responsible for national wildlife refuges, ecological services offices, federally endangered species, anadromous fish, migratory birds, international agreements, and federal fish and wildlife law enforcement (Sparling, 2014).

The USFWS is organized in a similar manner to the DOI. It is a decentralized, top-down hierarchical bureaucracy. It is led by a director and then there are a variety of other deputy directors. The USFWS consists of twelve divisions or offices within the larger department. They are the Wildlife and Sport Fish Restoration Programs, National Wildlife Refuge System, Migratory Birds, Fish and Aquatic Conservation, Ecological Services, International Affairs, Law Enforcement, Science Applications, External Affairs, Management and Administration, Information Resources and Technology Management, and the National Conservation Training Center (USFWS, 2020d).

The Law Enforcement Division is also a hierarchical bureaucracy. It is headed by a chief. Underneath the chief in the hierarchy is the Division of Special Operations, the Clark R. Bavin National Forensics Laboratory, the Division of Technical and Field Support, and the Regional Special Agents in Charge (USFWS, 2020d). There are two types of law enforcement officers in the Law Enforcement Division of the USFWS: special agents and wildlife inspectors. When fully staffed, there are 261 special agents and 140 wildlife inspectors. Law enforcement officers are assigned to one of eight regions across the United States and territories, with the main headquarters in Washington, D.C. (USFWS, 2020b). In addition to the special agents and wildlife inspectors in the Division of Law Enforcement, conservation officers are also present within the USFWS in the National Refuge Division.

The National Refuge Division is also a hierarchical bureaucracy. Similar to the Division of Law Enforcement, the National Refuge Division is also headed by a chief. Under the chief in the hierarchy is the Division of Natural Resources and Conservation Planning, Division of Realty, Division of Visitor Services and Communication, Division of Refuge Law Enforcement, Division of Information Technology and Management, and Division of Budget, Performance and Workforce (USFWS, 2020d). Officers that work in the National Refuge Division are fully certified federal law enforcement officers, but are only responsible for law enforcement on National Wildlife Refuge land (USFWS, 2020c). See Figure 4.2 for the USFWS organizational chart.

National Park Service

The NPS is another agency housed within the Department of the Interior. The NPS has responsibilities for national parks such as Yellowstone National Park, national historical areas, such as Gettysburg National Military Park, national monuments such as the Lincoln Memorial in Washington D.C., scenic parkways, and scenic lake shores and seashores. The amount of area that the NPS is responsible for is the equivalent of two states the size of Florida (Hughes & Chavez, 2019). The NPS employs approximately 20,000 permanent, temporary, and seasonal employees (NPS, 2020a; Sparling, 2014).

Similar to the USFWS and consistent with the larger DOI, the NPS is a hierarchical bureaucracy. It is headed by a director and there are three deputy directors. One deputy director is responsible for Congressional and External Relations, one is responsible for Management and Administration, and the third deputy director is responsible for Operations. Each of these deputy directors have a variety of divisions or offices under their supervision. The deputy director for Operations is responsible for the division that houses the law enforcement arm of the National Park Service in addition to seven other divisions. The law enforcement park rangers of the NPS are located under the Visitor and Resource Protection Directorate. This directorate is further divided into Fire and Aviation Management, the Office of Public Health, the Office of Risk Management, the Regulations and Special Park Uses Division, the U.S. Park Police, the Wilderness Stewardship Division, and the Law Enforcement, Security and Emergency Services Division.

4.2. U.S. Fish and Wildlife Service Organizational Chart

Credit: *U.S. Fish and Wildlife Service*

Ethics Office	Native American Liason	Diversity & Inclusive Mgmt

Dep. Dir. Operations

Chief L.E.	A.D. Science Apps	A.D. External Affairs	A.D. Mgmt. & Admin.	A.D. Info. & Tech.	Dir. NCTC
Special Operations		Congress & Legis. Affairs	JAO Ops.	Info. and Tech. Mgmt.	Training
Forensics Lab		Public Affairs	Aquis., Prop. & Project Mgmt.	Privacy	Education
Tech. & Field Support		Marketing Comm.	Human Capital	Cyber Security	Knowledge & Tech.
Special Agents in Charge		Partner & Intergov. Affairs	Policy, Econ., Risk Mgmt.	FOIA	Facility Ops.
				Operations	
				Policy & Planning	

The NPS is also decentralized in that there are 12 regions throughout the United States and its territories (NPS, 2020b).

The Law Enforcement, Security and Emergency Services division is further divided into five divisions: Emergency Services, Investigative Services, Law Enforcement Operations, the Law Enforcement Training Center, and the Office of Professional Responsibility (NPS, 2020b). Traditional park rangers are located in the Law Enforcement Operations division, but officers are also located in the Investigative Services division. They serve as special investigators that investigate crimes within the national parks and are similar to traditional law enforcement detectives (NPS, 2020c).

NPS law enforcement officers are also located in the US Park Police Division within the Visitor and Resource Protection Directorate. The U.S. Park Police are different from the regular law enforcement rangers of the NPS. The US Park Police have jurisdiction in any national park and are located in the Washington D.C., New York City, and San Francisco metropolitan areas (United States Park Police (2020a). They are also a hierarchical bureaucracy and are headed by a chief and an assistant chief. Under the chief is the Office of Professional Responsibility and Office of Business Services. There are three divisions located underneath the assistant chief: the Homeland Security Division, Field Operations Division, and Services Division. The Homeland Security Division is further divided into Intelligence and Counter Terrorism, the New York Field Office, and the Icon Protection Division. The Field Operations Division is responsible for the Patrol branch, the Criminal Investigations Unit, and the San Francisco Field Office. The Services Division is responsible for the administrative functions of the organization (United States Park Police, 2020b). See Figure 4.3 for an organizational chart of the US Park Police.

Bureau of Land Management

The Bureau of Land Management (BLM) is another agency within the DOI that has conservation officers. The BLM controls more land than any other federal agency. It manages approximately 248 million acres of land, which is the equivalent of about 12% of the entire United States. They allow their land to be used for a variety of purposes, including timber harvesting, mining, livestock grazing, and recreation.

4.3. U.S. Park Police Organizational Chart

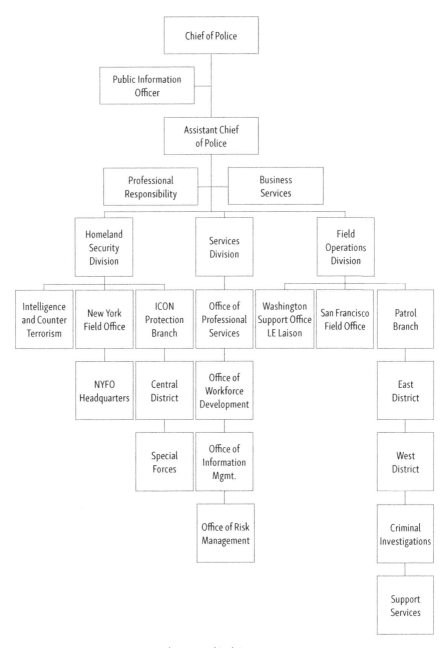

Credit: *National Park Service*

The development of energy resources is one of the BLM's main priorities. BLM has approximately 10,000 employees (Sparling, 2014).

Like other agencies within the DOI, the BLM is a hierarchical bureaucracy. However, unlike many other federal agencies, the headquarters for BLM is not in Washington, D.C. Most of the land that is controlled by BLM is in the western United States. Because most of the land and therefore employees are mostly in the western states, BLM moved its headquarters from Washington, D.C., to Grand Junction, Colorado. Some of the employees that are responsible for Washington, D.C., based operations, such as legislative duties, remained in Washington, but most of the other staff moved, including the director (BLM, 2020a). The BLM is headed by a director and there is also an assistant director. Underneath the director and assistant director in the hierarchy are multiple divisions. Each of these divisions has their own director and hierarchy. One of these divisions is Law Enforcement and Security (BLM, 2020b). Like the other agencies within the DOI, the BLM is decentralized and has employees stationed throughout the United States, but mainly in the western states. Even though the BLM has most of its land responsibilities and employees in the western states, there are still 12 regions throughout the United States (BLM, 2020c). Therefore, it may not be as decentralized as other federal agencies, but it is still decentralized.

The Law Enforcement and Security division is organized similarly to the larger BLM in that it is a hierarchical bureaucracy. It is led by a director and two deputy directors. Each of the five regions has a special agent in charge of that region. Additionally, there is Director of Public Affairs and Communication and an Office of Professional Responsibility (BLM, 2020d). Underneath the special agent in charge positions are approximately 200 uniformed officers. Additionally, there are approximately 70 criminal investigators that work for the BLM (BLM, 2020d). Even though the larger BLM parent organization is organized into 12 regions, the Law Enforcement and Security Division is divided into five law enforcement regions. How the regions are organized emphasizes the disproportionate nature of BLM's landholdings. Region 1 is the state of California. Region 2 is Alaska and Washington State, Oregon, and Idaho. Region 3 is Nevada and Utah. Region 5 is Arizona, New Mexico, Texas, and Oklahoma. Region 4 is the remainder of the United States (BLM, 2020d).

Department of Agriculture

United States Forest Service

The final organization that will be discussed in this chapter is the United States Forest Service (USFS). This federal agency also employs conservation officers. However, unlike the USFWS, NPS, and BLM, the USFS is not housed within the Department of the Interior. The USFS is housed within the United States Department of Agriculture (USDA). The Department of Agriculture has been in existence since 1889 and has approximately 100,000 employees (USDA, 2020a). The USDA is led by a secretary, a deputy secretary, and three assistant secretaries. Under the deputy secretary are eleven offices and eight undersecretaries in charge of various divisions. The Under Secretary for Natural Resources and Environment is the division that houses the USFS (USDA, 2020b). In addition to the USFS, the USDA houses 29 different federal agencies (USDA, 2020a).

The USFS is responsible for the management of 192 million acres of land across 44 states in the United States as well as Puerto Rico and the Virgin Islands and has approximately 35,000 employees (Sparling, 2014; USFS, 2020a). The leader of the USFS is known as a chief and there are four deputy chiefs—one for each of the four main divisions of the USFS. The four divisions or branches are the National Forest System, State and Private Forestry, Research and Development, and International Programs. Each of those divisions or branches then has its own hierarchy and bureaucracy. The National Forest System consists of four levels in its hierarchy. The National Forest System is divided into nine regions. Each region is supervised by a regional forester. Each region is then divided into national forests and grasslands. There are 155 national forests and 20 grasslands. Each national forest and grassland is supervised by a forest supervisor. Each national forest and grassland is then divided into ranger districts. Each ranger district is supervised by a district ranger (USFS, 2020b).

The Law Enforcement and Investigations Division of the USFS is organized similarly. This division is supervised by a director that reports to the chief of the USFS. The Law Enforcement Division is also organized in relation to the nine regions of the USFS. A special agent in charge is assigned to each region. Each region is then further divided into zones, and special agents are assigned to the zones depending on the workload of each zone. Directly under each special agent in charge are two supervisors—one for the investigative division and one patrol commander to supervise the enforcement operations. Then underneath these two supervisors in the hierarchy are either the investigators or patrol personnel respectively. The division's approximately 600 employees are then assigned to one of the nine regions (USFS, 2020c).

CONCLUSION

While there is variation in how conservation law enforcement agencies are organized, they are government agencies and generally adhere to a bureaucratic structure. This structure allows for task specialization and otherwise organizes the work of the organization. The most common arrangement is for conservation law enforcement officers to be housed within a larger department of natural resources, where they are one of the divisions within the larger organization. Within their division, they have a hierarchy that delineates the command-and-control structure, where each level of organization has specific tasks for which they are responsible. The types and frequency of their tasks will be influenced by how their particular organization is organized. At the federal level, there are multiple agencies that are responsible for conservation law enforcement. Even though they participate in conservation law enforcement, they are not all housed within a singular organization that specializes in conservation law enforcement. Regardless, they too are government agencies and adhere to a bureaucratic structure.

DISCUSSION QUESTIONS

1. The most common arrangement is for conservation officers to be housed within larger departments of natural resources or conservation, instead of departments of public safety. What are the advantages of conservation officers being housed in a non-law enforcement agency such as a department of natural resources? What are the disadvantages? What would the advantages be for conservation officers to be housed within a law enforcement-oriented department of public safety? What are the disadvantages? Which is the best arrangement—a department of natural resources or department of public safety? Explain.

2. The protection of natural resources is a complex enterprise in the United States, which includes multiple federal agencies as well as at least one state-level agency in each state. In addition, there are also some local agencies that manage municipal parks, etc. Is this the best arrangement for the protection of natural resources? Is it too complicated? If this is the best arrangement, then explain why. If not, then explain why it is not the best arrangement and what would be a better arrangement.

Key Terms

Bureaucratic structure: A formal organizational structure that creates a hierarchy or chain of command and is characterized by formal roles, rules, and regulations that coordinate the organization's activities.

Commission: A group of people with administrative authority. Similar to a board of directors.

Formalization: A characteristic of a bureaucracy related to the number of rules and regulations present in the organization. An organization with a high degree of formalization will have many rules and regulations.

Horizontal complexity: A characteristic of a bureaucracy that is related to how wide the organization is. Organizations will have various subunits at different levels of the organization. How many subunits occur at a particular level is related to its horizontal complexity.

Organizational hierarchy: An organizational structure based on levels of authority. Those with more authority are located higher in the organization than those with less authority. It is directly related to a chain of command where supervisors are located above subordinates.

Spatial complexity: A characteristic of a bureaucracy related to how an organization is organized throughout a geographic area. The number of components of the organization that are spread out over a given area is related to its spatial complexity.

Vertical complexity: A characteristic of a bureaucracy that is related to how tall the organization is. An organizational hierarchy consists of levels of authority within an organization. The more levels that exist is related to its vertical complexity.

References

Association of Fish and Wildlife Agencies (AFWA). (2010). *A comparison of the organizational structure of state fish and wildlife agency commissions and boards.* California Fish & Wildlife Strategic Vision Management Assistance Team. https://vision.ca.gov /docs/Management_Assitance_Team.pdf.

Bean, M. J. (1978). Federal wildlife law. In H. P. Brokaw (Ed.), *Wildlife and America: Contributions to an understanding of American wildlife and its conservation* (pp. 279–289). U.S. Government Printing Office.

Bernhardt, D. (2019). Departmental overview. https://www.doi.gov/ sites/doi.gov/files/uploads/fy2020_bib_dh005.pdf.

Blau, P. M., & Scott, W. R. (2003). *Formal organizations: A comparative approach.* Stanford University Press.

Blevins, K. R., & Edwards, T. D. (2009). Wildlife crime. In J. M. Miller (Ed.), *21st century criminology: A reference handbook. Volume 1* (pp. 557–563). Sage.

Bolman, L. E., & Deal, T. E. (2003). *Reframing organizations: Artistry, choice and leadership* (3rd ed.). Jossey-Bass.

Bureau of Land Management (BLM). (2020a). Headquarters move west. https://www.blm.gov/office/national-office/hq-move-west.

Bureau of Land Management (BLM). (2020b). Organization chart. https://www.blm.gov/about/organization-chart.

Bureau of Land Management (BLM). (2020c). Law enforcement headquarters. https://www.blm.gov/office/law-enforcement-headquarters.

Bureau of Land Management (BLM). (2020d). What we do. https:// www.blm.gov/programs/public-safety-and-fire/law-enforcement /what-we-do.

Colorado Department of Parks and Wildlife (CDPW). (2020). Operation game thief. https://cpw.state.co.us/aboutus/Pages /OGT.aspx#:~:text=Operation%20Game%20Thief%20was%20 pioneered,in%20more%20than%20700%20convictions.

Criscoe, M. C. (1999). North Carolina Wildlife Resources Commission patrol wildlife detector canine program. *Proceedings of the Southeast Association of Fish and Wildlife Agencies Annual Conference, USA, 53*, 480–487.

Dunlap, T. R. (1988). *Saving America's wildlife.* Princeton University Press.

Falcone, D. (2004). America's conservation police: Agencies in transition. *Policing: An International Journal of Police Strategies & Management, 27*(1), 56–66.

Giblin, M. J. (2014). *Organization and management in the criminal justice system: A text/reader.* Sage.

Hughes, T., & Chavez, K. (2019). Death on the trail: More Americans visit national parks, but fewer rangers on patrol. *USA Today.* https://www.usatoday.com/story/news/nation/2019/06/29/national-parks-rangers-vanishing-putting-visitors-risk/1503627001/.

Iowa Department of Natural Resources. (2020). Volunteer opportunities. https://www.iowadnr.gov/About-DNR/Volunteer-Opportunities.

Katz, D., & Kahn, R. L. (1978). *The social psychology of organizations* (2nd ed.). John Wiley.

Keefe, J. F. (1987). *The first 50 years.* Missouri Department of Conservation.

Kenney, D. J. & Alpert, G. P. (1997). A national survey of pursuits and the use of police force: Data from law enforcement agencies. *Journal of Criminal Justice, 25*(4), 315–323.

Krause, T. (2012). *Returning river otters to their natural habitat. Thank you Mr. Sevin sir.* National Animal Interest Alliance. http://www.naiaonline.org/articles/article/returning-river-otters-to-former-habitat-thank-you-mr.-sevin-sir#sthash.26RFMdFc.dpbs.

Lord, J. K., & Cheng, A. S. (2006). Public involvement in state fish and wildlife agencies in the U.S.: A thumbnail sketch of techniques and barriers. *Human Dimensions of Wildlife, 11*, 55–69.

Maguire. E. R. (2003). *Organizational structure in American police agencies: Context, complexity and control.* State University of New York Press.

Management Assistance Team. (2010). *A comparison of the organizational structure of state fish and wildiife agency commissions and boards.* Association of Fish and Wildlife Agencies.

McIver, S. B. (2003). *Death in the Everglades: The murder of Guy Bradley, America's first martyr to environmentalism.* University Press of Florida.

Missouri Department of Conservation (MDC). (2020). Contact and engage. https://mdc.mo.gov/contact-engage.

National Park Service (NPS). (2020a). Frequently asked questions. https://www.nps.gov/aboutus/faqs.htm.

National Park Service (NPS). (2020b). Organizational structure of the National Park Service. https://www.nps.gov/subjects/uspp/office-of-the-chief.htm.

National Park Service (NPS). (2020c). What we do: Investigations and more. https://www.nps.gov/orgs/1563/investigations-and-more.htm.

Nelson, C., & Verbyla, D. (1984). Characteristics and effectiveness of state anti-poaching campaigns. *Wildlife Society Bulletin, 12*(2), 117–122.

New Mexico Department of Game and Fish (NMDGF). (2020). Operation game thief. http://www.wildlife.state.nm.us/enforcement/operation-game-thief-overview/.

New York Department of Environmental Conservation (NYDEC). (2005). *Standing watch—125 years of conservation law enforcement in New York State.* https://www.dec.ny.gov/regulations/2744.html.

Nurse, A. (2013). Privatising the green police: The role of NGOs in wildlife law enforcement. *Crime, Law and Social Change, 59*, 305–318.

Oregon State Police. (2020). Division of fish and wildlife. https://www.oregon.gov/osp/programs/fw/Pages/default.aspx.

Palmer, C. E., & Bryant, C. F. (1985). "Keepers of the king's deer" Game wardens and the enforcement of fish and wildlife law. In C. D. Bryant, D. J. Shoemaker, J. K. Skipper, & W. E. Snizek (Eds.), *The rural work force: Non-agricultural occupations in America.* (pp. 111–137). Bergin & Garvey Publishers Inc.

Pepper, S. M. (2003). Law enforcement management in conservation outreach programs in Alabama. *Proceedings of the Southeast Association of Fish and Wildlife Agencies Annual Conference, USA, 57*, 357–363.

Perrow, C. (1986). *Complex organizations: A critical essay* (3rd ed). McGraw-Hill.

Scott, W. R. (1992). *Organizations: Rational, natural and open systems* (3rd ed.). Prentice Hall.

Scott, W. R., & Davis, G. F. (2007). *Organizations and organizing: Rational, natural and open systems perspectives.* Pearson.

Smith, L. J. (2010). The organizational environment and its influence on state criminal justice systems within the United States and the offender re-integration process. In S. Stojkovic, J. Klofas, & D. Kalinich (Eds.), *The administration and management by criminal justice organizations: A book of readings* (5th ed., pp. 19–38). Waveland Press Inc.

Sparling, D. (2014). *Natural resource administration: Wildlife, fisheries, forests and parks.* Elsevier.

Stojkovic, S., Kalinich, D., & Klofas, J. (2015). *Criminal justice organizations: Administration and management* (6th ed.). Cengage.

Thom, R. H., & Wilson, J. H. (1983). The natural divisions of Missouri. *Natural Areas Journal, 3*(2), 44–51.

TRAFFIC. (2019). *Combatting wildlife crime linked to the Internet: Global trends and China's experiences.* https://www.traffic.org/site/assets/files/12352/combating-wildlife-crime-online-chinas-experiences.pdf.

Trefethen, J. B. (1975). *An American crusade for wildlife.* Winchester Press.

United States Department of Agriculture (USDA). (2020a). About the US Department of Agriculture. https://www.usda.gov/our-agency/about-usda#:~:text=The%20U.S.%20Department%20of%20Agriculture%20(USDA)%20is%20made%20up%20of,across%20the%20country%20and%20abroad.

United States Department of Agriculture (USDA). (2020b). USDA organizational chart. https://www.usda.gov/sites/default/files/documents/usda-organization-chart.pdf.

United States Department of the Interior (USDOI). (2020a). About our employees. https://www.doi.gov/employees/about.

United States Department of the Interior (USDOI). (2020b). Departments and bureaus. https://www.doi.gov/bureaus.

United States Fish and Wildlife Service (USFWS). (2013). Federal Aid in Sport Fish Restoration Act. https://www.fws.gov/laws/lawsdigest/FASPORT.html.

United States Fish and Wildlife Service (USFWS). (2020a). About the U.S. Fish and Wildlife Service. https://www.fws.gov/help/about_us.html.

United States Fish and Wildlife Service (USFWS). (2020b). About Service law enforcement. https://www.fws.gov/le/about-le.html.

United States Fish and Wildlife Service (USFWS). (2020c). Refuge law enforcement. https://www.fws.gov/refuges/lawEnforcement/index.php.

United States Fish and Wildlife Service (USFWS). (2020d). U.S. Fish and Wildlife Service national organizational chart. https://fws.gov/offices/org-chart.html.

United State Forest Service (USFS). (2020a). Agency organization. https://www.fs.usda.gov/about-agency/organization.

United States Forest Service (USFS). (2020a). Understanding the Forest Service. https://www.fs.usda.gov/main/prc/legal-administrativeresources/forestservice.

United States Forest Service (USFS). (2020b). USDA Forest Service law enforcement and investigations. https://www.fs.fed.us/lei/organization.php.

United States Park Police. (2020a). Proudly serving since 1791. https://www.nps.gov/subjects/uspp/index.htm.

United States Park Police. (2020b). United States Park Police organizational structure. https://www.nps.gov/subjects/uspp/office-of-the-chief.htm.

White, T. H. (1995). The role of covert operations in modern wildlife law enforcement. *Proceedings of the Southeast Association of Fish and Wildlife Agencies Annual Conference, USA, 49*, 692–697.

Wilson, J. Q. (1989). *Bureaucracy: What government agencies do and why they do it.* Basic Books.

Five

LEGAL ASPECTS OF CONSERVATION LAW ENFORCEMENT

The laws pertaining to fish and wildlife are convoluted, to say the least. In the United States, people pursuing outdoor interests, and those who are responsible for enforcement of the law, are frequently subject to the rules of international agreements and treaties, federal laws, state laws, and the search authority of law enforcement that exhibits substantial variation between each state. Some states offer greater protections to their residents than are offered by the US Constitution, some offer relatively similar protections, while others have expanded search authority for fish and wildlife officers that may or may not extend beyond conventionally conceived constitutional rights (Haden & Israel, 2015; McLain, 2018). The following chapter highlights major international and US laws pertaining to the protection of wildlife and novel state laws that do the same. Additionally, the chapter concludes with examinations of state laws expanding conservation officer search authority, and a brief critical assessment of constitutional implications.

INTERNATIONAL AGREEMENTS AND TREATIES

The United States is party to many international agreements, covenants, and treaties that are designed to preserve or conserve natural resources and offer protection from damage to the natural environment. The US has bilateral or multilateral agreements with other nations on a host of important concerns. For example, the Trilateral Committee for Wildlife and Ecosystem Management is an agreement between the United States, Mexico, and Canada that involves numerous provisions to protect natural resources in North America. The international cooperation even involves mutual training for law enforcement personnel on issues related to border areas. Similar agreements have been developed with China (the US-China Nature Conservation Protocol), Russia (the US-Russia Environmental Agreement), and Japan (the US-Japan Migratory Bird Convention). In general, these agreements provide for research funding and research expertise in order to allow for the protection of vulnerable species across the world (USFWS, 2020a).

In addition to these bilateral or multilateral agreements, the US has also entered into multinational species conservation acts, or laws that seek to preserve or conserve a specific species that is often located in distinct geographic regions, and where the state exercising sovereignty over that region agrees to special assistance and resources from the US, which is often a consumer of animals and products exported from less wealthy nations. For example, the African Elephant Conservation Act of 1989 provides funding for protection of elephants, with substantial funds provided by the USFWS. A great deal of these funds are spent on research grants, habitat preservation and protection, construction projects that mitigate human-wildlife conflict, and funding for community rangers, law enforcement, and rapid response teams designed to proactively prevent poaching in vulnerable, at-risk, or ecologically important elephant populations (USFWS, 2020b). The US has entered into similar agreements worldwide, including the Asian Elephant Conservation Act, Great Ape Conservation Act, Marine Turtle Conservation Act, and the Rhino and Tiger Conservation Act.

Perhaps the most well-known, and most significant, international treaty ratified by the United States with respect to the maintenance of biodiversity is the Convention on International Trade in Endangered Species of Wild Fauna and Flora (**CITES**). CITES is an agreement voluntarily entered into by States in an effort to make sure the international trade in plant and animal specimens does not threaten the survival of those species. In 1973, representatives from 80 countries met in Washington, DC, to approve the language present in CITES, and the agreement became binding to member countries in 1975. To date, 183 member parties have officially joined CITES to control international trade of vulnerable species, as well as species that resemble threatened or endangered species (CITES, 2020).

The logic of how CITES can help ensure the survival of endangered and threatened species is to control trade in specimens between consumer countries (generally those with higher wealth, such as the US) and producer countries (generally countries low in wealth but high in biodiversity). As some countries have built increasing wealth, demand for luxury goods has increased in those nations. For example, China has increasingly moved from a producer nation to a consumer nation. This highlights that a party's role as a consumer or producer is not fixed, but is dependent upon the supply and demand for animal specimens in any given nation (Reeve, 2002).

Trade in plant and animal specimens is typically controlled through a permitting system. Permitting allows export nations to monitor the harvest for external consumption (CITES does not engage in permitting for specimens that remain in a nation), which in turn promotes the sustainable use of species. Additionally, import permits are also required to bring regulated species into a nation (Reeve, 2002).

There is rarely any quota system attached to the import and export of species, but the harvest numbers allow for Scientific Authorities to inform member parties about the consequences their actions are likely to have on wild populations. Thus, if an exporting nation produced a large number of exotic birds, the Scientific Authority would alert this nation that their behavior may be detrimental to the existing bird populations. Similarly, the United States, which is the largest importer of exotic birds in the world, may elect to place quotas or moratoriums on the importation of birds if importing behavior is detrimental to bird stocks in export countries (CITES, 2020).

CITES also employs a tiered system, which places restrictions on the types of permits that can be obtained for a specific species. The highest level of protection is that provided to Appendix I species. These species are those whose existence is threatened by the opening of trade in specimens. Under CITES, the trade of wild-caught specimens in this category is prohibited, and captive-bred individuals are protected under similar guidelines as Appendix II, which requires both export and import permits. In addition to the permits, the Scientific Authority advising the export country must offer a finding that trading in the captive specimens does not offer a threat to the wild specimens existing in that nation (CITES, 2020; Reeve, 2002).

For Appendix II species, there is generally a request made by exporting countries that species be listed in order to protect wild populations that may be negatively impacted by international trade. According to the convention, only export permits are required for trade in these species. However, specific nations may elect to require import permits via their domestic law in order to assist in the protection of vulnerable species. Appendix III species also require export permits issued by the exporting nation's Management Authority, but generally these permits are required to ensure that specimens are legally obtained and humanely packed for shipment (CITES, 2020).

US DOMESTIC LAWS

As noted, CITES does not impose laws that govern the behaviors of parties. Rather, parties are responsible for creating a legal framework within their country that promotes the proper use of plant and animal specimens. In the United States, this is notably achieved through domestic laws such as the **Endangered Species Act** (ESA), Marine Mammal Protection Act, Wild Bird Conservation Act (WBCA), **Lacey Act**, and the Pelly Amendment. Other domestic policies include the Migratory Bird Treaty Act, Migratory Bird Hunting and Conservation Stamp Act, and the Bald and Golden Eagle Protection Act (USFWS, 2020c).

Chronologically, one of the first large-scale legislative responses to the loss of biodiversity that occurred in the United States at the federal level was the Lacey Act of 1900 [16 U.S.C. §§3371–3378], commonly designated as the Lacey Act. The Lacey Act, as introduced by John Lacey, sought to preserve game, song, and other wild birds, prevent problematic introduction of exotic species, and supplement the state laws protecting wildlife that were already in existence.

The push for this law came in response to the commercialization of wildlife as a likely cause of extinction. During the late 1800s, several notable extinctions or near extinctions of species occurred. First, the passenger pigeon, which had once numbered in the billions (Fuller, 2014; Greenberg, 2014), was on its way to extinction (the last known passenger pigeon died in captivity in the Cincinnati Zoo in 1914). Similarly, other species which were marketable for their meat, including prairie chickens and American bison, were undergoing drastic reductions in their populations due primarily to market hunting (USFWS, 2020c; Hoch, 2015). Threats to species viability also came from hunting birds for their plumage. Great egrets and snowy egrets were killed by the millions each year in order to meet the demand of the millinery industry in places like New York, which produced hats for women's fashion (Serratore, 2018).

In accordance with these goals, the United States government created both criminal and civil penalties for the sale or trade of specimens that had been illegally harvested, possessed, transported, or traded. The act makes specific requirements about the packaging, documentation, and trafficking of specimens. Any interstate movement of wildlife or fish specimens must be plainly marked, labeled, or tagged according to regulation governing said activity or a civil fine may be assessed. Furthermore, producing false documents for interstate shipment of fish and animal parts may result in criminal sanctions, including felony offenses if the value of the item or items exceeds $350. Additionally, the Lacey Act provides for civil and criminal penalties for the transportation, possession, sale, or trade of illegal wildlife. This means that two criteria must be met for the trafficking violations to attach. First, the take, possession, transport, or trade must have violated state or federal law *and* the specimen must have been moved or obtained in violation of the Lacey Act. Civil penalties for a violation may not exceed $10,000, but felony criminal sanctions may involve up to five years in prison and up to $500,000 in fines for organizations that violate the act (USFWS, 2020c).

While the Lacey Act was certainly an early step in the right direction for addressing commerce in illegally taken animals, it fell well short of the protections required to preserve biodiversity both in the United States and abroad. The Lacey Act did not actively create laws that made it illegal to capture or harvest threatened or endangered species. Nor did it address threats from humans that were not directly consumptive, and arguably more damaging, such as habitat loss and the use of pesticides and herbicides (USFWS, 2020c). In response to increasing awareness of threats to charismatic species such as the whooping crane, and thoughtful scientific publications such as Rachel Carson's (1962) *Silent Spring*, the US government began modifying domestic policy to protect threatened and endangered wildlife from various existential threats.

Several protections were put into place by the federal government prior to the ESA (which Congress passed in 1973) that focused on preservation of habitat. In 1963, the Land and Water Conservation Fund (a fund established via the extraction of natural resources on federally held lands) included language specifying that the US government could use money generated by the program to acquire land essential to the preservation of endangered species (Goble et al., 2006). This was a change on two fronts, in that the protections expanded beyond the consumptive extraction of individual animals, and that it applied beyond traditionally conceptualized game species into wider protections for all threatened and endangered species (Goble et al., 2006). Similar expansions occurred under the 1966 Endangered Species Preservation Act and Endangered Species Conservation Act of 1969.

As noted by the US ratification of CITES, American prosperity and desire for exotic luxury goods represented a threat not only to species inside of US borders, but abroad. Thus, in 1973, to protect species native to the United States and those American residents contributed to depleting abroad, the ESA was passed nearly unanimously. The ESA helps to protect wildlife by listing species as threatened or endangered and providing concomitant recovery plans (Section 4), prohibiting trading of any endangered species (Section 9), and outlining both civil and criminal penalties for illegal trade or other violations that are injurious to endangered species (Section 11).

State Wildlife Laws

In the United States, the primary responsibility for managing wildlife rests in the power of the states. While the federal government does exert control over endangered species, interstate commerce, international trade, and fishing in federal waters, these interests are quite small compared to the widespread regulation necessary to ensure conservation of numerous game and nongame species. Given this responsibility, the resulting state laws have generally focused on regulating take of animals, responding to injurious damage caused by animals held in the state trust, habitat improvement, and disease control. While the challenges and resulting state laws are too numerous to mention, we give a brief synopsis of the goals associated with each body of law and subsequent examples of how states have sought to achieve these goals.

Regulating Take of Animals

As mentioned in Chapter Two, when the United States made its separation from England, the colonists and early Americans took a much more laissez-faire approach to the conservation of wildlife than did their European counterparts. The relics of these differences can still be seen in comparisons and contrasts between the North American and European models of conservation (Cooney, 2019), where wildlife in the United States is generally held as state property in the public trust and cannot be harvested and sold unless strictly regulated by the state, and wildlife in Europe is owned by the landowners and is permissible for sale.

Due to the overharvest of species by European settlers on the North American continent, one of the first areas to be regulated by state law was the elimination of market hunters and restrictions placed on the sale of wild game meat and other products such as bird plumes (Lund, 1980). Initial state laws focused on regulating the devices that could be used to harvest fish and game. While these laws did not specifically target the sale of game and associated products, it was clear that they were targeting the efficacy of market hunters and their ability to harvest copious specimens with little effort (Lund, 1980).

Eventually, state laws began to outright ban the sale of game. The turn of the twentieth century brought extinction and rapidly diminishing game stocks, along with more widespread economic success through the Industrial Revolution. The fact that many Americans had become wealthy enough to afford to buy farm-raised meat and poultry, without supply from wild game to defray the costs, meant that legal intervention banning the sale of wild meat could proceed without negatively impacting the nutrition of most residents (Lund, 1980). The severe curtailment of commercial interests in hunting (and to a lesser degree fishing), paved the way for these activities to be regulated as recreational rather than economic consumptive interests.

Following the movement into regulating the harvest of animals as recreational opportunities rather than industrial commercial opportunities, states began to also control the harvest by recreational hunters through licensure, harvest limits, and closed seasons. Despite the increased control of hunter and angler behavior through licensing, the greater benefit to both state governments and in turn wildlife has been the generation of revenue that these licenses produce (Lund, 1980). The sale of hunting and fishing licenses by states results in a great deal of income going to states, which makes enforcement of wildlife laws more effective through staffing of law enforcement agencies. Additionally, a national sales tax on hunting and fishing equipment provided through the **Pittman-Robertson Act and Dingell-Johnson Act**, which then provide a substantial amount of money for habitat, is tied to each state's generation of hunting and fishing license sales (USFWS, 2020d; Ducks Unlimited, 2020).

Licensing also provides for using hunters and anglers to achieve conservation-related goals by exerting control over the devices, times, dates, strategies, and types of animals that can be harvested in order to meet population goals while also allowing for significant opportunity to hunt and fish. One way that licensing allows for the control of populations while still permitting opportunity is via allowing more copious harvest of males, and restricting the harvest of females in instances where the number of females is the limiting factor in maintaining the number of individuals that are present in a population of animals (Lund, 1980). Thus, in some instances only males are permitted to be taken, or more males are permitted than females, or the number of females harvested is controlled through a lottery draw system (Michigan Department of Natural Resources, 2020a). In instances where animal populations are above goals, states may issue a seemingly unlimited number of permits to harvest females of a species, or even require the harvest of a specific number of females before a male can be harvested, as Wisconsin did with whitetail deer in its "earn-a-buck" program (Wisconsin Department of Natural Resources, 2020).

States have also sought to maximize opportunity by controlling the types of implements that can be used. For example, many states offer widespread or even unlimited numbers of archery permits to hunt game species such as elk, because the efficacy of hunting with archery devices is so low that many get the chance to hunt with little impact on the resource (Montana Fish, Wildlife & Parks, 2020). These seasons are also open during mating season, and firearm seasons in these same locations are generally issued through a lottery system and occur after breeding season (Montana Fish, Wildlife & Parks, 2020; Wyoming Game & Fish Department, 2020). States may also seek to control the efficacy of harvest through banning the use of bait, electronic calls, dogs, and specific types of decoys. Harvest can also be controlled through season length, time of day, and allowing or forbidding other interest groups, such as trappers, a specific amount of the overall harvest (Freyfogle & Goble, 2009; Lund, 1980).

Responding to Damage Caused by Wildlife Held in State Trust

Even though animals in the United States are held in the state trust, states are not liable for the damage caused by wild animals simply because they are owned by the state government (Freyfogle & Goble, 2009). As noted by Freyfogle and Goble (2009), the situations in which state governments have been held liable for damage by wild animals is really limited to only a few instances. These instances are typically when the state government fails to properly maintain state-owned property, which then becomes attractive to wildlife and said wildlife subsequently causes injury. The other instance is when wildlife is creating an obvious threat of injury or damage, and the state fails to warn citizens of the potential dangers present.

Despite the fact that states are not specifically liable for damage caused by wildlife, these states often engage in programs that permit the lethal control of wildlife to mitigate damage, work to modify human behaviors, or engage in action that increases tolerance for wildlife. In many states, animals causing damage are permitted to be killed either through blanket statements of the law or the issuance of **damage control permits** that allow for lethal responses to animals causing damage (Michigan Department of Natural Resources, 2020b; New York Department of Environmental Conservation, 2020). In some instances, states enter into agreements with the US Department of Agriculture and their Wildlife Services program, which then engages in lethal control of animals in more sensitive settings where permitting hunting would be problematic (USDA, 2020). Alternatively, some states engage in outreach programs to counsel interests having damage problems on how to modify their behavior to mitigate wildlife conflict (Gore et al., 2008). To increase public tolerance for animals that are causing damage, states will often orchestrate compensation programs to farmers and ranchers who experience damage and financial injury from wild animals (Wagner et al., 1997).

Disease Control

States have also engaged hunters to prevent the spread of disease among wildlife populations, and control their possible spread to other wildlife, farms, and humans. One example of an area that states have had to exert controls is on animal game farms, most commonly wild cervid (i.e., deer, elk) farms in the United States (Cosgrove, 2017). The main concern with operations on wild cervid farms is the spread of a disease known as Chronic Wasting Disease (CWD). In order to prevent the spread of CWD, states have taken actions such as forbidding the importation of any cervids into the state, outlawing possession of penned deer, banning deer baiting and feeding, and forbidding the interstate transport of specific parts of wildlife (typically portions of the central nervous system where the prions that cause CWD are likely to be found).

Police Authority to Search and Constitutional Law

In virtually all instances, before the police can enforce violations of the law via arrest, some form of investigation must occur prior to making the arrest. At the most basic level, these investigations are often comprised of gaining witness testimony, which may take the form of interrogations of potential suspects. It also usually includes questioning victims and witnesses for their testimony as well. The protection from self-incrimination was strongly established by the landmark SCOTUS case of *Miranda v. Arizona*, which required officers to inform criminal suspects of their rights prior to effecting an arrest. Most Americans are quite familiar with their protections from police intrusion into their lives via interrogation techniques and can identify that they "have the right to remain silent." Many may not understand that it applies to custodial interrogations, and that information offered not as a result of questioning may also be used. Additionally, police officers failing to "read" suspects their rights does not make an arrest illegal, it simply means the testimony obtained via interrogation is not admissible in court (Thomas & Leo, 2002).

There are also several exceptions or caveats to the protections offered under the Fifth Amendment with respect to self-incrimination. One way that protections received by citizens have changed since *Miranda* is that interrogations that occur prior to an actual arrest (e.g., taking a suspect into custody) are not protected under the Fifth Amendment. Similarly, police do not have to read a suspect their rights after taking them into custody, and evidence is suppressed only if it occurred because of interrogation. Thus, any spontaneous outbursts or statements that a suspect makes may be admissible, even if the officer did not inform the suspect of their rights (Thomas & Leo, 2002). In general, the Fifth Amendment applies to conservation officers in exactly the same way that it does to standard law enforcement officers, and even though many myths exist as to the authority of conservation officers with respect to their authority in investigations, the ability to compel personally incriminating testimony is generally not one of the concerns most frequently listed (LaCaze, 2014).

The authority of conservation officers to search persons, their vehicles, hunting blinds, ice fishing shanties, tents, recreational vehicles, cabins, and homes remains one of the most misunderstood areas of policing and research. The confusion among the public as to the search authority granted to wildlife law enforcement officers across the United States often leads to myths that are persistently offered by outdoorsmen and women as to how much authority conservation officers have. La-Caze (2014) has noted that some hunters sincerely believed that officers could search someone's vehicles, residence, or even freezers within a residence whenever they chose, to uncover evidence of violations of fish and game laws. While LaCaze (2014) noted that this was largely exaggerated, the fact remains that officers tasked with protecting natural resources do in fact have some search authority that is not granted to conventional police officers, but legal scholars disagree as to whether this authority is in violation of constitutional protections (Haden & Israel, 2015; McLain, 2018).

Conservation Officer Search Authority

When examining the legal authority of conservation officers to conduct searches of persons, private property, vehicles, and dwelling homes, a great deal of confusion exists, and frequently myths are provided by sportspersons to fill in the gaps. Those who enjoy outdoor pursuits such as hunting and fishing are frequently under the impression that conservation officers enjoy unlimited authority to search hunters and anglers, private property, boats and cars, tents, and even homes. A reason that these myths persist is that there is little national case law articulating exactly what behaviors are appropriate or inappropriate for conservation officers. Given the unique circumstances and challenges of their work, state courts and legislatures have often provided the guidance, leaving a patchwork nation of what behaviors are admissible or inadmissible for officers. The truth is a much more complex issue, which we address in focusing in on the least protected (but still protected) private property, followed by vehicles, temporary shelters, cabins, and domiciles.

Conservation Officer Search Authority on Open Private Lands

An additional explanation for why conservation officer authority may be subject to so many myths, is that the public is not well informed about what search authority conventional police officers possess. Police officers are permitted to conduct searches on open private property, but the confines of where conventional officers might search, and where conservation officers might search, could be vastly different.

In the 1924 case *Hester v. United States*, SCOTUS established what has become referred to as the "**open fields doctrine**." Essentially, this case determined that protections from unreasonable search and seizure do not apply to private lands, even if those lands are posted as "no trespassing," fenced, or both, which was affirmed in the court case *Oliver v. United States* (1984). The only areas of open private property that are protected under the Fourth Amendment are what is considered the curtilage of one's dwelling home. Essentially, this is the small yard encompassing an area around a house. This had been determined not to include areas surrounding garages, barns, or sheds that are often found on private property outside of the area immediately surrounding one's home (*United States v. Dunn*, 1987). Therefore, the United States Constitution holds that police officers in general have a great deal of authority to search private property, and that crossing fences, walking past "no trespassing" signs, and moving deep into large tracts of open private lands are not an authority unique to conservation officers, but that doing so may simply be more unique to conservation officer-related tasks.

Alternatively, some states actually do permit conservation officers more search authority on open private lands, or at least articulate specifically that this authority exists for those who enforce fish and game laws. For example, the state of Texas provides explicitly in their state laws that conservation officers may enter posted, fenced, or other locations where the public is excluded. More expansively, Texas permits game wardens to search containers or receptables (e.g., coolers) that commonly hold fish and game to check for illegal harvest of natural resources (Overturf, 2019; TEX. STAT. §12.103; TEX. STAT. §12.104). While not allowing for any expanded search authority, Florida and Pennsylvania also provide unmistakable language giving conservation officers permission to search posted private lands (FLA. STAT. §379.3311[e] [2019]; 34 Pa. Stat. And Cons. Stat. Ann. §901).

Alternatively, states do have the option of offering more protection from search and seizure by legal authorities than is offered under the US Constitution. In one instance, the expansion of legal protections from unreasonable search and seizure by law enforcement officers in Montana actually resulted from the actions of a conservation officer and the ensuing legal case. Case law in Montana now dictates that residents may expect to have privacy even in areas that are beyond the curtilage of their homes, if barriers or signage indicate that no one is permitted to enter without some evidence of illegal activity (*State v. Bullock*, 1995).

In the court case that established these protections in the state of Montana (*State v. Bullock*, 1995), three poachers killed a bull elk illegally, and then moved the carcass to an area near a cabin and garage that was down a driveway nearly 100 yards off of a forest service road, past a gate that was open at the time. Officers drove 60 yards down the driveway, through the open gate but past clearly marked no trespassing signs, before they were able to see the illegally taken elk. Thus, in Montana, illegal activities must be visible from publicly accessible areas, and residents can have an expectation of privacy on private property irrespective of the confined curtilage of their home. This expansion of protections (or diminishment of officers' search authority) exists in a similar form in Oregon (*State v. Dixson*, 1988), New York (*People v. Scott*, 1992), Vermont (*State v. Kirchoff*, 1991), and Washington (*State v. Johnson*, 1994). In these states, there would still not be a difference in the authority to search open public lands between conservation and general officers, but the increased restrictiveness of the authority to search open private lands may more greatly affect the ability of conservation police to fulfill the law enforcement portion of their role than traditional police officers.

Drawing upon these state laws and SCOTUS interpretations of constitutional protections provided by the Fourth Amendment, there is really not any indication that conservation officers are restricted from entering any type of open private property, or that this authority somehow is more expansive than that provided to all sworn law enforcement officers in the United States where they have jurisdiction. Conservation officers likely spend more time investigating on open private lands for violations of fish and game laws, and this may attach a perception among hunters and anglers that this authority is more expansive. In reality, the authority is not an extension of search authority, but conservation officers are simply more likely to exercise their abilities to search "open fields" given their role. When discussion of officer search authority moves to more protected areas such as vehicles and dwelling homes, it becomes apparent that conservation officers may be granted more authority under state laws.

Conservation Officer Search Authority of Persons

The authority to search persons or containers is another area in which police officers and conservation officers have ostensibly different authority, although the source of this authority often hinges upon the more expansive duties of COs to enforce hunting and fishing laws, which is a highly regulated activity.

In general, citizens in the United States are not required to provide identification to law enforcement unless they are driving, flying, or there is reasonable suspicion that the person is engaging in criminal activity (*Hilbel v. Sixth Judicial District Court of Nevada*, 2004). Additionally, when officers have reasonable suspicion that a crime has taken or is about to take place, officers are permitted to engage in a "pat down" search, which is often referred to as a "*Terry* **stop**," as this authority was upheld in the SCOTUS case *Terry v. Ohio* (1968).

Despite the restrictions placed upon conventional police officers, conservation officers are almost universally permitted to stop and check the licenses of hunters and anglers who are engaged in their respective activity to ensure that they are legally licensed in their pursuit. Alternatively, the SCOTUS case *Delaware v. Prouse* (1979) explicitly stated that drivers could not be stopped simply to determine that they were legally licensed to drive, but the concurring majority opinion directly stated that this restriction should not apply to conservation officers who are inspecting the licenses of those engaged in hunting and fishing.

Furthermore, most states permit conservation officers to inspect the bags, coats, and backpacks of individuals who are engaged in outdoor recreational pursuits such as hunting and angling (Overturf, 2019). Among the few exceptions, states such as Colorado and Wyoming permit officers to see all harvested fish and wildlife. Other states such as Ohio require suspicion, but then permit officers to search any place when they suspect wildlife has been taken illegally (Overturf, 2019). Other states (e.g., Kansas, Utah, Vermont) do not explicitly give officers the authority to search bags, coats, or containers without probable cause, but do explicitly permit officers to check equipment, apparatuses, and weapons used in pursuit of wildlife, or in the case of Kansas, allow inspection of licenses or other evidence by officers (Overturf, 2019).

Conservation Officer Search Authority of Vehicles

One of the most useful tools that an officer can use to initiate an investigation, and the most common way that residents in the United States have interactions with police officers, is through traffic stops (Davis et al., 2018). However, unlike entering unobtrusively onto private property, a traffic stop is more invasive and is considered a seizure under Fourth Amendment protections. Because of this intrusion, SCOTUS has held that police officers must be able to articulate reasonable suspicion in order to stop a motorist (*United States v. Arvizu*, 2002). This means that officers cannot stop any vehicle that they would like, or have a hunch is involved in illegal activity (like can be done with open fields), but that specific facts must be stated that would reasonably lead a person to believe that some violation of the law has occurred. One of the major Supreme Court cases that has upheld these protections specifically mentioned conservation officers, one of the few SCOTUS cases that has commented on conservation law enforcement.

In *Delaware v. Prouse* (1979), a patrol officer initiated a traffic stop to ensure that a motorist was legally licensed to operate a vehicle. Upon initiating the stop, the officer smelled marijuana and stated that they observed drugs in plain view. The court later determined that officers cannot simply stop motorists to check if they are legally licensed to drive, but that they must have reasonable suspicion of a violation. However, in their concurring opinion, Justices Blackmun and Powell specifically state that this decision should not prevent game wardens from fulfilling their duty of examining hunters and anglers to ensure that they are properly licensed (*Delaware v. Prouse*, 1979; Haden & Israel, 2015; McLain, 2018).

In many states, the authority of wildlife law enforcement to initiate traffic stops of vehicles that are travelling is more expansive than what has been decided in SCOTUS decisions. Specifically, case law in the state of California has given game wardens the authority to stop and question drivers who they have observed engaging in outdoor pursuits, but where no reasonable suspicion of any legal violations is present. In the case of *People v. Maikhio* (2011), two game wardens observed Maikhio fishing on a pier, but did not observe any legal violations. The officers initiated a traffic stop several blocks from the pier and directed Maikhio to display all fish and game that he had harvested on the pier (i.e., an illegally harvested spiny lobster). The Supreme Court of California opined that as long as the officers had reasonable suspicion that someone had been engaged in the act of hunting or fishing, the officers were permitted to stop the vehicle as an administrative search, that the car could be stopped, and that the driver must produce their hunting or fishing license as well as any harvested specimens (*People v. Maikhio*, 2011).

In a similar case, the state of Iowa upheld the authority of conservation officers to initiate traffic stops of hunters without reasonable suspicion of any illegal activity. In this case, Keehner was using a spotting scope and pair of binoculars to "glass" fields, which is an activity commonly associated with hunting, poaching, birdwatching, scouting, and examination of crop production. Upon the initiation of the traffic stop, Conservation Officer Rowley identified a loaded rifle in the truck, which was a violation of state law. The court determined that Iowa conservation officers have the legal authority to ask people who are engaged in hunting to produce a hunting license, and that Rowley had reasonable suspicion that Keehner was engaged in hunting, which permitted a traffic stop to inspect his hunting license (*State v. Keehner*, 1988). As noted in *Delaware v. Prouse* (1979), traffic stops to inspect for driving licenses are not permitted, but in Iowa stops to inspect for hunting licenses are.

Alternatively, other states have specifically affirmed that the protections from unreasonable seizure articulated in *Arvizu* apply to hunters or anglers who are actively engaging in outdoor pursuits in vehicles on roadways. The state of West Virginia in *State v. Legg* (2000) found that officers were not permitted to stop any vehicles in the woods or travelling the roadways near a common hunting area to conduct a "game survey." Officers indicated that they were under the impression that they had the legal authority to stop any vehicle in order to inspect for the possession of game animals, weapons, or hunting licenses, without reasonable suspicion of a legal violation. Contrary to what was at the time a West Virginia state law, the court held that conservation officers were not permitted to randomly stop any vehicle they chose in order to conduct a game survey. The state of Colorado decided that conservation officers must have reasonable suspicion of some legal violation before stopping a motor vehicle (*People v. Coca*, 1992), as has the state of New Mexico (*State v. Creech*, 1991). Similarly, the state of Illinois held in *State v. Levens* (1999) that reasonable suspicion of some illegal activity is required for a traffic stop (Butterfoss & Daly, 2004).

Unlike the roving stops, or stops of people who are obviously engaged in outdoor pursuits, the Supreme Court has allowed for the use of roadblock checkpoints in order to identify illegal behaviors that are imminently threatening, or to search for contraband in situations where there is little reasonable alternative, such as border crossings. In *Michigan Dept. of State Police v. Sitz* (1990), SCOTUS upheld the use of sobriety checkpoints. The majority opinion argued that the limited intrusion into motorists' privacy, coupled with the compelling state interest of protecting people from drunk drivers, made the use of these seizures constitutional. Additionally, the court specified that law enforcement must use some framework to determine which vehicles will be stopped to check for sobriety (e.g., stop every car, stop every sixth car), in order to mitigate the effect that officer biases might have on the burden of intrusion for citizens (*Michigan Dept. of State Police v. Sitz*, 1990).

The Supreme Court has subsequently clarified the boundaries of what types of roadblocks are permissible, and the anticipated violations that can be considered when establishing a checkpoint. In *City of Indianapolis v. Edmond* (2000), Indianapolis police officers initiated the use of checkpoints in order to search motorists for drug contraband. According to SCOTUS, this use of checkpoints was not constitutional, and represented too significant of an intrusion into the lives of motorists in the area. The significant difference, according to the courts, is that possession of drugs or associated paraphernalia is not markedly different than just simply searching for evidence of crime in general. Additionally, while drugs do have significant public health consequences, the threat to the public of a motorist possessing narcotics is not nearly as imminent a threat to public welfare as an intoxicated motorist.

In what might seem contrary to the *Edmond* decision, several states have upheld the use of roadblock checkpoints by conservation officers in order to search for contraband natural resources. Generally, these courts have focused on cases that allow checkpoints to achieve certain objectives. Namely, the checkpoint must achieve some compelling state interest, the checkpoint should be minimally intrusive and not engender fear and surprise among law-abiding motorists, and the agents must have a systematic protocol in place to prevent bias (e.g., stopping every car, stopping every *nth* car). The state courts of California (*People v. Perez*, 1996), Idaho (*State v. Thurman*, 1999; see also *Tanner v. Idaho*, 2019, for a case where checkpoints were upheld federally), Maine (*State v. Sherburne*, 1990), Mississippi (*Drane v. State*, 1986), Nebraska (*State v. Geissinger*, 1990), New Hampshire (*State v. Baldwin*, 1984), North Dakota (*State v. Albaugh*, 1997), Oregon (*State v. Tourtillott*, 1980), and South Dakota (*State v. Halverson*, 1979) allow these search strategies in situations where there is no immediate threat to human life. Similarly, checkpoint seizures to explore for hunting and fishing violations have been approved federally, generally involving enforcement near the entrances of national parks or federal wildlife areas (*U.S. v. Hunnicutt*, 2006; *U.S. v. Fraire*, 2009). Rarely do game law violations threaten public safety in the same way as intoxicated drivers, yet state courts have permitted these intrusions in contrast with SCOTUS decisions on the implementation of checkpoints. Similar checkpoint or suspicion-less stops of boaters have been approved in Illinois (*People v. Butorac*, 2013), Louisiana (*State v. McHugh*, 1994), and Minnesota (*State v. Larsen*, 2002).

In Oregon, the Oregon Supreme Court decided in the case *State v. Tourtillott* (1980) that the Oregon State Police Game Division was permitted to establish checkpoints that examined hunter compliance with the law, check for proper hunting licenses, and determine the rate of hunter success during deer season. In instances where the driver was not apparently involved in hunting, the officer would request a driver's license. In *Tourtillott*, a driver who was not engaged in hunting activity, and where no reasonable suspicion was evident, was subjected to enforcement action for driving with a suspended license. The state upheld her conviction and affirmed the use of checkpoints by wildlife officers for these types of enforcement actions. Similar behavior by officers engaged in wildlife enforcement, and then taking enforcement action for an expired motor vehicle safety inspection sticker and subsequent driving while license revoked, was upheld in the South Dakota case of *State v. Halverson* (1979).

Other state courts, such as Colorado, Nevada, and Utah, have not explicitly decided on the constitutionality of checkpoints for fish and game violations, but they are permitted under statute (C. R. S. §33-6-111; NV Rev. Stat. §501.375 [2014]; Utah Code 23-27-301). In other states (e.g., Iowa, Kansas, Kentucky, Montana, New York), there does not seem to be any expressed case law or state statute permitting the behavior, but evidence exists that conservation officers use checkpoints as an enforcement strategy fairly routinely (Farago, 2015). Still in other states (e.g., Maryland, Washington, Wyoming) there is evidence that checkpoints are used to combat the spread of invasive species (Beitzel & Edwards, 2015; Landers, 2017; Wyoming Game & Fish, 2020).

Conservation Officer Search Authority of Residences

In the United States, the locations in which people live have almost exclusively received the most protection under the Constitution and SCOTUS decisions. In nearly all instances, law enforcement must obtain a warrant in order to legally search someone's domicile. The generally recognized exceptions to warrant requirements are consent by the party involved, hot pursuit, public safety, and the limited area of the home incident to arrest when an arrest occurs in a dwelling (see *Agnello v. U.S.*, 1925; *Chimel v. California*, 1969). Outside of these exceptions, general law enforcement must obtain a warrant to search someone's home.

Unlike the expansiveness granted conservation officers in their legal authority to search vehicles, most states have not expanded the authority to include warrantless searches of dwellings, homes, or similar temporary living arrangements. The ephemeral nature of where people sleep while engaging in outdoor pursuits has created certain legal challenges for where conservation officers are legally allowed to search.

Throughout various cases, federal and state courts have determined that Fourth Amendment protections of dwellings/homes do extend to semi-fixed, temporary living arrangements such as tents (*State of Washington v. Pippin*, 2017; *U.S. v. Gooch*, 1993), but do not necessarily apply to more mobile and highly regulated recreational vehicles such as motorhomes (*California v. Carney*, 1985). In the *Carney* case, the more stringent Fourth Amendment protections were only withdrawn while the motorhome was acting as a conveyance in that it was operating on the road or had the potential to engage in imminent movement. The court explicitly stated that these vehicles would be treated more along the lines of a domicile when they are being used in a manner that indicates residential purposes. One could reasonably conclude that a motorhome which is on leveling jacks and hooked up to water, electric, and septic would not be treated the same as a motorhome actively driving.

Despite these clear legal proscriptions against engaging in warrantless searches of temporary dwelling homes, several states (i.e., Delaware, Florida, Nebraska, Nevada, New Hampshire, and New Mexico) have explicit statutes that permit these types of behaviors. Recently, the state of Idaho repealed a state statute permitting this behavior (Idaho Code §36-1303, "Repealed by 2019 Session Laws, ch. 270, sec. 1, eff. 7/1/2019."). Although many of these statutes clearly violate the Constitution, the states vary in how far officer authority is permitted to expand. For example, the Delaware statute (Del. Code. Ann. 7 §111) reads:

> Fish and Wildlife Agents may search and examine any person, conveyance, vehicle, game bag, game coat or other receptacle for protected wildlife, and in the presence of an occupant of any camp or tent, may search and examine without warrant such camp or tent for protected wildlife, when the Secretary or the Fish and Wildlife Agent has reason to believe and has stated to the suspected person or occupant the reason for believing that any of the laws relating to protected wildlife have been violated, and may seize and possess (take) any protected wildlife illegally in possession. This section shall not authorize the entering of a dwelling house without first procuring a search warrant.

Clearly, this statute seeks to authorize searches of camps or tents while explicitly excluding dwelling homes. Nebraska, Nevada, and New Mexico have employed quite similar language in their state laws, although not explicitly exempting dwelling homes.

Alternatively, the New Hampshire statute authorizes explicit entry only into temporary ice fishing shelters "so-called fish house or bob-house" (N.H. Rev. Stat. §206:26), which may or may not serve as a temporary residence. Similarly, the state of Minnesota decided in *State v. Larsen* (2002) that "fish houses" were not a place where conservation officers were permitted to engage in searches absent any suspicion of wrongdoing. However, that same court did not hold the state law (Minn.Stat. §97A. 215) permitting officers to "enter and inspect" fish houses or shanties was unconstitutional, nor did the court determine that a warrant was required. The court simply stated that "we do hold that these constitutional protections must be read into the 'at reasonable times' language," which would seem to indicate a warrant would not be required.

Perhaps the most expansive search authority over dwelling structures given to conservation officers is provided by the state of Florida. The statute (FLA. STAT. §379.3311) providing this authority reads:

> Arrest upon probable cause without warrant any person found in the act of violating any such laws or, in pursuit immediately following such violations, to examine any person, boat, conveyance . . . or any camp, tent, cabin, or roster, in the presence of any person stopping at or belonging to such camp, tent, cabin, or roster, when such officer has reason to believe, and has exhibited her or his authority and stated to the suspected person in charge the officer's reason for believing, that any of the aforesaid laws have been violated at such camp.

While we could not locate any caselaw examining whether this portion of the statute has been upheld as constitutional or not by the courts of Florida or the United States, it certainly seems to provide for warrantless searches of fixed domiciles (including stick-built structures with enclosed walls and locked doors) upon reasonable suspicion following a warrantless probable cause arrest. The way that this statute is written certainly seems to fall into an area that is not constitutional.

Other states have specifically clarified exactly what legal authority conservation officers have to search structures. In Maryland, state statute (Md. Code, Natural Resources §4-1204) explicitly states that when engaging in various warrantless searches with respect to fishing enforcement, that the state "does not permit entering a dwelling house without first procuring a search warrant." Similarly, Montana permits warrantless searches of tents, but only if those tents are not being utilized as dwellings (Mont. Code Ann. §87-1-506[b]).

Necessity of Expanded Search Authority

Based upon review of the state statutes, and case law at the state and (limited) federal level, it would be difficult to argue that conservation officers do not enjoy some expanded search authority, in some instances, in some states. While this statement is certainly not universal to all states, types of searches, and respective permutations, it still requires some consideration as to the necessity of these searches.

Some legal scholars focusing on this issue, such as McLain (2018), make a compelling argument that not only is the search authority granted to conservation officers in Missouri necessary, but that it is not outside the bounds of the Constitution as practiced in that state. McLain argues that the Fourth Amendment protections offered to residents of the United States are not violated, but that search authorities offered to Missouri conservation agents are within the scope of these protections. McLain (2018) provides careful consideration of the reasonableness of hunting- and fishing-related inspections, the compelling state interests, the level of intrusion, and the consent to inspection in highly regulated activities.

Other legal scholars have argued the opposite based largely upon the facts that we have stated in this chapter. As noted, conservation officers in some states such as California and Iowa are permitted to stop hunters and anglers without any reasonable suspicion of them having committed a legal offense. Similarly, states authorize by statute the legal authority to search containers inside of vehicles without probable cause to do so; however, many states permit conservation officers to search these containers without any evidence that laws protecting wildlife have been broken (Haden & Israel, 2015). Due to the expansiveness of this authority, Haden and Israel (2015) also offer a compelling argument that perhaps conservation officers enjoy an authority to search that expands beyond conventional conceptualizations of the Fourth Amendment.

CONCLUSION

The preceding chapter offered a concise review of international agreements, federal laws, and state laws that have been enacted for the protection of fish and wildlife in the United States. Additionally, this chapter offered substantial comparisons between states in the authority that they give conservation officers to conduct searches. As evidenced in many of the state laws, conservation officers generally enjoy an expanded authority to search hunters and anglers over conventional police and citizens who are not engaged in outdoor pursuits, as a result of the challenges associated with uncovering violations and the importance of protecting nature. The degree to which this expanded authority is unconstitutional is disputed by reputable legal scholars (Haden & Israel, 2015; McLain, 2018), and little case law at the national level has provided any guidance as to whether these more expansive state laws are in line with constitutional protections.

DISCUSSION QUESTIONS

1. In some states, the state legislature (with input from the state agency responsible for the management of fish and wildlife) drafts and passes laws pertaining to hunting and fishing, while in others, the state agency that is responsible for the management of the wildlife and fisheries is granted rulemaking authority to enact regulations under a more general state statute that grants them this authority. The argument for the state legislature enacting the laws is that they represent the people of the state and therefore they pass laws that are favored by their constituents. The argument for allowing the agency to enact regulations through the rule-making process is that they are more qualified to know what regulations should be enacted, and it also removes political influence from the management of the state's natural resources. Which method is the best method for the management of a state's natural resources? What are the advantages and disadvantages to the two systems? Explain.

2. Look up two state-level departments of natural resources and examine their sections on hunting and fishing regulations. Compare

and contrast the information on the two websites. How comprehensive are the sections? Are they easy to find and understand? Do they provide links to the statutes that govern the regulations? Do they provide areas for public input on regulations? Report on the similarities and differences between the two websites.

Key Terms

CITES: The Convention on International Trade in Endangered Species of Wild Flora and Fauna (CITES) is a 1973 agreement between governments across the globe that seeks to ensure international trade in endangered animals and plants does not threaten their survival.

Damage Control Permits: Site-specific permits that allow landowners and designees to use lethal controls with the intention of limiting damage to property, often agricultural croplands.

Endangered Species Act: The Endangered Species Act (ESA) is a 1973 law passed by the United States Congress that seeks to protect endangered and threatened flora and fauna, as well as the ecosystems they depend upon.

Lacey Act: The Lacey Act, which was passed in 1900 by the US Congress, became the first federal law in the US seeking to protect wildlife. The law restricts trade in animals, their parts, or products produced from them, particularly when that trade involves the violation of US, Indian, or state laws.

Open Fields Doctrine: Resulting from the SCOTUS case *Hester v. United States*, the court ruled that the Fourth Amendment did not require warrants or probable cause to search private property such as pastures, woods, water, or vacant lots. This has been the prevailing understanding following the decision.

Pittman-Robertson Act: Also known as the Federal Aid in Wildlife Restoration Act, this law created an eleven percent excise tax on firearms, ammunition, bows, and crossbows. In its current format, the law funds the acquisition, improvement, and access to habitat, as well as animal reintroductions and surveys. The funds may also be used for hunter safety.

Terry **stop**: Established by the SCOTUS case of *Terry v. Ohio*, this type of detainment allows police officers to stop, question, and frisk citizens when the officer has reasonable suspicion to believe that a crime has been committed.

References

Agnello v. United States, 269 U.S. 20 (1925).

Beitzel, W. R., & Edwards, G. C. (2015). Opinions of the Attorney General. https://dnr.maryland.gov/waters/bay/Documents/AIS/OAGOpinion_InvasiveSpecies.pdf.

Butterfoss, E. J., & Daly, J. L. (2004). *State v. Colosimo*: Minnesota angler's freedom from unreasonable searches and seizures becomes "the one that got away." *William Mitchell Law Review, 31*(2), 527–554.

California v. Carney, 471 US 386 (1985).

Carson, R. (1962). *Silent spring.* Houghton Mifflin.

Chimel v. California, 395 U.S. 752 (1969).

City of Indianapolis v. Edmond, 531 U.S. 32 (2000).

Colorado Revised Statutes, CO Rev Stat §33-6-111 (2016). https://law.justia.com/codes/colorado/2016/title-33/wildlife/article-6/part-1/section-33-6-111.

Convention on International Trade in Endangered Species of Wild Flora and Fauna (CITES). (2020). https://cites.org/eng/disc/text.php.

Cooney, R. (2019). A comparison of the North American model to other conservation approaches. In S. P Mahoney & V. Geist (Eds.), *The North American model of wildlife conservation* (pp. 148–155). Johns Hopkins University Press.

Cosgrove, M. (2017). Chronic wasting disease and Cervidae regulations in North America. Michigan Department of Natural Resources. http://cwd-info.org/wp-content/uploads/2017/08/CWDRegstableState-Province.pdf.

Davis, E., Whyde, A., & Langton, L. (2018). *Contacts between police and the public, 2015.* US Department of Justice, Office of Justice Programs, Bureau of Justice Statistics.

Delaware Code, Ann. 7 §111, https://delcode.delaware.gov/title7/c001/index.html.

Delaware v. Prouse, 440 U.S. 648 (1979).

Drane v. State, 493 So. 2d 294 (1986).

Ducks Unlimited. (2020). Celebrating 80 years of the Pittman-Robertson Act. https://www.ducks.org/conservation/public-policy/celebrating-80-years-of-the-pittman-robertson-act

Farago, R. (2015, October 17). Question of the day: You OK with "wildlife checkpoints"? https://www.thetruthaboutguns.com/question-of-the-day-you-ok-with-wildlife-checkpoints/.

Florida Fish and Wildlife Conservation—Police powers of commission and its agent, FLA. STAT. §379.3311[e] [2019]. http://www.leg.state.fl.us/statutes/index.cfm?App_mode=Display_Statute&Search_String=&URL=0300-0399/0379/Sections/0379.3311.html.

Freyfogle, E. T., & Goble, D. (2009). *Wildlife law: A primer.* Island Press.

Fuller, E. (2014). *The passenger pigeon.* Princeton University Press.

Goble, D. D., Scott, M., & Davis, F. W. (2006). *The Endangered Species Act at thirty.* Island Press.

Gore, M. L., Knuth, B. A., Scherer, C., & Curtis, P. D. (2008). Evaluating a conservation investment designed to reduce human-wildlife conflict. *Conservation Letters, 1*(3), 136–145.

Greenberg, J. (2014). *A feathered river across the sky: The passenger pigeon's flight to extinction.* Bloomsbury.

Haden, E. R., & Israel, A. K. (2015). The Fourth Amendment, game wardens and hunters. *Cumberland Law Review, 46*(1), 79–101.

Hester v. United States, 265 U.S. 57 (1924).

Hilbel v. Sixth Judicial District Court of Nevada, 542 US 177 (2004).

Hoch, G. (2015). *Booming from the mists of nowhere: The story of the Greater Prairie-Chicken.* University of Iowa Press.

Idaho Code §36-1303, Repealed by 2019 Session Laws, ch. 270, sec. 1, eff. 7/1/2019. https://casetext.com/statute/idaho-code/title-36-fish-and-game/chapter-13-enforcement-and-application-of-fish-and-game-law/section-36-1303-repealed.

LaCaze, K. (2014). Facts behind the fiction. *Louisiana Sportsman.* https://www.louisianasportsman.com/hunting/facts-behind-the-fiction/.

Lund, T. A. (1980). *American wildlife law.* University of California Press.

Maryland Code, Natural Resources §4-1204 (2014). https://law.justia.com/codes/maryland/2014/natural-resources/title-4/subtitle-12/section-4-1204/.

McLain, T. R. (2018). The constitutionality of fish and wildlife related searches and seizures conducted by conservation agents in Missouri. *Saint Louis University Law Journal, 62*(3), 713–737.

Michigan Department of Natural Resources. (2020a). 2020 antlerless deer digest. https://www.michigan.gov/dnrdigests.

Michigan Department of Natural Resources. (2020b). Deer management assistance permits. https://www.michigan.gov/dnr/0,4570,7-350-79134_82777-293283--,00.html.

Michigan Dept. of State Police v. Sitz, 496 U.S. 444 (1990).

Minnesota Statutes, §97A. 215 (1987). https://www.revisor.mn.gov/statutes/cite/97A.215.

Montana Code Annotated, §87-1-506[b]). https://leg.mt.gov/bills/mca/title_0870/chapter_0010/part_0050/section_0060/0870-0010-0050-0060.html.

Montana Fish, Wildlife & Parks. (2020). Hunt regulations. https://fwp.mt.gov/hunt/regulations.

Nevada Revised Statutes—Powers and duties of game wardens, sheriffs, and other peace officers, NV Rev. Stat. §501.375 [2014]. https://law.justia.com/codes/nevada/2014/chapter-501/statute-501.375/.

New Hampshire Revised Statutes, §206:26 (Amended by 2017, 206:11, eff. 9/8/2017), https://casetext.com/statute/new-hampshire-revised-statutes/title-18-fish-and-game/chapter-206-fish-and-game-commission/conservation-officers-superintendents-of-hatcheries-and-other-employees/section-20626-powers.

New York Department of Environmental Conservation. (2020). Deer management assistance program. https://www.dec.ny.gov/animals/33973.html.

Oliver v. United States, 466 U.S. 170 (1984).

Overturf, R. (2019). Keeping it regulatory: Examining state statutes pertaining to searches for fish and wildlife violations. http://dx.doi.org/10.2139/ssrn.3323431.

Pennsylvania Powers and duties of enforcement officers, 34 Pa. Stat. And Cons. Stat. Ann. §901, https://www.legis.state.pa.us/WU01/LI/LI/CT/HTM/34/00.009.001.000..HTM.

People v. Butorac, 2013 IL App (2d) 110953.

People v. Coca, 829 P.2d 385 (1992).

People v. Maikhio, 51 Cal. 4th 1074, 253 P.3d 247, 126 Cal. Rptr. 3d 74.

People v. Perez, 59 Cal.Rptr.2d 596 (Cal.Ct.App. 1996).

People v. Scott, 79 N.Y.2d 474, 583 N.Y.S.2d 920, 593 N.E.2d 1328 (1992).

Reeve, R. (2002). *Policing international trade in endangered species: The CITES treaty and compliance.* Routledge.

Serratore, A. (2018, May 15). Keeping feathers off hats—and on birds. *Smithsonian Magazine.* https://www.smithsonianmag.com/history/migratory-bird-act-anniversary-keeping-feathers-off-hats-180969077/.

State v. Albaugh, 1997 ND 229, 571 N.W.2d 345.

State v. Baldwin, 124 N.H. 770 (N.H. 1984).

State v. Bullock, 901 P.2d 61, 75–76 (Mont. 1995).

State v. Creech, 806 P.2d 1080 (New Mex. 1991).

State v. Dixson, 766 P.2d 1015 (1988).

State v. Halverson, 277 N.W.2d 723 (1979).

State v. Johnson, 75 Wn. App. 692 (Wash. Ct. App. 1994).

State v. Keehner, 425 NW 2d 41 (Iowa 1988).

State *v.* Kirchoff, 156 Vt. 1, 587 A.2d 988 (1991).

State v. Larsen, 650 N.W.2d 144 (Minn. 2002).

State v. Legg, 151 S.E.2d 215 (West Virg. 1966).

State v. Levens, 306 Ill. App. 3d 230, 233, 713 N.E.2d 1275, 1278 (1999).

State v. McHugh, 630 So. 2d 1259 (1994).

State v. Pippin, 403 P.3d 907, 913 (Wash. Ct. App. 2017).

State v. Sherburne, 571 A.2d 1181 (Maine 1990).

State v. Thurman, 996 P.2d 309, 314 (Idaho Ct. App. 1999).

State v. Tourtillott, 618 P.2d 423 (1980).

Tanner v. Idaho Department of Fish & Game, 2019 U.S. Dist. LEXIS 172950 (D. Idaho Oct. 3, 2019).

Terry v. Ohio, 392 U.S. 1 (1968).

Texas Parks and Wildlife Code, TEX. STAT. §12.103 (1975 & Amended 1995). https://texas.public.law/statutes/tex._parks_and_wild._code_section_12.103.

Texas Parks and Wildlife Code, TEX. STAT. §12.104 (1975 & Amended 1991). https://texas.public.law/statutes/tex._parks_and_wild._code_section_12.104.

Thomas III, G. C., & Leo, R. A. (2002). The effects of *Miranda v. Arizona:* "Embedded" in our national culture? *Crime and Justice: A Review of Research, 29,* 203–271.

United States v. Arvizu, 534 U.S. 266 (2002).

United States v. Dunn, 480 U.S. 294 (1987).

United States v. Fraire, 575 F.3d 929 (9th Cir. 2009).

United States v. Hunnicutt, No. 1:05mj241 (W.D.N.C. Jan. 13, 2006).

US Department of Agriculture (USDA). (2020). Wildlife services. https://www.aphis.usda.gov/.

US Fish & Wildlife Service (USFWS). (2020a). International affairs. https://www.fws.gov/international/.

US Fish & Wildlife Service (USFWS). (2020b). African Elephant Conservation Act of 1989. https://www.fws.gov/international/wildlife -without-borders/multinational-speicies-conservation-acts -african-elephant.html.

US Fish & Wildlife Service (USFWS). (2020c). Endangered species. https://www.fws.gov/endangered/laws-policies/.

US Fish & Wildlife Service (USFWS). (2020d). Wildlife & Sport Fish Restoration Program. https://www.fws.gov/wsfrprograms /subpages/grantprograms/wr/wr.htm.

U.S. v. Gooch, 6 F.3d 673 (9th Cir. 1993).

Utah Code Title 23 Wildlife Resources Code of Utah, Utah Code 23-27-301, https://le.utah.gov/xcode/Title23/Chapter27/23-27-S201 .html.

Wagner, K. K., Schmidt, R. H., & Conover, M. R. (1997). Compensation programs for wildlife damage in North America. *Wildlife Society Bulletin*, *25*, 312–319.

Wisconsin Department of Natural Resources. (2020). A chronology of Wisconsin deer hunting: From closed seasons to record harvests. https://dnr.wi.gov/topic/hunt/documents/deer4page.pdf.

Wyoming Game & Fish Department. (2020). 2020 Wyoming hunt planner. https://wgfd.wyo.gov/.

Six

JOB ENTRY REQUIREMENTS FOR CONSERVATION LAW ENFORCEMENT

The **standard minimum requirements** for entry into a position as a police officer have long been debated among police leadership and scholars alike (Kelling & Moore, 1988). Issues such as height and weight requirements, physical fitness standards, educational requirements, testing, criminal background checks, prior drug use, tattoo policies, and pre-employment training have all been in flux. Some, such as height and weight standards, have been essentially eliminated due to judgements declaring the practices discriminatory. Others, such as physical fitness requirements, tattoo policies, and prior drug use have been revised in many jurisdictions to open the applicant pool amid calls for diversity and challenges to fill positions to authorized strength. Across the board, training standards have continually increased, and while educational standards have not increased remarkably, the average educational level of sworn police officers in the United States has increased steadily over time.

In terms of the recruitment, minimum entry standards, and training of natural resources police in the United States, investigations into these topics has been much more limited. While some research has investigated these topics (Patten et al., 2015; Rossler & Suttmoeller, 2018, 2021), there has not been a comprehensive discussion as to how the recruitment, minimum entry standards, and training procedures for conservation officers tracks with their specialized mandate

153

as well as the broader role they are expected to fulfill. The following chapter examines the recruitment process, minimum entry standards, and training protocols for the 50 state agencies, as well as federal natural resources officers, in the United States.

RECRUITMENT

In terms of recruitment in the twenty-first century, it appears that most conservation departments have not been required to engage in any active recruitment strategies beyond hosting a website that directs potential applicants to job openings. Pursuing a career as a conservation officer is a competitive endeavor. Given the limited number of positions that are available each year (Tobias, 1998) conservation agencies have not been required to, or at least have not sought to engage in more active and creative recruitment strategies in the way that traditional police agencies have been forced to in order to fill their ranks (Orrick, 2008).

The natural motivations to become a conservation officer (Eliason, 2017) have provided agencies with a highly qualified and motivated work force that is not accessed by most traditional departments. Despite this highly competitive environment, some agencies have developed creative recruiting strategies to build their personnel. The state of Delaware holds a Natural Resources Police Basic Youth Academy, which gives youths 12–15 years of age some insight into the work of Fish and Wildlife Natural Resources Police and provides youths with both their hunter and boater safety certificates (Delaware DNREC, 2021).

While filling law enforcement positions with qualified applicants has not seemed to be much of a challenge for conservation agencies, increasing the diversity of hires has. Policing, in general, has been a field that has long been dominated by white and male employees, and increasing diversity has been outlined nationwide as a goal for local police agencies (Gupta & Yang, 2016; Ramsey & Robinson, 2015). Across the United States, representation of Black and African American officers has only increased from 9 to 12 percent over the three decades between 1985 and 2015. Similarly, the representation of female police hovers near 12 percent (Reaves, 2015).

In a nationwide survey of conservation officers, Rossler and Sutt-moeller (2021) found that there is far less diversity in terms of the representation for officers of color and women. As reported in their findings, only about six percent of conservation officers in the 15 state agencies they studied identified as female, while about three percent reported that they were a race other than white. Rossler and Suttmoeller (2021) offered some speculative reasons for why recruitment might be a challenge, including the lack of will in the United States to develop an outdoor interest in female youths and youths of color (US Department of Interior, 2011).

Certainly, the more passive recruiting strategies used by conservation departments in an attempt to diversify their ranks has not produced the desired outcomes. Efforts such as putting women and officers of color on their public facing literature is a good first step, but there needs to be a more active approach that would motivate people beyond white outdoorsmen to become conservation police officers. This recruitment approach would need to overcome not only the long-standing barriers that keep people of color and women out of police work (e.g., historical mistreatment by the police, lack of support from social networks, problematic police behavior such as use of force and racial profiling, racial discrimination, sexual harassment, discriminatory tests of physicality) (Chappell & Lanza-Kaduce, 2010; Kringen & Kringen, 2014; Matthies et al., 2012; Perrott, 1999; Rossler et al., 2019; Rossler et al., 2020; Schuck, 2014), but must also overcome the barriers that people of color and women experience when trying to learn or embrace outdoor pursuits (e.g., racism, sexism, lack of mentoring, access, equipment) (Responsive Management/National Shooting Sports Foundation, 2017; OutdoorAfro, 2021; Wachter, 2020).

BONA FIDE OCCUPATIONAL QUALIFICATIONS

Given that conservation officers are law enforcement personnel, individual states, as well as police agencies, are permitted to establish minimum occupational standards. In order for these thresholds to be permissible, the standards must represent **bona fide occupational qualifications** (BFOQ), and not be simply used as an exclusionary tool to screen out candidates differentially (e.g., height requirements screen out a far greater proportion of the female population compared to males). While all states or agencies establish some pre-employment standards, the presence or absence of a particular standard, as well as the actual threshold, vary considerably. In addition, standards may also shift based on the age or sex of a candidate.

Some of the most common pre-employment standards for aspiring officers include age, vision, physical agility, strength, and endurance tests. Nearly all agencies also require their candidates to pass a written test, as well as a criminal background check. In addition to these standards, some police agencies will also include hurdles that may more accurately be described as screening processes for general suitability and suitability for the specific agency. These generally include polygraph examinations, psychological condition, general physical condition, and the oral board or personal interview. In terms of age, most police agencies allow for recruits to begin their police careers between the ages of 21 and 35 years of age. Exceptions do exist for both younger and older age brackets as well; for example, the states of Montana and Wisconsin allows troopers to begin their application process as soon as they turn 18 years old (Montana DOJ, 2021; Wisconsin State Patrol, 2021), as do the states of Louisiana and Rhode Island for state police officers (Louisiana State Police, 2021; Rhode Island State Police, 2021). Some, such as the state of Florida, require trooper applicants to be 19 years old (Florida Highway Patrol, 2021), while the state of Washington requires those seeking employment in state patrol be at least 19½ years old at the time of their application (Washington State Patrol, 2021). In terms of the upper age limit, some police agencies do not set an upper age limit. One of the most iconic police agencies, the New York City Police Department (NYPD), allows recruits to take their entrance exam at 17 ½ years old, and permits candidates to test up until age 34. They also allow military veterans to subtract up to six years from their age in the application process, meaning they have until their 41st birthday to apply (NYPD, 2021).

In terms of age requirements for conservation police, the Florida Fish and Wildlife Commission (FWC) requires officers be 18 years old at the time of application, and 19 by the date of hire (Florida FWC, 2021). The state of Montana sets the age bar at 18 years of age, but requires a bachelor's degree in biology, criminal justice, or a related field, which likely precludes those who are under 20 years of age (Montana Fish, Wildlife & Parks, 2021). Similar thresholds can be found in Louisiana (Louisiana Wildlife & Fisheries, 2021). Unlike with state patrol, the state of Washington requires Department of Fish and Wildlife (WDFW) officers to be at least 21 years of age (WDFW, 2021).

Duties requiring officers to frequently serve as witnesses have set the standards for vision high as well. Many departments still require uncorrected vision no worse than 20/70. This may also be coupled with requirements to possess what would be considered normal color vision and depth perception as well. Contemporarily, these standards have allowed for vision to be corrected to 20/20 through the use of glasses or contact lenses. Legal challenges have often rendered the requirement illegal in many instances, as it excludes many otherwise qualified candidates without any evidence that it is a BFOQ for becoming a police officer (Novak et al., 2017). Despite indications that these requirements may be waning, a variety of vision requirements still exist for employment as a conservation officer across the US. The state of Washington requires WDFW officers to have 20/40 vision, whether that is corrected or uncorrected (WDFW, 2021), Florida and Montana require 20/100 uncorrected and corrected to 20/20 (Florida FWC, 2021), California requires 20/40 uncorrected and corrected to 20/20 (California Department of Fish and Wildlife, 2021), and Georgia requires 20/60 correctable to 20/40 for Department of Natural Resources Law Enforcement Division officers (Georgia Department of Natural Resources, 2021).

Physical Agility, Strength, and Endurance Testing

Physical agility tests generally involve some form of sprint, shuttle run, obstacle course, or other type of explosive athletic demand. Research evidence has continuously indicated that screening tools such as these are poor reflections of the demands placed upon police and are therefore not job related (Lonsway, 2003). Research has also indicated that their inclusion continues. These requirements have also been shown to be discriminatory and detrimental to the recruitment of female candidates (Rossler et al., 2020; Todak, 2017).

Despite these noteworthy criticisms, physical agility, strength, and endurance testing remains institutionalized, with many states instituting minimum physical standards for all law enforcement recruits. Many states ascribe to the physical test established by Peace Officers' Standards and Training (POST). Alternatively, other states establish their own boards for standards and training, such as the Illinois Law Enforcement Training & Standards Board (ILETSB), which uses the POWER test, the Michigan Commission on Law Enforcement Standards (MCOLES), which establishes its own standards, and the Kentucky Law Enforcement Council (KLEC), which claims that its five-item battery reflects "the underlying constructs required to perform police duties, as evidenced by a validated job-task analysis" (Kentucky Law Enforcement Council, 2021).

The work environment of conservation officers is substantively different from that of patrol officers who operate in urban or rural areas. There are precious few conventional patrol officers who will be asked to operate an all-terrain vehicle, hike up a mountain and hike down carrying an injured person, wade a stream, operate a boat, raft through whitewater, or rescue a duck hunter from icy water in November (Forsyth & Forsyth, 2009). In line with more conventional police agencies, about 80 percent of conservation agencies require some form of distance run or endurance test, and about three-quarters of identified agencies required some form of upper-body strength test (Rossler et al., 2021). Considering the job tasks of officers who protect natural resources, physical tests required by conservation agencies seem well tailored. As reported by Rossler and colleagues (2021), around 56 percent of state natural resource law enforcement departments require a swim test, which is a component that is rarely required of law enforcement officers with differing duties. Additionally, the state of Hawaii has a requirement that candidates be able to hike one mile in 20 minutes, which is closely tied to their work environment, but an unusual requirement compared to other police agencies across the US.

Written Test

Written tests as pre-employment screening tools can take one of two forms in the US. On one hand, the assessments can be used as a pass-or-fail tool to determine whether an applicant has the requisite abilities to pass academy coursework and carry out the necessary duties of a patrol officer, including notetaking and report writing. Alternatively, written exams have also been used to rank order candidates based upon their scores (Gaines & Falkenberg, 1998; Gottfredson, 1996; Novak et al., 2017).

One common criticism levied at the pass-fail option is that the written exams often lack the validity to differentiate candidates who have a high likelihood of successfully completing the academy and becoming effective officers from those who have a substantively lower likelihood. Essentially, the problem that frequently occurs is tests are too easy and therefore do a poor job of screening out candidates who are unlikely to be successful (Gaines & Falkenberg, 1998). Tests that encourage a larger sample to pass from the population of candidates are also not especially useful if they do so by omitting components that effectively assess the ability of candidates to complete job-related tasks (Gottfredson, 1996). Conversely, due to structural racism, simply making the exam significantly more challenging to screen out a large portion of candidates or rank-ordering candidates based upon exam performance can often eliminate candidates of color who would make perfectly suitable officers if they had not been screened out by a poorly conceived written exam protocol.

This process is well documented by Ridgeway and colleagues (2008), who conducted an extremely thorough analysis of the San Diego Police Department's (SPPD) recruitment process. Their evaluation of the written exam used by SPPD found that 40 percent of applicants fail the exam, and although retaking the exam is permissible it is not common. Of those who passed the exam, none were eliminated from the academy due to an inability to keep pace with their academic coursework requirements. Ridgeway et al. (2008) perceptively note that this likely means the threshold for passing is set too high, and that recalibrating the pass-fail threshold could allow more qualified applicants to continue the process without deleterious consequences. Despite these recommendations, Ridgeway et al. (2008) noted significant push back on that idea from SPPD, noting that it would be viewed as lowering standards. This is an interesting approach to take during what has been frequently identified as a "cop-crunch" era, where the number of open positions far exceeds the number of qualified applicants for police careers.

For departments of natural resources and akin agencies, the written test is a common feature of the hiring process. Of the 50 state conservation law enforcement agencies, only seven could be identified as not explicitly listing a written exam as part of their hiring process (i.e., Arizona, Arkansas, Colorado, Delaware, Hawaii, Indiana, Mississippi, Nevada, and New Jersey). Within these states, the educational standards are quite high for law enforcement in general, and within conservation policing, specifically. Arizona and New Jersey specifically call for a minimum of a bachelor's degree and indicate that the degree major must be in a hard science closely tailored to the work of the organization, such as wildlife science, biology, or other similar program from an accredited university (Arizona Game & Fish Department, 2021; New Jersey Division of Fish & Wildlife, 2021). Similarly, Colorado requires a bachelor's degree, while Delaware and Mississippi require the equivalent of an associate degree or equivalent work experience (Colorado Parks & Wildlife, 2021). Certainly, these credentials surpass simple reading comprehension and writing tests in the eyes of most in society. Perhaps the lowest thresholds exist in Hawaii and Indiana, which require a high school diploma and one year of general experience, or assess writing proficiency in the academy, respectively. Given these requirements, it seems that nearly all states use a written exam to assess candidate proficiency, or some equivalent design early in their hiring process.

While nearly every state uses an exam, the content of these exams can vary quite significantly. Some states, such as California, Massachusetts, Nebraska, New York, North Carolina, and Texas utilize police civil service exams, generalized POST tests, or tests of basic adult education in order to screen applicants. Other states, such as Kansas and Wyoming, include questions about conservation-specific issues in their exams (Kansas Department of Wildlife & Parks, 2021; Wyoming Department of Game & Fish, 2021). Wyoming even goes so far as to ask questions pertaining specifically to Wyoming state law (e.g., which species are designated as small game animals).

States may also apply their exam scores to the selection process through a variety of different methodologies. One of the most sophisticated strategies used by conservation departments to apply scores in a meaningful way, and to eliminate potential differences that do not reflect useful differences in candidates, is to engage in band scoring. This process is used by the state of Alabama in their selection of conservation officers. Candidates are lumped into similarly scoring thresholds on each individual exam session, and then department personnel have the ability to choose candidates based upon these rankings. So, all candidates in band 1 are considered "tied," and slight variations in test scores do not reflect meaningful differences in the selection process. Additionally, Alabama still maintains a minimum score threshold, where candidates would not be placed in a band, as they do not meet the minimum score threshold (Alabama State Personnel Department, 2021).

Oral Interview, Psychological Examination, Medical Evaluation, and Polygraph

Among most police agencies nationwide, and among conservation law enforcement agencies, oral interviews, psychological examinations, and medical evaluations appear to be quite common steps in the hiring process. Oral interviews may serve a number of purposes in a conservation law enforcement hiring process. At the most basic level, these tests are designed to assess whether the candidate has the requisite skills, knowledge, and abilities to engage in effective verbal communication. Conservation police work involves a great deal of community-facing oral communication, whether that be investigating criminal activity, participating in game surveys, teaching hunter safety courses, or engaging in other outreach (Minnesota Department of Natural Resources, 2021).

Oral interviews can also assess whether the candidate has the requisite behavioral skills to engage in conservation work, while also ensuring that they would be a good fit in the culture of the organization and reflective of its values and mission. For example, the state of Alaska, which employs state troopers who operate under a specialized bureau for conservation law enforcement, utilize an oral interview that includes between 10 and 15 behavioral scenario-based questions. The interview lasts around 45 minutes, and participants are scored based upon the perceptions of three troopers of varying ranks (Alaska Department of Public Safety, 2021). Similarly, the state of Minnesota conducts panel interviews with three members that involve questions which are not law enforcement specific but are designed to ensure suitability with the mission and values of the organization. New Hampshire indicates that their oral board tests candidates on their knowledge, skills, and abilities. Candidates are scored on criteria such as judgement, critical thinking, maturity, and discretion.

In addition to interviews with conservation department personnel or civil service agencies, conservation police recruits, like other police recruits, are frequently subjected to mental health screenings through the use of written psychological exams, interviews with psychologists, or both. Commonly used written test instruments include the Minnesota Multiphasic Personality Inventory (MMPI), the California Personality Inventory (CPI), and the Inwald Personality Inventory (IPI), which was the only instrument designed specifically to assess compatibility with police work (Texas Law Enforcement Management and Administrative Statistics Program, 1994). Overall, these instruments are not especially effective at predicting on-the-job performance of police officers, but rather simply identifying obvious psychological issues (Burbeck & Furnham, 1985; Travis, 1994; Varela et al., 2004). Agencies also use these instruments more or less to screen out candidates rather than to select in, which does little to contribute to identifying suitability and predictive power of choosing the best candidates. Their use perpetuates the cycle of hiring mediocre candidates (Metchik, 1999).

As in many aspects of their organizations, state conservation agencies are largely ahead of the curve in terms of their professionalization, and this extends to the pre-employment screening process. An additional area where this professionalism is exhibited is in the use of both written and in-person psychological evaluations by trained psychologists. For example, the Wisconsin Department of Natural Resources uses written and in-person psychological screenings after conditional employment offers are made. Used in this manner, the screening is less likely to screen out exceptional candidates, and the process includes the perspectives and judgements of a licensed professional, rather than scores on a written test with a questionable history of validity in predicting job performance.

Psychological exams are standard fare for most police departments, due to the civil liability associated with the authority to make arrests and use force (including lethal force) on members of the public. Police departments are subject to significant civil liability if they engage in negligent or inadequate hiring practices. In one instance, a jury awarded the estate of a former city mayor (Bert Reeves of Cottageville, South Carolina) $97.5 million as compensation for his death at the hands of a troubled police officer who had been fired from several different agencies (Elmore, 2016). Of course, fit within the organization is also important, but appropriate hiring standards (that include legally defensible indicators) are the reason that departments utilize such stringent criteria.

Medical evaluations are also used by virtually every conservation agency within their hiring process. These medical evaluations usually serve three purposes. The initial purpose is to ensure that the candidate is physically able to complete tasks related to law enforcement. This portion of the testing process usually includes the hearing and vision standards that were mentioned earlier in this chapter. Second, if departments require a drug test to screen the officer for illegal substances, it usually occurs at this stage. In addition to ensuring that officers can sense the appropriate stimuli and testify to what they witnessed, as well as ensuring they have not recently used banned substances, conservation departments also frequently administer health evaluations. This is to ensure that officers do not possess any physical defects that could result in them collecting disability for an extended period of time rather than performing the functions for which they were employed. Conservation agencies are notoriously understaffed, and the loss of an officer to injury or chronic illness can be quite devastating to the organization, as would the disability payments or lawsuits that might arise from these issues. The work of COs is incredibly physically demanding, and any indications that an officer might suffer from common issues such as back, knee, or cardiovascular problems is usually addressed during this medical screening (Massachusetts Public Employee Retirement Administration Commission, 2021).

One final commonly used tool of the pre-hiring process for conservation law enforcement positions is the polygraph examination.

The lie detector test is used by some agencies, but not by others. In general, the goal of a polygraph is to verify the statements that applicants made on their application materials. For example, the state of Alaska, which operates their Wildlife Troopers under the state police, uses the polygraph for uncovering behaviors such as criminal activity, other inappropriate behavior, drug use, or any falsifications or omissions on the application forms (Alaska Department of Public Safety, 2021). Similarly, California indicates that they use the polygraph to verify the existing documents, as does Arizona for documents and personal statements (Arizona Game & Fish Department, 2021; California Department of Fish and Wildlife, 2021).

Education

Given the broad occupational requirements placed upon conservation officers, it comes as little surprise that the minimum educational standards for conservation officers are higher, on average, than the educational standards found in the rest of policing. Nationwide, less than one percent of traditional law enforcement agencies require police officers to obtain a bachelor's degree; in fact the number has been explicitly identified as 37 local agencies out of over 12,500 local agencies estimated to be in existence (Bruns, 2010). Contrary to these expectations, about 40 percent of conservation and natural resource-oriented law enforcement agencies require a four-year degree if no relevant work experience is included. Another 13, or 26 percent require an associate degree (Patten et al., 2015). While some may argue that the numbers could be somewhat lower, as conservation agencies do allow for some substitutions for relevant work or military experience, about 16 percent of agencies require an associate degree or approximately 60 credit hours, and 24 percent require a bachelor's degree, without exception (Rossler et al., 2021).

In addition to the minimum educational achievement criteria, some agencies also express preferences or requirements for certain curricula or degrees. For example, the state of Kansas indicates that a bachelor's degree is a bona fide occupational requirement, with no substitutions permitted, and they express a preference that the degree be in natural resources. Similarly, New Mexico also requires a bachelor's degree, and the disciplines preferred include natural resource management or science, wildlife management or science, fisheries management or science, animal or agricultural science, biology, environmental science, forestry or forestry management, zoology, ecology, criminal justice, or wildlife law enforcement. Other states, such as Missouri, Montana, Oklahoma, Tennessee, Utah, and Wyoming, express nearly identical requirements.

In lieu of higher education as a bona fide occupational requirement, other state agencies allow for substitutions that take the place of education should that experience be absent. Some examples include Arkansas, which allows candidates to substitute two years of law enforcement experience or four years of active military experience for the qualification of a bachelor's degree. In some instances, these qualifications can be used in combination in order to satisfy requirements for previous experience that approximate the earning of a four-year degree. States such as West Virginia, Pennsylvania, New York, New Hampshire, Mississippi, Louisiana, Kentucky, and Illinois utilize a combination of educational and experiential requirements to satisfy the minimum educational requirements.

In addition to requirements of, or substitution for, a bachelor's degree, those states requiring a minimum of an associate degree also place strict curricula requirements on their incoming candidates' educational achievement. The states of California, Louisiana, New Jersey, and Ohio mandate that the minimum educational standards of an associate degree or 60 hours of college credit must include a core focus on natural resource or criminal justice curricula. The natural resources background is generally mentioned first, and thresholds are usually in the area of 18 to 24 credits focused on biological or resources sciences, criminal justice, or a combination of the two.

TRAINING

As highlighted by this point in the chapter, the hiring process for police officers is a long task that requires many arduous hurdles (Orrick, 2008). These steps and standards are even more challenging for those who choose to become conservation officers, as conservation departments typically require more education and physical testing than general service police agencies do. Given the specialized tasks of COs, the pre-employment training process can also be quite extensive. In general, the pre-employment training of law enforcement occurs in two phases, the first being the police academy, with the second phase consisting of field training.

Virtually every police agency in the United States requires officers to complete some form of academy training. Academies usually come in two forms, with one being residential (e.g., the cadets sleep in barracks for most of the time, with leave for short periods such as weekends) and the other being part-time academies (e.g., cadets are permitted to go home or stay in off-campus housing during the academy). Academies differ quite substantially in the duration that they require officers to attend, but the commitment is generally in the three-to-six-month range, with the average academy duration being about 19 weeks long (Reaves, 2009). In most academies, recruits obtain training on skills that are universal to policing, such as report writing, operating patrol vehicles, and application of criminal and constitutional law. During the process, cadets generally must pass academic tests on the curricula they cover, as well as driving and operational tests, shooting scenario tests, and continued participation in physical training.

Natural resources agencies vary in their size, responsibilities, and resources. This variation may also lead to different pre-employment training models that are employed by agencies. As noted by Rossler and colleagues (2021), conservation agencies employ one of three models of academy training for officers, which they termed basic only, specialized, and hybrid academies. For about a third of state conservation agencies operating in the United States, the department uses an external police academy that does not offer conservation-specific curricula (Rossler et al., 2021). Essentially, the cadets' academy experience mirrors those of other police officers, and they attend the academy with police officers who will go on to work in conventional police departments; these officers then begin their field training without an additional training component.

The most popular academy training model used by conservation agencies is what Rossler and colleagues (2021). have termed the "hybrid" model. Under the hybrid model, agencies require recruits to attend an academy that is much like the basic model, where policing skills are learned alongside recruits who will not be employed by a conservation agency. Following the successful completion of their police academy training, recruits then attend a shorter series of training sessions prior to engaging in their period of field training. This model is used by the Iowa Department of Natural Resources to train their recruits. After attending their initial basic training at the Iowa Law Enforcement Academy, Iowa recruits then attend the Probationary Conservation Officer Academy and Field Training Program (Iowa Department of Natural Resources, 2021).

Finally, just under 20 percent of agencies operate their own stand-alone academy to train conservation officers prior to their field training period. States with historically strong hunting and fishing traditions such as Michigan and Pennsylvania are included in this list, as are states that have shown a strong dedication to conserving natural resources, such as Missouri (Shurr, 2019). Finally, two states, Alaska and Oregon, completely house their officers responsible for natural resource protection under their respective departments of public safety. Alaska Wildlife Troopers (AWT) complete the public safety academy curriculum along with Alaska State Troopers, as well as the field training program that all troopers must complete. From there, assignment as AWT can happen one of two ways. First, they may indicate preference during the hiring process in the final week of testing or bid to the AWT division following two years of service (Alaska Department of Public Safety, 2021). Similarly, Oregon State Troopers assigned to the Fish & Wildlife division attend recruit school with other troopers, and then receive specialized training in curriculum areas such as horse packing, environmental crimes, meat inspection, four-wheel drive patrol, commercial fishing operations, and restaurants, as well as outdoor survival and navigation (Oregon State Police, 2021).

Notable differences can also be identified both within and between academy types designed to service, or specifically train conservation officers. The role of conservation officers, as we have frequently mentioned, requires them to enforce laws, make identifications, and operate equipment that would be rather unusual for most conventional police officers (Eliason, 2006; Rossler & Suttmoeller, 2018). Some significant differences have been found between academies that report they have the capacity to train natural resource officers (NRO), and those who do not. Rossler and Suttmoeller (2018) report that NRO-equipped academies are significantly more likely to offer training on marine patrols, all-terrain vehicle operations, and methamphetamine laboratories (i.e., meth labs). One thing to consider is that this research examined all academies and compared them based upon their capacity to train NRO recruits; it did not specifically dive into the curricula that are found in academies specialized to produce conservation officers.

Fortunately, the Michigan Department of Natural Resources (DNR) has provided some behind-the-scenes insight into the training curriculum of specialized conservation officer academies through their blog detailing all 23 weeks of the 2018 recruit school (Michigan DNR, 2021). Much like conventional police academies, recruits in Michigan engage in significant physical training. However, unlike most conventional police academies, the DNR places heavy emphasis on water skills, including exposing recruits to freezing ice baths and engaging in submerged vehicle rescue scenarios. This type of curriculum is important, given that the state has over 11,000 inland lakes, and borders every great lake with the exception of Lake Ontario (Michigan Department of Natural Resources, 2021). In week two, recruits are introduced to organizational tactics that allow them to transition quickly from motor vehicle to other forms of patrol, such as marine, ATV, and snowmobile. They also receive detailed training on how to operate these various patrol vehicles later in the academy class. Of course, more conventional content such as report writing and radio communication are also covered; however, the events are often scenario based and focused on issues such as hunting and fishing violations (Michigan Department of Natural Resources, 2021).

Recruits in the Michigan DNR also focus on generalized legal issues such as Fourth Amendment curricula related to search and seizure, but again the scenario-based training involves situations on requesting a search warrant when a harvested deer has been observed in a garage that then closed. Officers are trained in legal areas that they may commonly encounter including domestic violence, motor vehicle code, and public disorder crimes. Much more specialized training is required to cover laws specifically related to hunting, fishing, trapping, and general outdoor recreation. Recruits cover laws specific to each of several big game species including deer, elk, bear, and turkey criminal cases. They also cover the investigation of crimes related to protected species in Michigan that may be poached (e.g., moose, wolf) and how the legal and enforcement environment differs from that of game species. The academy covers laws and practices required of individuals in the outdoor industry, such as taxidermists. Hazardous materials and laws governing other environmental crimes are covered in the academy training (Michigan Department of Natural Resources, 2021).

Michigan DNR CO recruits are exposed to significant training in investigatory techniques, some of which would be common in any accredited academy across the country, while others are quite specific to conservation law enforcement. Some of the more conventional topics include suspect, witness, and victim questioning, including the observation of nonverbal cues, which are presented by a police psychologist. Recruits cover evidentiary techniques such as sketching scenes, digital crime scenes, and photographing evidence. The academy training covers narcotics and other dangerous drugs, field sobriety and breathalyzer tests, fingerprinting, and preliminary death investigations, with many of these topics covered by subject matter experts employed by nearby traditional police departments. Other topics are highly specific to the work of conservation officers, including the recovery of bullets from gutted deer, animal necropsies to determine cause of death for game animals, obtaining tissue samples from gut piles, engaging in blood trail identification and tracking, and utilizing the searchers' cube to locate contraband items that may have been disposed of along a trail (Michigan Department of Natural Resources, 2021).

Use-of-force techniques (including minimal use of force), arresting techniques, survival tactics, firearm training, and marksmanship are also topics that recruits receive extensive training on, but which are certainly not unique to the work of COs. However, recruits in the Michigan DNR academy receive specific training on the handling of hunting contacts. This is an especially important aspect of DNR training curricula, because while most outdoorspeople are not violent, COs will frequently encounter armed suspects (doubly true while investigating hunting concerns), and they need to maintain control and personal safety while investigating legal violations. Beyond these concerns, they also must maintain a sense of procedural justice while interacting with hunters and anglers who do not pose a threat (i.e., the typical response from a conventional police officer to discovering a person is armed would likely be inappropriate for conservation officers). COs must receive extensive training on assessing violations for armed hunters and managing these encounters professionally, in order to maintain their safety and the legitimacy of their profession (Michigan Department of Natural Resources, 2021).

Conservation officer recruits are given training on contemporary police topics such as cultural issues and managing encounters with people recording or live streaming their behavior. In the Michigan DNR academy, recruits deal with accusations of racial profiling when requesting a fishing license from an angler, as well as confronting their own implicit biases. Recruits are exposed to the concepts of institutional bias and personal bias and are given examples of the consequences that these issues can cause for both citizens and officers. In addition to bias and racial profiling training, conservation officers in Michigan also receive tribal cultural training through interactions with representatives from several tribes in Michigan. Tribal hunting and fishing rights have long been established by treaty in Michigan, resulting in specific regulations for various parts of the state, and for tribal and non-tribal users. Michigan conservation officers work closely with tribal law enforcement and must also manage cultural conflicts that arise between tribal members and other members of the public over appropriate use of natural resources (Michigan Department of Natural Resources, 2021).

Plant, fish, bird, mammal, and other nongame species identification skills are also important for conservation officers, and these skills are practiced through various scenarios and skill-building exercises (Michigan Department of Natural Resources, 2021). Recruits are tasked with identifying both intact and processed fish parts. They are tested on these skills with identification tests of the curricula throughout the academy.

Survival skills are also important to learn. Like conventional police officers, Michigan provides academy curricula in the areas of first aid and cardiopulmonary resuscitation (CPR). Of course, more in depth and specialized training is included in the academy curricula as well. COs learn skills such as knot tying, making bed-like devices to extract injured persons from wilderness areas and other rugged landscapes, fire starting, shelter building, and the characteristics and behaviors of people who become lost in order to recognize and anticipate what they might do in order to assist locating them during a search and rescue. They receive training in orienteering to expand their search and rescue and survival skills (Michigan Department of Natural Resources, 2021).

Conservation officers receive training specific to hunting, fishing, and other outdoor equipment. Unlike most conventional police, conservation officers must be versed in various types of firearms, as the type of firearm may be legal or illegal for a specific activity or season, and officers may be called upon to safely handle a weapon if it has been used in a crime. Officers must be able to distinguish between semi-automatic, bolt, pump, lever, or break action firearms, as well as whether those arms use an external magazine, and safe operation of each type. Officers may also encounter black powder and other muzzleloader equipment and must be able to identify these weapons to determine compliance with state laws (Michigan Department of Natural Resources, 2021).

In addition to the curricula in Michigan, still other states may engage in training that more appropriately reflects the outdoor heritage of that state. Agencies in the Western United States may train in horseback riding and packing. Somewhat surprisingly, Arizona wildlife managers engage in high-risk water pursuits and live-fire training exercises out on the water.

SPECIALIZED MODELS:
BIOLOGIST/ENFORCEMENT HYBRID

Within specific conservation departments, officers may not be strictly focused on law enforcement, but may occupy a hybrid role that places them in the capacity of biologists with law enforcement powers. Two notable states that embrace this model are Colorado and Arizona. In Colorado, the members of Parks and Wildlife who have law enforcement authority are referred to as district wildlife managers (DWM). To fulfill this role, Colorado requires applicants for the position to have earned a bachelor's degree while majoring in a hard science that provides a proper baseline of knowledge for their specific role (e.g., biology, environmental science, forestry).

Once this minimum educational standard (or relevant fieldwork substitution) has been met, the candidate will then be required to pass a POST-certified police academy, with the basic curricula on arrest law, use of force, witness questioning, and civil liability. After graduating from the academy, the recruits are required to attend training that includes both a classroom and field component on issues related to wildlife, including resource management, habitat, public relations, and resource-specific law enforcement. This process also includes becoming a certified hunter safety instructor (Colorado Parks & Wildlife, 2021).

After their training has been completed, district wildlife managers engage in a wide variety of tasks and have an expansive role. Of course, like all personnel with law enforcement authority over natural resources, these employees engage in tasks such as investigating wildlife law violations, taking enforcement action on these violations, seizing equipment and other evidence used in the crimes, and properly disposing of illegally taken specimens. Additionally, DWMs engage in public outreach sessions with schools, civic groups, and outdoor-focused clubs, as well as teaching hunter education and providing consultations to landowners on issues such as habitat and human–wildlife conflict. Furthermore, DWMs also work to apply management plans, including the collection of data on habitat, which aids in protection of native flora and fauna in a different capacity than selective law enforcement does (Colorado Parks & Wildlife, 2021). The Arizona Game and Fish Department (AZGFD) makes similar requirements of their wildlife managers, but also include listed responsibilities of making hunt recommendations, as well as conducting fish and game surveys (Arizona Game & Fish Department, 2021).

REQUIREMENTS FOR FEDERAL CONSERVATION
LAW ENFORCEMENT

While likely the most commonly identified federal law enforcement positions are with the US Fish & Wildlife Service (USFWS), many other agencies include law enforcement bureaus that are tasked with protecting natural resources and possess arrest powers. Some of these agencies include the National Parks Service (NPS), the Bureau of Land Management (BLM), the US Forest Service (USFS), the Environmental Protection Agency (EPA), and the National Oceanic and Atmospheric Administration (NOAA). In general, the requirements listed for recruits in many of these positions include being between 21 and 37 years of age at the time of entrance to duty, having US citizenship, and for males, registering with the Selective Service System.

Like most state agencies identified in this chapter, applicants to these federal positions will also be required to pass a medical screening, as well as pass a physical fitness test and psychological screening exam. A background check on qualified applicants is also conducted. Those who apply are also viewed favorably if they have a four-year degree in wildlife management, criminal justice, or a closely related degree major. In the USFWS, special agents are required to qualify with firearms to standard, and requalification with arms is required annually. USFWS special agents are also required to have periodic medical examinations in addition to fitness testing, and some may even be required to provide annual financial disclosures (USFWS, 2021a).

Most federal law enforcement officers begin their training at the Federal Law Enforcement Training Center (FLETC) in Glynco, Georgia. In 2005, agencies responsible for protecting natural resources at the federal level (e.g., US Park Police [USPP], NPS, USFWS, USFS, BLM, Tennessee Valley Authority [TVA], and the National Marine Fisheries Service [NMFS]) conducted the Curriculum Development Conference (CDC) to develop an integrated training program. The CDC established the Land Management Police Training Program (LMPT), which then dissolved standalone training curricula such as the US Park Police Integrated Training Program, the National Park Ranger Integrated Training Program, and the Natural Resources Police Training Program. The LMPT is now used for the entry-level training required of federal law enforcement officers responsible for the protection of natural resources (Federal Law Enforcement Training Centers, 2021).

The LMPT provides a standard curriculum, including focused topics necessary for general law enforcement personnel, including emergency response driving, report writing, firearm training, conflict management, and arrest techniques. Other, more specialized topics include training on hazardous materials, scenario training at trail heads, wildlife viewing areas, hunter encounters, campsites, and marijuana grow operations. Trainees will also get practice in conducting laboratory exercises, and even get to participate in a Continuing Case Operation, where the process of a single case is practiced from the incident to courtroom testimony (National Parks Service, 2020).

For USFWS special agents, the 20-week training session includes curricula on criminal investigation and wildlife law, including rules of evidence, surveillance techniques, waterfowl identification, crime scenes, and report writing (USFWS, 2021b). After FLETC, USFWS special agent hopefuls complete a 44-week field training program. Recruits seeking to become EPA special agents with the Criminal Investigations Division (CID) will spend eight weeks at FLETC obtaining basic law enforcement and criminal investigator training. After this session, an additional eight weeks of training is required focusing on conducting investigations and coverage of environmental laws (Environmental Protection Agency, 2021).

CONCLUSION

Overall, several conclusions can be drawn from the information provided in the preceding chapter. First, conservation agencies have actually lagged traditional police agencies in terms of their ability to attract a more diverse candidate pool of recruits to conservation police positions. While conservation agencies do not generally have the same struggles that traditional agencies do in attracting qualified applicants, their more passive recruitment efforts, coupled with a lack of diversity among outdoor hobbyists, has produced a less diverse workforce than traditional policing.

Second, the bona fide occupational requirements of conservation officers closely track those of traditional police agencies, with some exceptions. Issues such as the use of written tests, oral interviews, physical examinations, physical fitness tests, background investigations, and polygraph examinations are very similar to those employed by local police agencies. Some exceptions, however, include the requirements to pass a swimming test or assessing the ability of candidates to hike.

Third, the educational standards required of police employed by conservation agencies far surpasses the average minimum standard set in traditional police agencies. There is a much higher expectation for educational achievement, with roughly 40 percent of agencies requiring a four-year degree if no relevant work experience is available for substitution. Additionally, many agencies expressly state preferences for specific degree majors such as those in the natural sciences or criminal justice. This is particularly true of states such as Colorado and Arizona, where officers function in both a biologist and law enforcement capacity.

Finally, the training for conservation officers, for the most part, appears to be quite specialized relative to the general police training models used by most municipal police agencies. States such as Michigan use a specialized academy, where conservation issues are thoroughly integrated into every aspect of their scenario-based and classroom training. Recruits in Michigan also spend a great deal of time on water-based training, which is closely aligned with the fishing and boating heritage of the state. Other states, such as Iowa and Arizona, utilize a hybrid model, where they send recruits to a traditional police academy and then implement a secondary pre-employment training session before commencement of field training. This represents substantial evidence that the training of conservation police is closely aligned with their work responsibilities.

DISCUSSION QUESTIONS

1. Go online and find the minimum basic job requirements for four conservation law enforcement agencies—one from the West, one from the East, one from the South, and one from the Midwest.

Compare and contrast the minimum basic job requirements. Think about possible reasons why the requirements may be different. How does this impact recruitment efforts?

2. Three different models of training academies were discussed within the chapter. Create a list identifying positive and negative attributes of each type of academy relative to their effectiveness at training conservation law enforcement officers. Which model is the most effective? Why would agencies choose one model over another?

Key Terms

Bona fide occupational qualifications: A quality or attribute that an employer may consider when making decisions on hiring an employee that could be considered discriminatory if it were not necessary to perform a particular job.

Standard minimum requirements: The minimum requirements that a prospective officer must meet before applying for a position as a conservation officer.

References

Alabama State Personnel Department. (2021). Candidate Information Guide. Conservation Enforcement Officer, Trainee, 70798. Written examination. https://personnel.alabama.gov/Documents/HTPGuides/101993_G.pdf

Alaska Department of Public Safety. (2021). Alaska State Troopers: Recruit interview. https://dps.alaska.gov/AST/Recruit/Interview

Arizona Game & Fish Department. (2021). Become a Game Ranger. www.azgfd.com/agency/employment/wildlifemanager

Bruns, D. (2010). Reflections from the one-percent of local police departments with mandatory four-year degree requirements for new hires: Are they diamonds in the rough? *Southwest Journal of Criminal Justice, 7*(1), 87-108.

Burbeck, E., & Furnham, A. (1985). Police officer selection: A critical review of the literature. *Journal of Police Science and Administration, 13*, 58–69.

California Department of Fish and Wildlife. (2021). Fish and Wildlife Warden career: Minimum qualifications. http://wildlife.ca.gov/Enforcement/Career/Qualifications

Chappell, A. T., & Lanza-Kaduce, L. (2010). Police academy socialization: Understanding the lessons learned in a paramilitary-bureaucratic organization. *Journal of Contemporary Ethnography, 39*(2), 187–214.

Colorado Parks & Wildlife. (2021). District Wildlife Manager. https://cpw.state.co.us/aboutus/Pages/Jobs-District-Wildlife-Manager.aspx

Delaware Department of Natural Resources and Environmental Control (DNREC). (2021). Natural Resources Police Youth Academy. https://dnrec.alpha.delaware.gov/fish-wildlife/police/youth-academy/

Eliason, S. L. (2006). Factors influencing job satisfaction among state conservation officers. *Policing: An International Journal of Police Strategies & Management, 29*(1), 6–18.

Eliason, S. L. (2017). Becoming a Game Warden: Motivations for choosing a career in wildlife law enforcement. *Journal of Police and Criminal Psychology, 32*(1), 28–32.

Elmore, C. (2016, December 9). Jury awards $97.5M in fatal shooting of Cottageville ex-mayor. Cottageville mayor says Price was laid off because of 'budget constraints.' Lawsuit filed in Cottageville shooting that took former mayor's life. Suit accuses former Cottageville officer of unethical conduct. Civil proceedings underway in former Cottageville mayor's slaying. *The Post and Courier.* https://www.postandcourier.com/archives/jury-awards-m-in-fatal-shooting-of-cottageville-ex-mayor/article_d95aea6c-f299-5ef2-8a60-a423084330ec.html

Environmental Protection Agency (EPA). (2021). Criminal enforcement: Special agents. https://www.epa.gov/enforcement/criminal-enforcement-special-agents

Federal Law Enforcement Training Centers. (2021). Land Management Police training. https://www.fletc.gov/land-management-police-training

Florida Fish and Wildlife Conservation Commission (FWC). (2021). Minimum qualifications for law enforcement positions. myfwc.com/get-involved/employment/law-enforcement/minimum-qualifications

Florida Highway Patrol. (2021). Requirements. beatrooper.com
/requirements

Forsyth, C. J., & Forsyth, Y. A. (2009). Dire and sequestered meetings:
The work of game wardens. *American Journal of Criminal Justice,
34*, 213–223.

Gaines, L. K., & Falkenberg, S. (1998). An evaluation of the written
selection test: Effectiveness and alternatives. *Journal of Criminal
Justice, 26*(3), 175–183.

Georgia Department of Natural Resources. (2021). Qualifications for
employment. gadnrle.org/qualifications-employment

Gottfredson, L. S. (1996). Racially gerrymandering the content of
police tests to satisfy the U.S. Justice Department: A case study.
Psychology, Public Policy, and Law, 2(3/4), 418–446.

Gupta, V., & Yang, J. R. (2016). *Advancing diversity in law enforcement.* U.S. Department of Justice and U.S. Equal Employment
Opportunity Commission.

Iowa Department of Natural Resources. (2021). Conservation law enforcement. https://www.iowadnr.gov/About-DNR/dnr-staff-offices
/conservation-law-enforcement

Kansas Department of Wildlife & Parks. (2021). KDWP Jobs & Employment Information. https://ksoutdoors.com/KDWP-Info/Jobs

Kelling, G., & Moore M. (1988). From political reform to community:
The evolving strategy of police. In J. R. Greene & S. Mastrofski
(Eds.), *Community policing: Rhetoric or reality?* (pp. 3–25). Praeger.

Kentucky Law Enforcement Council (2021). Physical Agility Test
Prep. https://klecs.ky.gov/physical-agility-prep

Kringen, A. L., & Kringen, J. A. (2014). Identifying barriers to Black
applicants in police employment screening. *Policing, 9*(1), 15–25.

Lonsway, K. (2003). Tearing down the wall: Problems with consisten-
cy, validity, and adverse impact of physical agility testing in police
selection. *Police Quarterly, 6*(3), 237–277.

Louisiana State Police. (2021). Join Louisiana's finest. http://lsp.org
/recruit.html

Louisiana Wildlife & Fisheries. (2021). Become an agent. www.wlf
.louisiana.gov/page/become-an-agent

Massachusetts Public Employee Retirement Administration Commission. (2021). Medical standards for municipal police officers.

https://www.mass.gov/doc/medical-standards-for-municipal
-police-officers-perac/download

Matthies, C. F., Keller, K. M., & Lim, N. (2012). *Identifying barriers to diversity in law enforcement agencies*. RAND Corporation.

Metchik, E. (1999). An analysis of the "screening out" model of police officer selection. *Police Quarterly, 2*(1), 79–95.

Michigan Department of Natural Resources (DNR). (2021). 2018 Recruit School blog. https://www.michigan.gov/dnr/0,4570,7-350 -79136_79772_81097_81107---,00.html

Minnesota Department of Natural Resources. (2021). Conservation Officer careers and hiring information. www.dnr.state.mn.us /enforcement/careers/index.html

Montana Department of Justice (DOJ). (2021). Recruitment: Applicant info. dojmt.gov/highwaypatrol/recruitment-applicant-info/

Montana Fish, Wildlife & Parks. (2021). Law enforcement: Warden hiring. fwp.mt.gov/aboutfwp/enforcement/warden-hiring

National Parks Service (NPS). (2020). NPS law enforcement ranger training and employment process. https://www.nps.gov/aboutus /nps-law-enforcement-ranger-training-and-employment-process. htm

New Jersey Division of Fish & Wildlife. (2021). Employment. www .state.nj.us/dep/fgw/employ.htm

New York City Police Department (NYPD). (2021). Hiring process. www1.nyc.gov/site/nypd/careers/police-officers/po-hiring.page

Novak, K., Cordner, G., Smith, B., & Roberg, R. (2017). *Police & society* (7th ed.). Oxford University Press.

Oregon State Police. (2021). Fish and Wildlife Division. https://www .oregon.gov/osp/programs/fw/Pages/default.aspx

Orrick, W. D. (2008). *Recruitment, retention, and turnover of police personnel: Reliable, practical, and effective solutions*. Charles C. Thomas.

OutdoorAfro. (2021). Outdoor Afro: Our stories. https://outdoorafro .com/stories/

Patten, R., Crow, M. S., & Shelley, T. O. (2015). What's in a name? The occupational identity of conservation and natural resource-oriented enforcement agencies. *American Journal of Criminal Justice, 40*, 750–764.

Perrott, S. B. (1999). Visible minority applicant concerns and assessment of occupational role in the era of community-based policing. *Journal of Community and Applied Social Psychology, 9*, 339–353.

Ramsey, C. H., & Robinson, L. O. (2015). *Final report of the President's Task Force on 21st Century Policing.* Office of Community Oriented Policing Services.

Reaves, B. A. (2009). *State and local law enforcement training academies, 2006.* US Department of Justice.

Reaves, B. A. (2015). *Local police departments, 2013: Personnel, policies, and practices.* US Department of Justice, Bureau of Justice Statistics.

Responsive Management/National Shooting Sports Foundation. (2017). *Hunting, fishing, sport shooting, and archery recruitment, retention, and reactivation: A practitioner's guide.*

Rhode Island State Police. (2021). Minimum qualifications. risp .ri.gov/academy/jobdescription

Ridgeway, G., Lim, N., Gifford, B., Koper, C., Matthies, C. F., Hajiamiri, S., & Huynh, A. K. (2008). Strategies for improving officer recruitment in the San Diego Police Department. RAND Corporation. https://www.rand.org/pubs/monographs/MG724.html

Rossler, M. T., Rabe-Hemp, C. E., Peuterbaugh, M., & Scheer, C. (2020). The influence of gender on perceptions of barriers to a police patrol career. *Police Quarterly, 23*(3), 368–395.

Rossler, M. T., Scheer, C., & Suttmoeller, M. J. (2019). Perceptions of barriers and patrol career interest among African-American criminal justice students. *Policing: An International Journal, 42*(2), 421–440.

Rossler, M. T., & Suttmoeller, M. J. (2018). Is all police academy training created equally? Comparing natural resource officer and general police academy training. *The Police Journal: Theory, Practice and Principles, 91*(2), 107–122.

Rossler, M. T., & Suttmoeller, M. J. (2021). Conservation officer perceptions of academy training: Resource specific and general policing tasks. *Policing: A Journal of Policy and Practice, 15*(2), 980–994.

Rossler, M. T., Foster, J.T., & Suttmoeller, M. J. (2021). *The influence of conservation agency resources on officer entry and training requirements.* Manuscript submitted for publication.

Schuck, A. M. (2014). Female representation in law enforcement: The influence of screening, unions, incentives, community policing, CALEA, and size. *Police Quarterly, 17*(1), 54–78.

Shurr, A. (2019, April 30). Lawmakers consider whether conservation tax should be renewable. *Missouri Times.* https://themissouritimes.com/lawmakers-consider-whether-conservation-tax-should-be-renewable/

Texas Law Enforcement Management and Administrative Statistics Program. (1994). *TELEMASP Bulletin, 1*(7).

Travis, M. A. (1994). Psychological health tests for violence-prone police officers: Objectives, shortcomings, and alternatives. *Stanford Law Review, 46,* 1717–1770.

Tobias, M. (1998). *Nature's keepers: On the front lines of the fight to save wildlife in America.* John Wiley & Sons Inc.

Todak, N. (2017). The decision to become a police officer in a legitimacy crisis. *Women & Criminal Justice, 27,* 250–270.

U.S. Department of the Interior, U.S. Fish and Wildlife Service, and U.S. Department of Commerce, U.S. Census Bureau. (2011). 'National Survey of Fishing, Hunting, and Wildlife-Associated Recreation.'

United States Fish & Wildlife Service (USFWS). (2021a). How do I become a federal wildlife officer? https://www.fws.gov/refuges/lawenforcement/career-information.php

United States Fish & Wildlife Service (USFWS). (2021b). About service special agents. https://www.fws.gov/le/special-agents.html

Varela, J. G., Boccaccini, M. T., Scogin, F., & Stump, J. (2004). Personality testing in law enforcement employment settings: A metanalytic review. *Criminal Justice and Behavior, 31*(6), 649–675.

Wachter, P. (2020, September 2). Outdoor Afro founder Rue Mapp: 'The trees don't know that you're black.' *The Undefeated.* https://theundefeated.com/features/outdoor-afro-founder-rue-mapp-the-trees-dont-know-that-youre-black/

Washington Department of Fish and Wildlife (WDFW). (2021). Minimum qualifications and disqualifiers. wdfw.wa.gov/about/enforcement/jobs/requirements

Washington State Patrol. (2021). Be a Trooper. www.wsp.wa.gov/be-a-trooper

Wisconsin State Patrol. (2021). Minimum requirements. wsp.wi.gov
/Pages/Minimum-Requirements

Wyoming Department of Game & Fish. (2021). Game Warden exam.
wgfd.wyo.gov/game-warden-exam

Seven

OFFICER LAW ENFORCEMENT FUNCTIONS AND PATROL STRATEGIES

The management of wildlife and fisheries in the United States relies on the three pillars of research, management, and law enforcement. Without the enforcement of hunting, fishing, and trapping regulations, it would be difficult for wildlife and fisheries biologists to manage the natural resources in America (Morse, 1973). This important role in wildlife management has been filled by conservation officers. While conservation officers fill several different roles, their main role is law enforcement. While conservation officers are similar to traditional law enforcement officers in some respects, they are also quite different in others. This chapter will focus on the law enforcement aspects of the conservation officer job including, their role in the larger law enforcement community, their approach to natural resources law enforcement, and techniques that conservation officers use to fulfill their law enforcement role. One of the main differences between conservation law enforcement officers and traditional law enforcement officers is the environment and context within which they operate. Because of these differences, conservation law enforcement requires a different approach, so this chapter will highlight these differences and explain how conservation officers fulfill the important role of a law enforcement officer. Other aspects such as public relations and order maintenance will be covered in the subsequent chapter.

Conservation officers have existed in one form or another since around the sixth century (Trench, 1965). While the form that conservation officers have taken and the reasons why they are enforcing laws pertaining to hunting and fishing have changed over the years, the main role of conservation officers to enforce laws pertaining to hunting and fishing has not changed (Eliason, 2007; Falcone, 2004; Shelley & Crow, 2009).

In the United States, there are only approximately 6,000 conservation officers serving all 50 states (Patten et al., 2015), and hunters outnumber conservation officers approximately 10,000 to 1 (Tobias, 1998). The number provided by Tobias does not include the numbers of other types of outdoor recreationists that may pursue activities that fall under the purview of conservation officers, such as fishing, gathering, and boating, as well as unlicensed hunters and anglers (Rossler & Suttmoeller, 2021). Because of the relatively small number of conservation officers compared to those that participate in outdoor pursuits, compliance with rules and regulations is very important for effective resource management (Mayne, 2000). Successful promotion of compliance with natural resources regulations depends upon a mix of education, regulation, and enforcement (McGarrell et al., 2013). While this chapter focuses on the enforcement aspect of compliance, apprehension is only one aspect of achieving compliance (Hall, 1992). The educational aspects of compliance will be covered in a later chapter.

Traditionally, conservation law enforcement officers were tasked with enforcing laws pertaining to the protection of natural resources (hunting, fishing, etc.). However, in recent years, their role has expanded to a more general law enforcement role, which has included the enforcement of laws pertaining to more traditional crimes (Falcone, 2004). Even though they have begun to adopt a more generalized law enforcement role, the people that conservation law enforcement officers interact with are in much different environmental settings than are those encountered by traditional law enforcement officers (Eliason, 2007; Falcone, 2004; Patten & Caudill, 2013; Shelley & Crow, 2009; Sherblom et al., 2002). While traditional police officers are more likely to encounter citizens through traffic stops, calls for service, or domestic disputes, the citizens that conservation officers encounter are normally recreating outdoors by hunting, fishing, boating, hiking, watching wildlife, or any number of outdoor activities (Patten & Caudill, 2013; Shelley & Crow, 2009). Because of the nature of the activities that those conservation officers contact are participating in, the officer may utilize different law enforcement approaches when addressing law violations. Conservation officers must balance the task of ensuring that people enjoy their time recreating, with the enforcement of laws to ensure public safety and natural resources protection. This balance requires that conservation officers utilize both soft and hard enforcement when addressing violations (Pendleton, 1998).

SOFT AND HARD ENFORCEMENT

Soft enforcement is characterized by gaining compliance through informal methods of education, prevention, and community relations. Conversely, hard enforcement would be characterized by arrests and citations. Pendleton (1998) identified four common styles of soft enforcement: conciliatory enforcement, threat enforcement, non-enforcement, and covert enforcement.

Conciliatory enforcement is also known as "encouraging compliance" (Pendleton, 1998, p. 557). The goal of conciliatory enforcement is to ensure that the park visitor or recreation area user willingly complies with the regulations and enjoys their time at the park or recreation area. One of the strategies employed by an officer utilizing conciliatory enforcement is to prominently display the symbols of law enforcement such as a marked patrol vehicle, uniforms, and officer presence where they can be easily observed by the users. By displaying these symbols of authority, the area user is aware that the officer has the potential for taking enforcement action, even if it is indirectly (Pendleton, 1998). In addition to displaying the symbols of enforcement, conciliatory enforcement relies on face-to-face interaction between the officer and the recreational user. These interactions do not necessarily have to occur in the presence of a violation, but they may. An officer may simply stop to talk to a group to inquire if they are enjoying themselves or may engage someone actively violating a regulation. The tone of these conversations is friendly and informative, rather than in an accusatory or guilt-seeking tone. However, if the interaction occurs the presence of a violation, the officer may let them know that they have noticed the violation, but in a tone that allows for the user to correct their actions (Pendleton, 1998). This style encourages visitors to comply due to the friendly tone of the conversation, the information on how to correct the violation, and the still-present chance of formal enforcement now that the officer is aware of the violation and knows the visitor.

The next style identified by Pendleton (1998) was **threat enforcement** or "bluffing" for compliance (p. 559). Unlike conciliatory enforcement, threat enforcement does not prioritize the enjoyment of the visitor, but rather prioritizes the protection of the recreational area or the overall visitor experience. Compliance in this style is expected based on the threat or promise of formal enforcement actions if the visitor did not take immediate steps to rectify the offending behavior. Officers employing the threat enforcement style will also use the formal symbols of law enforcement such as marked vehicles and uniforms, but they are utilized as more than simply symbols. For example, the patrol vehicle may activate its emergency lights. Uniformed officers may openly display notebooks where they record information about those that are in violation of the regulations or may openly display ticket books or other symbols of formal law enforcement. Officers utilizing this style do not aim to be viewed as a "friend" of the park visitor, but rather as a police officer. This style portrays the visitor as a violator and the park or recreational area as the victim. Even though this style is more confrontational than conciliatory enforcement, the relationship between the officer and the person in violation does not always become overtly confrontational because the officer may explain that formal law enforcement action is one option that can be employed if the visitor does not correct their behavior. The visitor may often believe they have been provided a break and may even thank the officer for not taking formal enforcement action (Pendleton, 1998).

The third style of soft enforcement identified by Pendleton (1998) was non-enforcement. The goal of this style of soft enforcement was to avoid any potential law enforcement situation. This style was most often observed in remote areas but could potentially occur elsewhere.

Officers utilizing this style would oftentimes be working out of uniform or have their uniforms or other outward law enforcement symbols covered. Officers would simply ignore violations that they either witnessed or were made aware of. Sometimes officers would pass on information concerning violations to officers who were more law enforcement oriented but may also simply ignore the violations. Sometimes the decision to ignore a clear violation was dependent on the particular situation at the time of the violation, but it could also be a common part of an officer's work routine. Non-enforcement could also be utilized to gather information in exchange for not taking enforcement action. A final reason that a non-enforcement style may be utilized is due to an organizational edict based on political pressure. If the enforcement of a particular law is politically unpopular, officers may be directed to ignore those violations (Pendleton, 1998).

The final soft enforcement style identified by Pendleton (1998) is **covert enforcement** or "bargaining" for compliance (p. 563). This style does not take visitor enjoyment or the violator's enjoyment into account. The goal of this style is to protect the park/recreational area or the resource. This style is characterized by undercover work with few to no outward displays of traditional law enforcement symbols. Even though more extensive law enforcement measures are undertaken with this style, formal law enforcement action is still not necessarily the end goal of this method. Compliance is still the end goal. For example, officers utilizing this style may seize tents from a prohibited area. When the owners of the tents arrive at the park headquarters to inquire about their tents, they are encouraged to either leave the park or agree to comply with the regulations (Pendleton, 1998).

Soft enforcement can be viewed as both a proactive approach that attempts to predict, identify, and implement responses to potential violations and also as a reactive method of addressing particular situations. This type of enforcement realizes that formal punitive measures are not always required to gain compliance, even if it is not always voluntary compliance. Soft enforcement also allows for the officer to utilize discretion when distinguishing between the uninformed and the chronic offender. However, because soft enforcement does not rely on formal sanctions, over time, it may lose its effectiveness with frequent visitors to a recreational area. If there is no threat of actual formal punitive sanctions, then there may be a loss of compliance because there is no tangible reason to comply with directives or regulations. Therefore, even if soft enforcement is the preferred method of enforcement, hard enforcement should also be utilized when necessary (Pendleton, 1998).

Hard enforcement is the other style of enforcement that conservation officers may employ. While it is considered a more traditional policing strategy that utilizes more punitive sanctions such as arrests and citations as the method of gaining compliance than is soft enforcement, it is also commonly used by conservation officers to enforce laws pertaining to outdoor recreation (Pendleton, 1998). Conservation officers have traditionally focused exclusively on the laws pertaining to hunting and fishing (Forsyth, 1993, 2008; Palmer & Bryant, 1985). However, more recent scholarship has suggested that the law enforcement role of conservation officers is expanding to include more enforcement activities other than fish and wildlife law enforcement, and therefore they are beginning to more closely resemble traditional law enforcement officers (Eliason, 2007; Falcone, 2004; Pendleton, 1998; Shelley & Crow, 2009; Sherblom et al., 2002). The law enforcement role of conservation officers has expanded due at least in part to increased police powers. Over the last several decades the number of urban residents utilizing outdoor recreational areas for hunting, fishing, boating, and hiking has increased (Falcone, 2004). As a result of this increase in use, an increase in the number and type of crimes that were occurring in natural areas or outdoor spaces where citizens would recreate has occurred as well as an urbanization in the types of crimes that were taking place, including increased drug use and personal violence (Chavez & Tynon, 2000; Patten, 2012; Pendleton, 1998). These societal and social changes have led to an increase and broadening of the role of conservation officers (Eliason, 2007).

EXPANDED ROLE OF CONSERVATION OFFICERS

Additionally, historically, conservation officers were housed in smaller departments of conservation, but in the 1990s, many of these smaller departments of conservation expanded their form and function to include a variety of other types of outdoor recreation in addition to the more traditional hunting and fishing. When conservation officers were absorbed into these larger departments of natural resources, the scope of their duties expanded beyond the traditional role, which has led conservation officers to function and act more like a general service police agency than strictly a conservation-related agency (Falcone, 2004). As a result of this increased focus on traditional police work, conservation officers will commonly assist other agencies with the enforcement of various criminal laws (Eliason, 2007; Falcone, 2004). Even though conservation officers are increasingly expected to enforce laws that do not pertain to hunting or fishing, officers may continue to view the enforcement of hunting and fishing laws as their primary responsibility and enforce other laws when they encounter violations through their enforcement of conservation-related statutes (Eliason, 2007).

The most common types of violations conservation officers encounter that are not wildlife related are drug and alcohol offenses. For example, officers may encounter those that are in possession of illegal drugs (Blevins & Lanham, 2013; Eliason, 2007; McGarrell et al., 2013; Shelley & Crow, 2009; Sherblom, et al., 2002), driving or boating under the influence (Blevins & Lanham, 2013; Eliason, 2007; McGarrell et al., 2013; Shelley & Crow, 2009), or producing illegal drugs such as growing marijuana or producing methamphetamine (Blevins & Edwards, 2009; Eliason, 2007; Sherblom et al., 2002). Remote areas that are patrolled by conservation officers are commonly used for drug production and distribution (Cohen et al., 2007; Chavez & Tynon, 2000; Eliason, 2007; Swan, 2016; Weisheit et al., 1999).

Conservation officers also encounter a wide variety of other offenses, including traffic offenses, assaults, arson, domestic violence, rape/sexual assault, destruction of property, trespassing, burglary, stolen cars, firearms and other property, outstanding criminal warrants, extremist groups/domestic terrorism, and even murder (Blevins & Lanham, 2013; Chavez & Tynon, 2000; Eliason, 2007; Shelley & Crow, 2009; Swan, 2016).

While quite a bit of attention has been given to the types of violations that conservation officers encounter, very little attention has been given to strategies and techniques utilized by conservation officers to discover or detect law breakers. Generally, conservation officers are known for working independently and may be isolated from other officers or backup, which means they generally will work by themselves while on routine patrol (McGarrell et al., 2013; Sherblom et al., 2002). However, routine patrol is not the only way that conservation officers detect and apprehend violators. Violations may also be detected through a group patrol (McGarrell et al., 2013) or as it is more traditionally known, a saturation patrol (Piza, 2018).

Hunting and fishing violations may also be discovered through information gleaned from the public (McGarrell et al., 2013). Conservation officers receive phone calls reporting violations directly from the public, oftentimes at their homes (Calkins, 1970; Swan, 2016). Another way that conservation officers receive information about violations from the public is through citizen reporting programs (Nelson & Verbyla, 1984). The most common of these programs is Operation Game Thief that allows citizens to report a poaching violation through either a toll-free number, online reporting form (NMDGF, 2020) or an email (Colorado Department of Parks and Wildlife [CDPW, 2020). Currently, 49 states have adopted Operation Game Thief or a very similar program (CDPW, 2020). Working closely with the public is an example of the policing strategy known as community policing.

LAW ENFORCEMENT STRATEGIES

Community Policing

Community policing is a strategy that at its core emphasizes that officers should work closely with community residents and businesses, instead of only relying on themselves for crime control. As a result, crime prevention should be the focus of the police, rather than strictly law enforcement (Walker & Katz, 2013). There are four major dimensions to community policing: the philosophical dimension, the strategic dimension, the tactical dimension, and the organizational dimension (Cordner, 2015).

The philosophical dimension includes the main ideas or tenets of community policing. The three most important are: citizen input, a broad function, and personalized service. Community policing organizations subscribe to the belief that citizens should have access to policing agencies. The mechanisms through which agencies seek input from or involve the citizens within their jurisdiction varies. Some organizations may use public meetings or forums, call-in radio, and television shows to engage the public, while others may meet with various citizen advisory boards, business owners, or other community leaders. Strategies to seek citizen input can be tailored in size and scope to the organization's needs (Cordner, 2015).

The next important facet of the philosophical dimension of community policing is that community policing organizations embrace a wide police role. Even though police agencies may participate in a variety of activities that are not directly linked to law enforcement, agencies that do not employ a community policing philosophy may view their role in society as a narrow crime fighting role. Interestingly, historically the police role began very broadly and then narrowed over time, most likely due to the professional model and media representations of the police role. Even in agencies that view their role as a very narrow crime fighting role, police officers actually spend very little time dealing with serious and violent offenses and offenders (Cordner, 2015; Parks et al., 1999; Terrill et al., 2014). The broader view of community policing embraces these other non-enforcement activities that police officers are participating in such as order maintenance, social service, or other types of calls for assistance, or any number of other non-law enforcement activities (Cordner, 2015).

Personal service is another important aspect of the philosophical dimension of community policing. Personal service allows for policing activities to be adapted to local norms and values or for individual situations. Allowing for the officer to consider the local norms and individual circumstances when utilizing their discretionary decision making of whether to take formal enforcement action combats the common belief that government officials and especially law enforcement officers do not care about anyone and only want to enforce all laws as written in statute (Cordner, 2015). Allowing for local norms to influence decision making does not allow the community to decide exclusively what laws are enforced and which are not because there still needs to be some uniformity in policing across a wider jurisdiction.

The strategic dimension is another characteristic of community policing. This dimension is when the philosophy of community policing is implemented through policy, procedures, and programs. There are three main strategic considerations within this dimension: re-oriented operations, geographic focus, and an emphasis on prevention. Because community policing is predicated on increased interaction with citizens, the re-oriented operations strategic consideration focuses on a decreased reliance on patrolling by vehicles and more face-to face interactions (Cordner, 2015). While the adoption of the patrol vehicle by law enforcement agencies has allowed officers to more efficiently patrol and respond to calls, it had the unintended consequence of isolating officers from the citizens they serve (Walker & Katz, 2013). A community policing strategy attempts to reverse some of that isolation by focusing on increased face-to-face interaction with citizens.

Another strategic consideration of community policing is a geographic focus. This focus suggests that officers are more effective if they are responsible for a specific geographic area. Traditional law enforcement officers are subjected to regular reassignment to different beats. By having officers assigned to a particular geographic area, officers are able to become more familiar with the citizens of their area and the problems unique to that area. It also allows for citizens of that particular area to become familiar with the officers assigned to their area. This familiarity should help to build trust, confidence, and cooperation between the citizens and the law enforcement officers (Cordner, 2015).

The final strategic consideration is an emphasis on prevention and being proactive, rather than reactive. Instead of officers randomly patrolling their assigned areas or waiting for calls for service, officers should be engaging in directed enforcement activities, specific crime prevention efforts, problem solving, community engagement, or citizen interaction (Cordner, 2015, p. 487). Also, instead of simply addressing the obvious issues prevalent in their assigned areas, officers should be considering the underlying problems that are contributing to the issues present in their assigned district. Officers and policing organizations commonly value crime fighting over crime prevention, but citizens would most often rather have a crime prevented, than a crime solved (Cordner, 2015). Another aspect of prevention concerns police officers serving as role models and providing educational and other more social service-oriented programming in an effort to impact people's behavior that may lead to a decrease in crime.

The third dimension of community policing is the tactical dimension. The tactical dimension is characterized by the actual programs, practices, and behaviors implemented by the community policing organization. The three most important elements of this dimension are positive interactions, partnerships, and problem solving (Cordner, 2015). The nature of many aspects of police work leads to negative interactions between the police and the public. Community policing recognizes this fact and encourages officers to try to engage in positive interactions when possible to mitigate some of those negative interactions. Positive interactions can take many forms such as spending extra time on a call instead of rushing to complete the call and move on to the next call for service. Officers should view calls as an opportunity to provide quality service and result in a positive interaction between the police and the person making the call. Officers can also engage with people outside of enforcement interactions or calls for service by stopping and talking to citizens that are outside, business owners, schools, or any other people they come across through the course of their duties. Police should engage people, rather than simply watch them (Cordner, 2015).

Developing partnerships with the community is another characteristic of the tactical dimension of community policing. Law enforcement officers and agencies should seek out opportunities to create meaningful partnerships within the communities that they serve. This can take a variety of forms and will vary from community to community because every community is different. Officers should become involved in the community by partnering with community organizations, and agencies should actively seek input from communities regarding the types of issues that are important to those particular communities (Cordner, 2015).

Problem solving is the final characteristic of the tactical dimension. In addition to particular incidents that occur that must be investigated and addressed, officers should place an emphasis on addressing the causes of the incidents as well. This approach should not be limited to special projects but should be the standard operating procedure utilized by the agency and should be practiced by all members of the agency. It should incorporate community input and participation and involve collaboration with other agencies and organizations. All decisions should be made based on information collected in a systematic manner, rather than based on anecdotal or perceptual information (Cordner, 2015). The process for solving problems should consist of four steps: identification of the problem, analysis of the problem, identification of possible alternative solutions to the problem, and the implementation and assessment of the response to the problem. Traditional law enforcement responses should be considered within this process, but should not be the sole focus when determining possible solutions (Cordner, 2015).

The final dimension to community policing is the organizational dimension. To effectively implement community policing, agencies must structure their organizations accordingly. The three main aspects related to this dimension are agency structure, management, and information (Cordner, 2015). In order to accommodate the activities required for the successful implementation of community policing, organizations should decentralize so that authority and responsibility are more widely distributed. This will allow for all involved personnel to be more responsive and have more independence. Organizations should also flatten their hierarchies. Reducing the number of layers in an organization increases communication and efficiency. De-specialization will also increase an organization's efficiency and effectiveness. This will provide more resources to the delivery of community policing services to the community. The creation of teams to address problems should also be considered. Employees working as teams can increase efficiency of solving problems and increase quality. Finally, civilianization should be considered. If positions held by sworn personnel could be staffed by non-sworn personnel, agencies may save money and also better utilize sworn personnel (Cordner, 2015).

Management should also make modifications from a traditional bureaucratic structure to implement community policing more effectively. Agencies should become less reliant on formal rules, regulations, and procedures to allow for the flexibility that is required for effective community policing. Agencies should also modify their mission statements and participate in more mentoring and coaching of employees and strategic planning. Continuous strategic planning should take place so agencies can readily and effectively monitor their progress. Agencies should also empower their employees to take some risk and to be creative in their problem-solving approaches to community problems (Cordner, 2015).

The final characteristic of the organizational dimension of community policing is the management of information. Traditionally, law enforcement agencies have relied on empirical measures to measure success, such as number of arrests, number of calls adjudicated, etc. Community policing cannot generally be evaluated by these types of measures because community policing relies more on the quality of the interactions, rather than the number of interactions (Cordner, 2015). They also need to become more adept at collecting and analyzing the types of information that will be most advantageous for the implementation of community policing in that information should be collected at the neighborhood and community levels. They also need to improve their information collecting in terms of crime analysis and modify other systems to collect and analyze the information needed for community policing (Cordner, 2015) more effectively.

Problem-Oriented Policing

Problem-oriented policing is a versatile policing strategy that is commonly employed by law enforcement agencies. The basic premise of problem-oriented policing is to identify, understand, and address the various issues that result in citizens calling the police for assistance (Reisig, 2010). Goldstein (1979), considered to be the earliest advocate of problem-oriented policing, developed the SARA acronym that provided the basic outline for problem-oriented policing. The first stage, "Scanning," requires not only that the police attempt to define the problem, but also that the public wants the problem addressed. When defining the problem, police officers should try to be as precise as possible in labeling the problem instead of using broad criminological classifications (Reisig, 2010). For example, police should label computer thefts from the local college library as such instead of simply something more general such as theft. However, not all crimes are as geographically isolated as the previous example. If the problem/crime is occurring in a much broader geographic scope, they should still try to be as precise as possible. At this stage, the police also must determine whether they can effectively address the problem or if it is better addressed by a different agency.

The second step of SARA is "Analysis." During this stage, the police work to identify the size and scope of the problem, as well as the underlying causal process of the problem (Clarke & Eck, 2005). It is important at this stage to gather as much information as possible about the problem/crime. Police will often rely on official sources of information such as crime reports or calls for service. While these sources of information are important for determining the size and scope of the problem, officers should also utilize other sources of information as well, such as information from other agencies or organizations, residents, and any other sources that may provide essential information. It is important to gather as much information as possible because it is important to identify any underlying causes that may be contributing to the crime or reported problem (Reisig, 2010). In order to be thorough in collecting all relevant information, it may be helpful for the police to create teams that consist of officers, crime analysts, researchers, or anyone else that may be able to provide insights into the problem being investigated (Bynum, 2001; Reisig, 2010).

The third step of the SARA process is the "Response" stage. During this stage, the police will take all the relevant information and develop responses to the problem. Responses may vary based on the particular details associated with the problem. However, Goldstein (1979) cautions that the police should search for alternative responses that may provide more effective solutions than what the police have previously done or are currently doing. Responses could invoke traditional police responses that address issues related to the time and place that the problem is occurring, such as directed patrols and crackdowns, also known as "enforcement problem-oriented policing," or it may require a less law enforcement-oriented response, such as organizing local residents, agencies, and organizations to collaborate with the police, also known as "situational problem-oriented policing" (Braga & Weisburd, 2006, p. 146; Reisig, 2010).

The final stage of the SARA process is known as "Assessment." During this stage, the police should assess whether the responses implemented solved the problem, and if not, whether strategies should be modified in the future to more effectively address the problem (Reisig, 2010). One way they could do this would be to utilize an evaluation approach using research methodologies (Sherman, 1991). However, most police agencies do not have personnel trained in evaluation research methodologies, so agencies could partner with external evaluators such as a local university or could develop internal solutions to effectively evaluate their responses in an unbiased manner (Reisig, 2010; Scott et al., 2008). Problem-oriented policing is a common strategy utilized by conservation officers. It can be applied to many different types of wildlife crimes, such as illegal commercial fishing, illegal trapping, or deer poaching. For example, if there is a problem with commercial fishermen fishing in restricted areas or at restricted times, problem-oriented policing can be applied to scan, analyze, respond, and assess the situation (Lemieux & Pickles, 2020).

Hot Spots Policing

Hot spots policing is a patrol and crime prevention strategy that is utilized by conservation officers (Palmer & Bryant, 1985). The basic premise of hot spots policing is that crime is not evenly distributed across a particular area such as a city, but rather crime is clustered in certain areas or "hot spots" (Braga et al., 2012; Pierce et al., 1988; Sherman et al., 1989; Weisburd et al., 1992). If police officers can focus on certain risk factors that make crime more likely, they may be more effective at preventing crime than they could from participating in the random patrolling of large areas, responding to calls for service quickly, or making large numbers of reactive arrests (Braga, 2001; Clarke, 1992; Goldstein, 1990; Sherman, 1997; Wilson & Kelling, 1982). If policing attention can be focused on these particular areas with a high incidence of crime, then crime may be more efficiently addressed (Braga et al., 2012; Sherman & Weisburd, 1995; Weisburd & Green 1995). To be effective, policing strategies such as directed patrols, proactive arrests, and problem-oriented policing could be utilized to address these high-crime areas (Braga, 2008; Braga et al., 2012; Eck

1997, 2002; Weisburd & Eck 2004). Braga et al. (2012) analyzed 19 studies that examined the effects of hot spots policing techniques. The studies included in their meta-analysis contained police interventions that utilized problem-oriented policing strategies, and more traditional law enforcement strategies such as enforcement focused on drug offenses, increased gun searches and seizures, increased patrol, and zero-tolerance policing. They found that the police agencies that utilized problem-oriented policing strategies were more effective than those utilizing traditional law enforcement strategies, but overall, positive gains were realized by most of the studies included in the meta-analysis. Conservation officers utilize hot spots policing to patrol areas that exhibit high levels of hunting and fishing activity. For example, they may stake out areas known for a particular type of hunting such as deer or mourning doves (Palmer & Bryant, 1985).

Patrol and Investigative Techniques

Routine Patrol

Conservation officers also utilize **routine patrol** as a method of law enforcement. Patrolling has been a common practice of law enforcement agencies for many years. Routine patrol consists of officers patrolling their assigned area or beat. The main goal of routine patrol is for police to demonstrate that they are ever-present, and it therefore creates a deterrent effect on would-be criminals (Kelling et al., 2004). While traditional law enforcement patrol officers are assigned a beat, which is typically a certain section of a city or municipality, conservation officers are typically assigned to a particular county (Palmer & Bryant, 1985). Routine patrol for conservation officers consists of driving around their assigned area looking for people that are hunting, fishing, boating, or otherwise participating in activity that would fall under their jurisdiction. Conservation officers become familiar with their assigned districts and decide where to focus their patrol based on the particular time of year and the types of activities that would be occurring at that time. For example, if it is deer season, the conservation officer would most likely focus their patrol activities on areas where high levels of deer hunting would be occurring.

Choosing to patrol areas known for certain types of activities means that a conservation officer may not patrol their entire county or district every day but may focus on a particular area of their assignment on a particular day. While they are patrolling, they are looking for illegal activity, but also are participating in compliance checks, where they will check hunters or anglers to ensure they have the proper licenses, legal equipment for the activity in which they are participating, have properly tagged a game animal, or any number of other laws pertaining to hunting and fishing (Palmer & Bryant, 1985). Officers will utilize routine patrol during specific seasons, but they will also engage in routine patrol during times where they do not have any particular activities planned. During these times, they are engaged in watching for any types of activity that would fall under their jurisdiction (Palmer & Bryant, 1985). Most routine patrol by vehicle occurs utilizing a four-wheel drive truck or sport utility vehicle, but officers may also utilize all-terrain vehicles to patrol areas that are not accessible by a standard four-wheel drive vehicle (LaCaze, 2013). Most patrolling by conservation officers is conducted via a vehicle, but they also utilize other methods for patrolling (Palmer & Bryant, 1985).

Patrolling by Boat, Horseback, and Aircraft

In addition to patrolling by vehicle, conservation officers may also utilize boats for routine patrol. When patrolling by boat, officers are generally enforcing laws pertaining to angling and boating. They will conduct compliance checks for fishing licenses, the sizes and numbers of any fish the angler has in their possession, fishing equipment, boat registrations, personal floatation devices, and fire extinguishers (Palmer & Bryant, 1985). The goals of patrolling by boat are essentially the same as when patrolling by a vehicle on land, but the activity requires that the officers utilize a boat. Conservation officers will also utilize foot patrol because there are areas that are inaccessible by vehicle, and when looking for those that are engaging in hunting activity away from a roadway (Palmer & Bryant, 1985).

Officers may also engage in patrol on horseback (Calkins, 1970; LaCaze, 2013). Historically, horseback was a common patrol method. It was more routine before the use of all-terrain vehicles became commonplace. Horses were very good for transporting an officer into areas that were not easily accessed by vehicle. Horses allowed officers to quietly and efficiently access areas that were otherwise inaccessible. However, once all-terrain vehicles became mainstream, they replaced horses. Today's conservation officers do not generally utilize horses for patrolling, except for areas of the West that are still inaccessible by methods other than horseback (LaCaze, 2013).

Another method utilized by conservation officers is patrolling using aircraft (Glover, 1982; Palmer & Bryant, 1985; Rich & Shankle, 1988). Aircraft are an efficient and effective method of patrol for conservation officers and are utilized to enforce wildlife laws during both daytime and nighttime. Generally, the aircraft will be coordinating with several units on the ground. Nighttime patrols focus on illegal night hunting—normally attempts to take wildlife with the aid of an artificial light (Glover, 1982; Rich & Shankle, 1988). Spotlights that are used by violators are seen from the aircraft and then the coordinates are relayed to ground units, who respond to the area and conduct enforcement action (Rich & Shankle, 1988). Daytime patrols are utilized for enforcing laws related to small game hunting, trapping, closed season and big game hunting, waterfowl hunting, locating illegally baited duck blinds and fields used for dove hunting, and other types of closed season activity. Even if a violator realizes they were seen by the aircraft and attempts to escape, the aircraft can often follow their movements and guide a ground unit to their location. Aircraft can also be used by officers during search and rescue operations, which are an important non-law enforcement activity for conservation officers (Rich & Shankle, 1988).

Use of Canines

Another method that conservation law enforcement officers use to uncover wildlife violations and assist them with their duties is the use of canines. Canines began to be used for police work in the United States in the early 1900s and became commonplace beginning in the 1950s (Mitchell, 2019). Like traditional police agencies, conservation law enforcement agencies also utilize canines to assist conservation officers in their duties. The first canines for conservation law enforcement were used in New York in 1978 (Leavine, 1990). A variety of different breeds of dogs are used in conservation law enforcement, including Belgian Malinois, German Shepherds, and Labrador Retrievers (Anderson, 2013).

Dogs that assist conservation officers in their duties are trained to protect their handler, other officers, and the public; track suspects; perform area and building searches to find suspects; detect illegally taken wildlife, invasive species, firearms, bullet casings, and other evidence; assist in the arrest of suspects; locate lost or missing persons; and perform educational demonstrations and programs. The dogs are specially trained to detect various types of wildlife such as bear and bear gall bladders, deer, fish, elk, abalone, waterfowl, quagga mussels (California Department of Fish and Wildlife, 2020), and zebra mussels (Anderson, 2013).

Dogs are also used to help slow wildlife trafficking. The United States Fish and Wildlife Service uses dogs at international airports and other ports of entry to identify containers that may contain wildlife. Because of their tremendous ability to smell contraband, the dogs can much more quickly, efficiently, and effectively search a warehouse or shipping containers for wildlife than can a person (Heil, 2017). Other countries also use dogs to combat wildlife trafficking. Countries such as Kenya, Tanzania (African Wildlife Foundation [AWF], 2015), Botswana (Adhi, 2017) Cameroon, and Uganda (Sehmi, 2020) utilize canines to detect illegally taken rhino horns, ivory, and pangolin scales (Adhi, 2017). Additionally, the dogs are used to track poachers in the field that are attempting to take wildlife illegally (AWF, 2015).

Undercover/Covert Operations

In addition to more traditional and overt patrolling techniques to uncover violations of wildlife law, conservation officers will also utilize undercover or covert techniques. Covert operations have been used by conservation law enforcement officers since the 1930s, but the use of these types of investigations began to increase in popularity and frequency in the 1980s. Both state and federal agencies employ undercover or investigative units (White, 1995).

These types of investigations are not usually used to uncover traditional hunting and fishing violations such as permit violations or over limits, but rather normally target large-scale illegal commercialization of wildlife operations (White, 1995). These types of investigations are complex, expensive, and dangerous for the officers involved. Like more traditional covert law enforcement operations, conservation officers working in a covert capacity will assume new identities and then attempt to infiltrate the group participating in the illegal activity or gain acceptance by those that are the targets of the investigation (White, 1995). Further, since these investigations normally involve the commercial exploitation of fish and game, violations often occur across state lines, which requires cooperation between several state agencies and the United States Fish and Wildlife Service. Wildlife that was either illegally acquired and transported across state lines, or that is unlawfully sold across state lines, would be in violation of the Lacey Act, so it is important for these types of investigations to include the Fish and Wildlife Service (White, 1995).

However, not all investigations utilize the Fish and Wildlife Service and involve the commercialization and interstate or international movement of illegal wildlife. Some undercover investigations are in response to complaints from concerned citizens about a particular type of illegal hunting or fishing activity that is not easily addressed by traditional law enforcement methods (Simmons, 1996). For example, Operation Dalmatian was undertaken by the Texas Parks and Wildlife Department to address illegal deer hunting with the use of dogs. It was necessary to utilize covert techniques to address this problem because there were increased clashes between those who still wanted to hunt deer with dogs and property owners who would not allow the hunters or their dogs onto their land. Further complicating the issue is that some local jurisdictions placed unrealistic evidentiary demands on conservation law enforcement officers to prosecute individuals involved in this type of hunting, and efforts at intimidating witnesses and conservation officers was increasing, including one officer having his house burned (Simmons, 1996). Because of all these reasons, undercover methods were utilized. Gaining access to these types of groups is somewhat different than those involved in commercial trade because in commercial trade examples, a financial transaction can occur which assists the undercover officer in gaining acceptance to the group. These types of investigations require different methods to gain acceptance to the group because there isn't a type of transaction that can occur, but rather they must gain acceptance through relationship building (Simmons, 1996).

Regardless of the type of investigation, undercover investigations are dangerous, not only because the suspects do not want to be identified and apprehended, but also because they commonly are involved in other forms of criminality such as narcotics (Blissett & Wilson, 1998; White, 1995), stolen property, prostitution, burglary (Blissett & Wilson, 1998), stolen vehicles, counterfeiting, automatic weapons, and murder-for-hire plots (White, 1995).

Computer Investigations

Conservation officers across the world have made strides in addressing physical markets where illegal wildlife is sold and bartered. However, the Internet has opened an entirely new marketplace where wildlife and their parts can be bought and sold. Cyberspace makes it more difficult to identify those that are participating in the illegal wildlife trade and allows for just about anyone to become involved in the trade (Cleva, 2010). While more traditional markets for wildlife and wildlife parts have existed for many years, traffic in cyberspace or on the Internet started to become more active in the late 1990s. Since that time, international agencies as well as the United States Fish and Wildlife Service (USFWS) and state wildlife enforcement agencies have begun to monitor and address issues related to this illicit trade. However, the volume of the trade that takes place over the Internet is too great for all aspects to be investigated and addressed. In addition to the amount of trade that occurs, the laws where the items are located vary greatly, and there are jurisdictional issues related to online trade (Cleva, 2010).

In addition to international agencies such as INTERPOL, the USFWS has been working to improve its ability to address issues related to illegal online trade in wildlife and parts. In addition to becoming better equipped to address the many facets of the illicit wildlife trade, they also have worked to create partnerships with various other interested parties such as other international, federal, and state agencies, other countries, and members of the e-commerce business community (Cleva, 2010). The USFWS created an Intelligence Unit to help to address these issues as well as trained special agents in cybercrime techniques, open-source information gathering, officer safety on the Internet, collecting Web-based evidence, and topics related to the online trade of wildlife. In addition, they added computer forensics staff at the wildlife forensics laboratory in Oregon and trained selected officers in the seizure and analysis of computers and electronic media. Then, in 2009, they created a new unit comprised of special agents that were specialists in computer forensics and technology-assisted investigative skills.

In addition to the USFWS efforts within their agency, they have also created partnerships with a variety of stakeholders. They have developed collaborative relationships with companies such as eBay, PayPal, and other online auction site owners to not only educate them about the ramifications of the online wildlife trade, but also to enlist their help with ongoing criminal investigations. The USFWS has partnered with countries such as the United Kingdom, Canada, Australia, New Zealand, Germany, Belgium, Cameroon, and others to share information and collaborate on investigations. They also work closely with INTERPOL and the INTERPOL Wildlife Working Group. They have provided training on cybercrime investigations and Internet wildlife trafficking to various state wildlife agencies (Cleva, 2010).

While state-level conservation officers may not become involved in international investigations regarding the illegal wildlife trade, they may become involved in more localized investigations through classified ad websites, where local operators may be offering wildlife or wildlife parts for sale. For example, state authorities can become involved in cases targeting online retailers of illegal reptiles, unlicensed seafood dealers (Curtis, 2013), or the illegal sale of a fawn deer (White, 2016). Other types of violations uncovered by local authorities could be the unlawful online sale of hunting licenses such as in the case of three Colorado residents who sold guided hunts for big game and then used their resident Colorado hunting licenses to tag game taken by other hunters (OutdoorNews, 2011).

Forensics

Similar to traditional policing, **forensic analysis** of evidence is also used in conservation law enforcement. The basic elements of the use of forensics in conservation law enforcement is the same as in traditional law enforcement—to link a suspect, victim, and crime scene.

However, the main difference is that in conservation law enforcement, the victim is an animal, instead of a person. While many wildlife crimes result in the seizing of a whole animal or fish, other wildlife crime investigations result in the seizure of parts of an animal or animals that are not necessarily as readily identifiable as a whole carcass (Goddard, 1993). For example, cases could involve boots made from endangered sea turtles, items made from ivory, jewelry made of coral, shark fins, ginseng, or whether a piece of leather on a watchband is from a protected animal (Peak, 2017). Because the legality of the species involved is not readily identifiable, forensics must be used to determine the item's legality. Conservation officers are generally not able to complete the forensic analysis themselves and must submit the evidence to a forensics laboratory for analysis.

The USFWS established the Clark R. Bavin National Fish and Wildlife Laboratory in 1989 as the only comprehensive forensic laboratory dedicated to wildlife crimes. This laboratory not only serves the USFWS special agents and wildlife inspectors, but also conservation officers in all 50 states and the approximately 150 signatories to the United Nations Convention on International Trade in Endangered Species (CITES) treaty (USFWS, 2020). A wide variety of evidence items are submitted to the lab, including blood and tissue samples, bones, teeth, claws, talons, tusks, hair, hides, furs, feathers, leather products, poisons, pesticides, stomach contents, projectiles, weapons, and Asian medicines. These items are analyzed in one or more of the laboratory's five units: Chemistry, Criminalistics, Genetics, Morphology, and Pathology.

The Chemistry unit uses chemical and instrumental techniques to analyze submitted items. Common examinations include the testing of Asian medicinal products, the analysis of poisons and pesticides, identifying unknown materials, and identifying species. The Criminalistics unit uses microscopic, chemical, and instrumental techniques to analyze evidence such as wildlife parts and products, bullets, shell casings, shot pellets, fibers, paint, soil, and other physical identifiers. This unit commonly compares bullet and cartridge cases, identifies firearms, compares paint chips, and analyzes soil. The Genetics unit uses protein and DNA analysis to analyze unknown evidence. They will commonly identify and analyze blood and tissue samples, determine the gender and assign them to a family, genus, species, or other source, and also analyze blood and tissue samples to exclude them from a particular source. The Morphology unit uses visual and microscopic techniques to identify wildlife parts and products back to their original family, genus, or species source. Common analysis involves identifying a species or subspecies of hides for taxidermy or the leather or fur industry; identification of vertebrates that are found dead or based on animal parts used in jewelry, garments, leather goods, or artwork; species identification from hair, bone fragments, or stomach contents; and identifying the number of individual animals present in a collection of feathers, talons, or claws. They also can help to determine the time since death and determine the age and sex of submitted evidence. The Pathology unit conducts pathological evaluations of evidence using trace evidence such as bullets, pellets, or stomach contents. Common analysis consists of the evaluation of carcasses for gunshot wounds, poisoning, pollutants, electrocution, trap wounds, or other trauma that is not caused naturally. The also will conduct x-ray, gross, and microscopic evaluations of evidence (USFWS, 2020).

The use of forensics has increased since the establishment of the national laboratory in 1989 and eleven states currently also have forensic laboratories that can assist in wildlife crimes. Additionally, the National Oceanic and Atmospheric Administration also has a forensic laboratory that is dedicated to the analysis of marine species. The use of forensics has become more common and will most likely gain in importance as the technology available to investigators continues to advance.

CONCLUSION

Conservation officers utilize a variety of techniques and strategies to identify and apprehend those that are violating conservation laws. Employing a variety of overarching strategies or patrol techniques may increase the effectiveness of conservation officers at apprehending those violating natural resources laws. In addition to the more traditional aspects of patrol, increases in the use of computer technology and laboratory forensics also has increased the effectiveness of conservation officers in the United States and beyond at thwarting the illegal exploitation of natural resources.

DISCUSSION QUESTIONS

1. A conservation officer receives information that a large-bodied deer has been killed in a field next to a road. The head and meat have been removed and only the carcass remains. Over the next week, they receive more reports of similar occurrences within the same general geographic area. Outline how the officer could work to solve these crimes utilizing the following approaches:

   a. Community policing
   b. Problem-oriented policing
   c. Hot spots policing

2. Explain the differences between "hard" and "soft" enforcement. Explain why it is necessary for conservation law enforcement officers to utilize both. Should officers attempt to use both styles equally? Are there consequences to favoring one style over the other? What factors could be important in the officer's choice to choose one style over the other? Explain.

Key Terms

Community policing: An enforcement strategy that focuses on officer relationships with community stakeholders to solve crime and quality of life problems.

Conciliatory enforcement: An enforcement strategy characterized by encouraging area users to willingly comply with regulations and enjoy their time at the park or recreation area.

Covert enforcement: An enforcement strategy that employs undercover work with no outward displays of traditional law enforcement symbols.

Forensic analysis: An enforcement technique utilizing scientific investigative methods to link evidence to suspects.

Hard enforcement: An enforcement strategy that more closely resembles a traditional policing strategy that utilizes more punitive sanctions such as arrests and citations to gain compliance.

Hot spots policing: An enforcement strategy that directs police resources to areas where crime is more likely to occur, rather than large scale preventative patrol.

Non-enforcement: An enforcement strategy where the officer avoids potential law enforcement situations.

Problem-oriented policing: A versatile policing strategy that focuses on identifying, understanding, and then addressing the various reasons why citizens call the police for assistance.

Routine patrol: An enforcement strategy of a conservation officer patrolling their assigned district to demonstrate they are ever-present and create a deterrent effect. Also known as preventive patrol.

Soft enforcement: An enforcement strategy characterized by gaining compliance through informal methods of education, prevention, and community relations.

Threat enforcement: An enforcement strategy that uses the threat or promise of formal enforcement actions if someone does not correct their actions.

References

Adhi, G. (2017). These dogs are taking on wildlife trafficking in Botswana. African Wildlife Foundation. https://www.awf.org/blog/these-dogs-are-taking-wildlife-trafficking-botswana

African Wildlife Foundation (AWF). (2015). Sniffer dogs ready to combat wildlife trafficking. https:www.awf.org/news/sniffer-dogs-ready-combat-wildlife-trafficking

Anderson, D. (2013, August 9). Crime stoppers: DNR conservation officers and their dogs. *Star Tribune*. https://www.startribune.com/crime-stoppers-dnr-conservation-officers-and-their-dogs/218885221

Blevins, K. R., & Edwards, T. D. (2009). Wildlife crime. In J. M. Miller (Ed.), *21st century criminology: A reference handbook Vol. 1* (pp. 557–563). Sage.

Blevins, K. R., & Lanham, C. M. (2013). *Occupational roles and practices of Kentucky conservation officers*. Eastern Kentucky University. https://justicestudies.eku.edu/sites/justicestudies.eku.edu/files/files/Blevins%20SJRP%20Report%202012-2013.pdf

Blissett, S. R., & Wilson, G. K. (1998). A pipeline of smuggled Florida wildlife-Operation Brooklyn. *Proceedings of the Southeastern Association of Fish and Wildlife Agencies, USA, 52*, 501–505.

Braga, A. A. (2001). The effects of hot spots policing on crime. *The ANNALS of the American Academy of Political and Social Science, 578*(1), 104-125.

Braga, A. (2008). *Problem-oriented policing and crime prevention* (2nd ed.). Criminal Justice Press.

Braga, A., Papachristos, A., & Hureau, D. (2012). *Hot spots policing effects on crime.* The Campbell Collaboration.

Braga, A. A., & Weisburd, D. (2006). Problem-oriented policing: The disconnect between principles and practice. In D. Weisburd & A. A. Braga (Eds.). *Police innovation: Contrasting perspectives* (pp. 182–202). Cambridge University Press.

Braga, A., & Weisburd, D. (2010). *Policing problem places: Crime hot spots and effective prevention.* Oxford University Press.

Bynum, T. S. (2001). *Using analysis for problem-solving: A guidebook for law enforcement.* U.S. Department of Justice, Office of Community Oriented Policing Services.

California Department of Fish and Wildlife. (2020). K-9 program. https://wildlife.ca.gov/Enforcement/K9

Calkins, F. (1970). *Rocky mountain warden.* Alfred & Knopf Inc.

Chavez, D. J., & Tynon, J. F. (2000). Triage law enforcement: Societal impacts on National Forests in the West. *Environmental Management, 26*(4), 403–407.

Clarke, R. V. (1992). *Situational crime prevention: Successful case studies.* Harrow & Heston.

Clarke, R. V. & Eck, J. E. (2005). *Crime analysis for problem solvers in 60 small steps.* Center for Problem Oriented Policing.

Cleva, S. (2010). Untangling the net: U.S. Fish and Wildlife Service efforts to target Internet wildlife trafficking. *CITES World, 19.* https://cites.org/eng/news/world/19/4.php

Cohen, K., Sanyal, N., & Reed, G. E. (2007). Methamphetamine production on public lands: Threats and responses. *Society & Natural Resources, 20*(3), 261–270.

Colorado Department of Parks and Wildlife (CDPW). (2020). Operation game thief. https://cpw.state.co.us/aboutus/Pages/OGT.aspx#:~:text=Operation%20Game%20Thief%20was%20pioneered,in%20more%20than%20700%20convictions

Cordner, G. W. (2015). Community policing: Elements and effects. In R. G. Dunham & G. P. Alpert (Eds.), *Critical Issues in Policing* (Vol. 7, pp. 481–498). Waveland Press.

Curtis, H. P. (2013, October 3). Shrimp, lobsters and bearded dragons seized in statewide Craigslist sting. *Orlando Sentinel.* https://www.orlandosentinel.com/news/os-xpm-2013-10-03-os-craigslist-wildlife-sting-20131003-story.html

Eck, J. (1997, February). Preventing crime at places. In L. W. Sherman, D. Gottfredson, D. MacKenzie, J. Eck, P. Reuter, & S. Bushway, University of Maryland, Department of Criminology and Criminal Justice (Eds.), *Preventing crime: What works, what doesn't, what's promising* (pp. 7-1–7-62). NCJ 165366. Office of Justice Programs, U.S. Department of Justice.

Eck, J. (2002). Preventing crime at places. In L. Sherman, D. Farrington, B. Welsh, & D. L. MacKenzie (Eds.), *Evidence-based crime prevention* (pp. 241–294). Routledge.

Eliason, S. L. (2007). From wildlife specialist to police generalist? The scope of nonwildlife violations encountered by conservation officers. *Southwest Journal of Criminal Justice, 4*(2), 120–132.

Falcone, D. (2004). America's conservation police: Agencies in transition. *Policing: An International Journal of Police Strategies and Management, 27*(1), 56–66.

Forsyth, C. J. (1993). Chasing and catching the "bad guys": The game warden's prey. *Deviant Behavior, 14,* 209–226.

Forsyth, C. J. (2008). The game of wardens and poachers. *Journal of Rural Social Sciences, 23*(2), 43–53.

Glover, R. L. (1982). Effectiveness of patrol techniques for apprehending deer poachers. *Proceedings of the Southeastern Association of Fish and Wildlife Agencies, USA, 36,* 705–716.

Goddard, K. W. (1993). Wildlife forensics: A new approach to species conservation and preservation. *Proceedings of the Southeastern Association of Fish and Wildlife Agencies, USA, 47,* 752–756.

Goldstein, H. (1979). Improving policing: A problem-solving approach. *Crime and Delinquency 25,* 236–258.

Goldstein, H. (1990). *Problem-oriented policing.* Temple University Press.

Hall, D. (1992). Compliance: The mission of conservation law enforcement. *Proceedings of the Southeastern Association of Fish and Wildlife Agencies, USA, 46*, 532–542.

Heil, J. (2017). K-9's bark more powerful than their bite. United States Fish and Wildlife Service. https://www.fws.gov/cno/newsroom/featured/2017/k9_program/

Kelling, G. L., Pate, T., Dieckman, D., & Brown, C. E. (2004). The Kansas City preventive patrol experiment: A summary report. In S. E. Brandl & D. E. Barlow (Eds.), *The police in America: Classic and contemporary readings.* (pp. 237–256), Wadsworth.

LaCaze, K. (2013). Horses for conservation law enforcement. *Louisiana Sportsman.* https://www.louisianasportsman.com/general/horses-for-conservation-law-enforcement/

Leavine, W. E. (1990). Use of canines in conservation law enforcement. *Proceedings of the Southeastern Association of Fish and Wildlife Agencies, USA, 44*, 408–411.

Lemieux, A. M., & Pickles, R. S. A. (2020). *Problem-oriented wildlife protection.* Center for Problem-Oriented Policing. https://popcenter.asu.edu/sites/default/files/problem-oriented_wildlife_protection_lemieux_pickles_2020.pdf

Mayne, J. S. (2000). Specialization units and natural resources law enforcement. *Proceedings of the Southeastern Association of Fish and Wildlife Agencies, USA, 54*, 500–504.

McGarrell, E. F., Suttmoeller, M., & Gibbs, C. (2013). Great lakes fisheries law enforcement. In W. W. Taylor, A. J. Lynch, & N. J. Leonard (Eds.), *Great lakes fisheries policy and management: A binational perspective* (2nd ed., pp. 455–472). Michigan State University Press.

Mitchell, C. (2019). The beginning of the American K9 units: A brief history. National Law Enforcement Museum. https://lawenforcementmuseum.org/2019/08/26/the-beginning-of-american-k9-units-a-brief-history/

Morse, W. B. (1973). Law enforcement: One third of the triangle. *Wildlife Society Bulletin, 1*(1), 39–44.

Nelson, C., & Verbyla, D. (1984). Characteristics and effectiveness of state anti-poaching campaigns. *Wildlife Society Bulletin, 12*(2), 117–122.

New Mexico Department of Game and Fish (NMDGF). (2020). Operation game thief. http://www.wildlife.state.nm.us/enforcement/operation-game-thief-overview/

OutdoorNews. (2011, October 4). CO: Craigslist ad yields wildlife convictions. https://www.outdoornews.com/2011/10/04/co-craigslist-ad-yields-wildlife-convictions/

Palmer, C. E., & Bryant, C. D. (1985). Keepers of the king's deer: Game wardens and the enforcement of fish and wildlife law. In C. D. Bryant, D. J. Shoemaker, J. K. Skipper, & W. E. Snizek (Eds.), *The rural workforce: Non-agricultural occupations in America* (pp. 111–137). Bergin & Garvey Publishers Inc.

Parks, R. B., Mastrofski, S. D., DeJong, C., & Gray, K. (1999). How officers spend their time with the community. *Justice Quarterly, 16*(3), 483-518.

Patten, R. (2012). Drunk and angry is no way to enjoy the outdoors: An examination of game wardens and the use of force. *International Journal of Comparative and Applied Criminal Justice, 36*(2), 121–132.

Patten, R., & Caudill, J. W. (2013). Weekend warriors and sun block: Game wardens and the use of force. *American Journal of Criminal Justice, 38*, 410–421.

Patten, R., Crow, M. S., & Shelley, T. O. (2015). What's in a name? The occupational identity of conservation and natural resource oriented law enforcement agencies. *American Journal of Criminal Justice, 40*, 750–764.

Peak, K. J. (2017). Enforcing the laws of wildlife and recreation (Part One). *FBI Law Enforcement Bulletin.* https://leb.fbi.gov/articles/featured-articles/enforcing-the-laws-of-wildlife-and-recreation-part-one/layout_view

Pendleton, M. R. (1998). Policing the park: Understanding soft enforcement. *Journal of Leisure Research, 30*(4), 552–571.

Pierce, G., Spaar, S., & Briggs, L. (1988). *The character of police work: Strategic and tactical implications.* Center for Applied Social Research, Northeastern University.

Piza, E. L. (2018). The effect of various police enforcement actions on violent crime: Evidence from a saturation foot-patrol intervention. *Criminal Justice Policy Review, 29*(6-7), 611–629.

Reisig, M. D. (2010). Community and problem-oriented policing. *Crime & Justice, 39*(1), 1–53.

Rich, J. R., & Shankle, T. E. (1988). Aircraft in wildlife law enforcement. *Proceedings of the Southeastern Association of Fish and Wildlife Agencies, USA, 42,* 554–557.

Rossler, M. T. & Suttmoeller, M. J. (2021). Conservation officer perceptions of academy training: Resource specific and general policing tasks. *Policing: A Journal of Policy and Practice. 15*(2), 980-994

Scott, M., Eck, J., Knutsson, J., & Goldstein, H. (2008). Problem-oriented policing and environmental criminology. In R. Wortley & L. Mazerolle (Eds.), *Environmental criminology and crime analysis* (pp. 221–246). Willan.

Sehmi, H. (2020). Detection dogs help Uganda double down on illegal traffickers. African Wildlife Foundation. https://www.awf.org/blog/detection-dogs-help-uganda-double-down-illegal-traffickers

Shelley, T. O., & Crow, M. S. (2009). The nature and extent of conservation policing: Law enforcement generalists or conservation specialists? *American Journal of Criminal Justice, 34,* 9–27.

Sherblom, J. C., Keranen, L., & Withers, L. A. (2002). Tradition, tension, and transformation: A structuration analysis of a game warden service in transition. *Journal of Applied Communication Research, 30*(2), 143–162.

Sherman, L. W. (1991). Problem-oriented policing. By Herman Goldstein. *Journal of Criminal Law and Criminology, 82*(3), 690–707.

Sherman, L. W. (1997). Policing for crime prevention. In L. W. Sherman, D. C. Gottfredson, D. L. Mackenzie, J. E. Eck, P. Reuter, & S. D. Bushway (Eds.), *Preventing crime: What works, what doesn't, what's promising* (pp. 309–334). U.S. Department of Justice, National Institute of Justice.

Sherman, L., Gartin, P., & Burger, M. (1989). Hot spots of predatory crime: Routine activities and the criminology of place. *Criminology, 27,* 27–56.

Sherman, L., & Weisburd, D. (1995). General deterrent effects of police patrol in crime hot spots: A randomized controlled trial. *Justice Quarterly, 12,* 625–648.

Simmons, M. (1996). Operation Dalmatian—Covert investigation of dog deer hunting. *Proceedings of the Southeastern Association of Fish and Wildlife Agencies, USA, 50,* 665–675.

Swan, J. A. (2016). Thin green line: The heroic work of game wardens. *American Forests.* https://www.americanforests.org/magazine/article/thin-green-line-heroic-work-game-wardens/

Terrill, W., Rossler, M. T., & Paoline, E. A. (2014). Police service delivery and responsiveness in a period of economic instability. *Police Practice and Research, 15*(6), 490-504.

Tobias, M. (1998). *Nature's keepers: On the front lines of the fight to save wildlife in America.* John Wiley & Sons Inc.

Trench, C. C. (1965). Game preserves and poachers. *History Today, 15*, 259–268.

United States Fish and Wildlife Service (USFWS). (2020). Forensics Laboratory. https://www.fws.gov/lab/

Walker, S., & Katz, C. M. (2013). *The police in America: An introduction.* McGraw Hill.

Weisburd, D. (2008). *Place-based policing.* Police Foundation.

Weisburd, D., & Eck, J. (2004). What can police do to reduce crime, disorder, and fear? *Annals of the American Academy of Political and Social Science, 593*, 42–65.

Weisburd, D., & Green, L. (1995). Policing drug hot spots: The Jersey City DMA experiment. *Justice Quarterly, 12*, 711–736.

Weisburd, D., Maher, L., & Sherman, L. (1992). Contrasting crime general and crime specific theory: The case of hot spots of crime. In F. Adler & W. S. Laufer (Eds.) *New Directions in Criminological Theory* (Vol. 4, pp. 45–69). Transaction Press.

Weisheit, R. A., Falcone, D. N., & Well, L. E. (1999). *Crime and policing in rural and small-town America.* Waveland.

White, C. (2016). Woman allegedly tried to sell captured baby deer on Craigslist for $300. *Law and Crime.* https://lawandcrime.com/crazy/woman-allegedly-attempts-to-sell-captured-baby-deer-on-craigslist-for-300/

White, T. H. (1995). The role of covert operations in modern wildlife law enforcement. *Proceedings of the Southeastern Association of Fish and Wildlife Agencies, USA, 49*, 692–697.

Wilson, J. Q., & Kelling, G. (1982). Broken windows: The police and neighborhood safety. *Atlantic Monthly, 3*, 29–38.

Eight

NON-LAW ENFORCEMENT AND OTHER DUTIES OF CONSERVATION OFFICERS

Conservation officers are known for their ability to enforce laws related to fish and game. As discussed in the previous chapter, conservation officers are most commonly associated with a law enforcement role. Historically, that role consisted primarily of enforcing laws related to hunting and fishing (Forsyth, 1993, 2008; Palmer & Bryant, 1985). However, that role has expanded to include responsibilities more commonly associated with traditional police officers and a more traditional policing role (Eliason, 2007; Falcone, 2004; Shelley & Crow, 2009; Sherblom et al., 2002). In addition to their more traditional law enforcement role, conservation officers also commonly participate in activities that are unique from those of traditional law enforcement officers, such as educational programming and public relations.

LAW ENFORCEMENT OFFICER POLICING STYLES

Mastrofski's Four Non-Crime Models

Law enforcement is the most well-known role that conservation officers hold, but like traditional police officers, conservation officers also participate in activities that would more closely align with a service role. Mastrofski (1983) reported that non-crime duties performed by law enforcement officers have been prevalent since the beginning of policing, but crime control activities are those for which the police are most well-known. He further stated that non-crime activities encompassed a large percentage of the work in which police officers engaged. While there may be some variation in the types of non-crime activities in which conservation officers participate as compared to traditional law enforcement officers, conservation officers regularly participate in non-crime activities. There are four different models that categorize and explain the various types of non-crime activities in which police officers participate. The first is the **crime prophylactic model**. This model explains that police intervention in non-crime matters is often in order to prevent non-crime incidents from becoming criminal incidents. Examples of activities that would fit this model would be domestic feuds, neighbor disagreements, and nuisance complaints (Mastrofski, 1983).

The second model proposed by Mastrofski (1983) is the **police knowledge model**. This model suggests that by the police participating in non-crime matters, they are exposed to a broader segment of the community than if they only handled criminal matters. This allows them to gain knowledge about the community at large and particular characteristics that are relevant to knowing their community such as individuals, places, and routines that may be helpful in preventing crime and solving cases. The opportunities for police officers to gather intelligence relative to crime in their communities is limited if they only are involved in criminal matters.

The **community cooperation model** is the third model presented by Mastrofski (1983). This model is centered on the belief that by participating in non-crime matters, the police demonstrate to the public that they can help the community as well as enforce the laws using coercion if necessary. Further, by participating in non-crime activities, the police are demonstrating to the public that they care for their well-being and that they should be treated in a civil manner. Further, this model encourages the police to engage and partner with the community in fighting crime and recognizing that citizens are coproducers of arrests, convictions and deterring criminal activity. The police may also benefit from this model as it may encourage citizens to cooperate with the police, provide information, testify in court, and participate in police crime fighting efforts. This model typically enjoys the most support from police administrators and scholars.

The final model presented by Mastrofski (1983) is the **social work model**. This model suggests that the police may have a role in steering people toward a life free from crime, and for them to internalize law-abiding norms. The extent to which the police are able to successfully rehabilitate people is suspect, and this theory does not enjoy much support among police professionals. In spite of this, departments do spend considerable time and resources on programs such as Police Athletic Leagues and school programs.

Wilson's Three Styles of Policing

Similar to Mastrofski's four different models of non-crime police activities, other scholars have identified a variety of different types of police officers based off their attitudes toward various aspects of their occupation. Officers vary in their views on the best ways to accomplish the goals of their department and to be an effective police officer (Muir, 1977). Wilson's (1968) seminal work on the different law enforcement styles remains one of the most comprehensive studies of different policing styles and the factors that influence those styles. He identified three main styles: watchman, legalistic, and service. Police officers all utilize these various styles at different times, but officers will have a main style that they utilize depending on their own personal attitudes and those of their department or local political climate. The **watchman style** emphasizes the maintaining of order over law enforcement and is more closely aligned with the order maintenance function of policing (Wilson, 1968). Order maintenance is characterized by the police managing minor offenses and disorder in order to address larger community problems and has always been considered a legitimate and desirable police function (Sousa & Kelling, 2014).

The **legalistic style** is a strict law enforcement function of the police and is characterized by the police viewing commonplace situations that may normally be considered order maintenance as a law enforcement situation. This does not mean that law enforcement action is always taken to resolve situations because an officer cannot sanction someone with a ticket or arrest if the situation is not breaking any law, but rather it means that they approach each situation as one that could result in a formal sanction until it is proven otherwise (Wilson, 1968). The legalistic style would more closely align with the previous chapter's discussion of law enforcement strategies.

The final style identified by Wilson was the **service style**. The service style is characterized by a department that takes both law enforcement and order maintenance functions seriously, but are less likely to impose formal sanctions for infractions. This style is more responsive to the community's preferences for how they would like their police department to function. Service-style police departments are more likely to participate in public relations and educational opportunities and be more community oriented (Wilson, 1968). This style is more closely aligned with the current conception of community policing (Hawdon, 2008).

Similar to traditional police officers, conservation officers employ all three policing styles. As discussed in the previous chapter, conservation officers are commonly associated with their role as law enforcement officers, but they also participate in order maintenance and service activities. Prior police research on the various styles of policing focuses almost exclusively on urban metropolitan police officers and departments, which may make it difficult to apply these styles to conservation officers, who fill a role that is quite different from urban metropolitan police departments and officers. Further complicating the discussion of policing styles of conservation officers is the political climates in which the different state departments of natural resources operate. Some state agencies are more political, where the directors of those agencies report directly to the state legislature, while others, such as the Missouri Department of Conservation, were created by a constitutional amendment, which makes them independent and not directly responsible to the state legislature (Keefe, 1987). So, while states such as Missouri enjoy some autonomy related to the management of natural resources, they are also still responsible to the citizens of Missouri in order to retain the sales tax revenue on which they rely. While the goals of the various department of natural resources are most likely quite similar, the political climates of the different states and different departments will influence the extent to which they employ the various policing styles (Wilson, 1968).

The previous chapter focused on the law enforcement role of conservation officers, which would more closely align with the legalistic style. This chapter will focus on the other aspects of the conservation officer role, such as order maintenance and service.

NON-LAW ENFORCEMENT ACTIVITIES

Order Maintenance and Service

Order maintenance is commonly associated with community policing (Sousa & Kelling, 2014), and the service style of policing is also associated with community policing and is commonly considered to be the role most closely aligned with community policing (Hawdon, 2008). Community policing is a strategy that emphasizes that officers should engage with and work closely with the communities that they serve. The three main tenets of community policing are that officers seek citizen input, accept a broad police role, and engage in personalized service. The police may seek public input through public meetings, meetings with specific interested groups, or any number of other community partnerships (Cordner, 2015). By forming community partnerships and engaging citizens, officers are no longer relying exclusively on themselves for crime control, but the citizens as well (Walker & Katz, 2013). Officers engaging in community policing should also accept a broad police role. By accepting a broader police role, officers are willing to engage in activities other than crime fighting, including order maintenance and service-style activities. Finally, police officers will engage in personalized services. Community policing officers can adapt to local norms and values and use their discretion as the best way for a situation to be adjudicated (Cordner, 2015). A more thorough discussion of community policing is presented in the previous chapter. Because conservation officers are oftentimes the most well-known and available member of their agency, a community policing orientation may be particularly important for them (McGarrell et al., 2013). Educating the public on various regulations is an important part of a conservation officer's duties. In addition, the relationships that conservation officers may form with various constituents may also increase the perceived legitimacy of regulations and therefore increase compliance. These relationships are also important because they may lead members of the public to report law violations to conservation officers that may not have been reported if the officer had not formed a relationship with those stakeholders. Further, the need for conservation officers to be good public educators has been identified as important by natural resources division chiefs (McGarrell et al., 2013).

Order Maintenance Activities

Like traditional police officers, conservation officers participate in order maintenance activities. Because of the difference in where conservation officers work, as compared to traditional metropolitan police, the types of order maintenance activities in which they participate is different. One common type of order maintenance activity in which conservation officers participate are landowner disputes or, as they are commonly known in the policing literature, disputes between neighbors. Certainly, two adjoining landowners could find any number of reasons to begin a dispute, but some are particularly salient to the discussion of the order maintenance role of conservation officers. Common order maintenance scenarios that conservation officers would address may be related to the placement of elevated stands that hunters sit in to hunt deer. One common situation is when a deer stand is located within sight of a residence of a non-hunter. The non-hunter may want the conservation officer to make the neighboring landowner remove the stand or move it to a place where they cannot see the stand and feel more comfortable. However, since the neighboring landowner has not broken any laws, the conservation officer may help to broker communications between the two landowners or may simply encourage the distressed landowner to contact their neighbor and attempt to resolve the situation. Another common order maintenance situation involves disputes over tree stands that are placed near a property line. These situations can become particularly contentious because the neighboring landowners may accuse the others of shooting at game across the property line or accusing the other of trying to sabotage their hunting spot. Additionally, this type of situation may become dangerous due to the proximity of the hunting locations on the adjacent lands. With some exceptions, most states do not have any laws requiring specified distances that hunting stands may be placed along property lines, so the landowners have not done anything illegal (LaCaze, 2015). The conservation officer may attempt to resolve the dispute, but it is also incumbent upon the landowners to attempt to reach a resolution as well. This is an example of Mastrofski's (1983) crime prophylactic model. This type of situation has the potential to devolve into criminal behavior such as trespassing, property damage, or even a physical assault if it is not managed.

Another common order maintenance situation in which conservation officers may be involved is with deer stands that are perceived to be too close to a public roadway. If people driving down a public road can see a deer stand near the road, they may contact the conservation officer to alert them to the proximity of the stand to the road. Unless the stand is located within the road right-of-way, the hunter most likely has not broken any laws (LaCaze, 2015). A situation where a deer or other animal was shot on one property and then crossed a property line before expiring is another common order maintenance situation that may require the involvement of a conservation officer. If the hunter does not have permission to be on the adjoining land, they cannot legally enter the land to retrieve the animal because they would be trespassing. These are often easily resolved by either the landowner allowing the hunter to retrieve the animal, or the landowner retrieving the animal for them and giving it to them. However, sometimes a conservation officer may also be called to try and resolve this conflict (Roznik, 2018). This type of situation would also fall under Mastrofski's (1983) crime prophylactic model. However, not all order maintenance situations revolve around the act of hunting.

A variety of other order maintenance situations are currently addressed by conservation officers. The improper disposal of animal parts and carcasses is a common order maintenance activity for conservation officers. Sometimes these parts and carcasses are dumped along roadways, in parking lots, or in other public areas. This is illegal activity, but normally it is impossible to determine who illegally disposed of the parts. In other cases, it may be legally disposed of on private land, but if it is visible to the public, the officer may receive calls complaining about the animal parts (LaCaze, 2015). This is an example of either Mastrofski's (1983) police knowledge model or the community cooperation model. By responding to reports such as these, the conservation officer may increase their knowledge of a particular area or may even discover an area that may require additional law enforcement attention. The community cooperation model applies because by responding to these calls, even though the chance of taking law enforcement action is small, the conservation officer is demonstrating to the community and the person that reported the incident that they take these matters seriously, and this may encourage either the person that reported the dumping or someone familiar with the situation to contact the conservation officer in the future regarding other issues.

Nuisance, Sick, and Injured Wildlife

Nuisance, sick, and injured wildlife are another type of concern that conservation officers must address (McKinzie, 1989; NACLEC, 2021; Sherblom et al., 2002). Conservation officers assist residents, businesses, and municipalities with wildlife that are causing a nuisance, are sick, or are injured. While almost any type of wildlife could fall into this category, common types of situations addressed by conservation officers include rabid animals, beavers flooding property or roadways, animals such as raccoons causing damage in gardens, animals such as opossums living under houses, armadillos causing damage, or deer or other wildlife injured in motor vehicle accidents (McKinzie, 1989; Sherblom et al., 2002). The conservation officer will generally either remove the animal themselves or may refer the resident or concerned citizen to an animal damage control company for assistance. Some conservation officers have also enlisted student organizations such as local chapters of the Future Farmers of America (FFA) to assist with some aspects of nuisance animal control (McKinzie, 1989). This order maintenance situation would fall under Mastrofski's (1983) community cooperation model. Sick and injured wildlife pose a risk to the community, and by assisting in these situations, the conservation officer is demonstrating to the community that they take their welfare seriously. Additionally, these types of contacts for conservation officers may also result in someone providing other types of law enforcement-related information later.

Anti-hunting Protests

A final example of an order maintenance situation that may be addressed by conservation officers are anti-hunting protests. Animal rights and anti-hunting activists may sometimes engage in protests during hunting season. There are multiple ways in which these groups may conduct their protests. If the hunt is occurring on public land such as a park or wildlife management area, protestors may stand outside the area carrying signs and banners. Other times, protestors may enter the woods and simply walk through the woods or make noise, by talking loudly, carrying radios, or otherwise making loud noises in an attempt to disrupt the hunting activity. While the protestors have a First Amendment right to protest hunting, federal and state law prohibits the actual interference with lawful hunting and fishing (Hessler, 1997). Conservation officers may have to protect the protestors' right to protest, while also preventing or mitigating confrontations between those that are pro-hunting and those that are anti-hunting. In situations where the protestors are interfering with lawful hunting and fishing, the officers may have to make arrests. This would be an example of Mastrofski's (1983) crime prophylactic model. When emotions are high, as they may be during a protest, there is a chance of physical or violent altercations. By effectively addressing these situations, the conservation officer can ensure that everyone's constitutional rights are respected, while also providing safety and security for those present.

Service Activities

In addition to law enforcement and order maintenance duties, conservation officers also participate in a variety of service-oriented activities. Conservation officers are often the most well-known and visible representatives of their agency and therefore must be skilled at public relations (McGarrell et al., 2013; Palmer & Bryant, 1985). While part of the conservation officer's job responsibilities involves enforcing laws and regulations related to hunting, fishing, and other outdoor pursuits, they also are responsible for educating the public about a variety of outdoor activities, such as hunting seasons and regulations, wildlife management, hunting safety, local outdoor recreation areas, and other outdoor pursuits. To reach the largest number of people possible, conservation officers will engage various forms of media including newspapers, radio, and television (Hailey, 1988; Hass, 2021; Pledger & Hailey, 1981; Tobias, 1998).

Public Relations

Conservation agencies may use public meetings to engage with the public (Lord & Cheng, 2006). Agencies may conduct meetings concerning proposed hunting and fishing regulations, changes to hunting or fishing regulations, management plans for various wildlife species, or management plans for public use areas owned or managed by the agency (MDC, 2020). While these meetings may not be conducted by conservation officers directly, conservation officers may participate directly in these meetings by conducting presentations, or indirectly by being available to answer questions from the public concerning the proposed regulations or management plans. These are another example of the types of public relations activities in which conservation officers may participate.

In addition to public relations activities (Hailey, 1988; Pledger & Hailey, 1981; Tobias, 1998), conservation officers also participate in educational activities (Falcone, 2004), interact with landowners concerning wildlife issues on their properties (Calkins, 1970; Pledger & Hailey, 1981; Sherblom et al., 2002), and conduct public meetings (Lord & Cheng, 2006). These activities are like those included in Mastrofski's (1983) social work model and Wilson's (1968) service style and are commonly associated with community policing (Hawdon, 2008).

Educational Programming

Conservation officers commonly participate in educational programs or activities. One of the most common educational programs traditionally involving conservation officers are hunting and boating safety programs (Falcone, 2004; Lawson, 2003; NACLEC, 2021; Palmer & Bryant, 1985; Pepper, 2003). Traditionally, these courses were conducted in person, and conservation officers would have a role in presenting the curriculum. However, this may be somewhat changing as more safety programs are moving online. Some programs are still offered in person, but others are either completely online, or partially online with an in-person skills test (Kalkomy, 2015). The in-person courses traditionally were taught by officers, certified volunteer instructors, or some combination of the two (Pepper, 2003).

In addition to safety programs, conservation officers also educate the public by providing programming for civic organizations, schools, and outdoor groups (Carpenter, 1984; Lawson, 2003; NACLEC, 2021; Palmer & Bryant, 1985; Pledger & Hailey, 1981). Educational programming for civic groups may include such topics as ecology, the value of natural heritage (Lawson, 2003), wildlife management, habitat conservation, sustainable use of natural resources, and the responsibility of passing on natural resources for future generations (NACLEC, 2021). Programming in the schools may consist of the conservation officer providing an in-person presentation or providing educational materials to educators and working with them on developing conservation- and outdoors-related curriculum. Some officers have worked to establish or were involved with conservation-related clubs at the schools within their assigned districts (Carpenter, 1984; Viverette et al., 2006; Wagner, 2019; Weinstein, 2006).

Conservation officers also participate in other less traditional educational programming. In addition to established nation-wide programs such as Project Wild and Becoming an Outdoor Woman (Pepper, 2003; Tobias, 1998), conservation officers also may be present at booths for boat shows, regional and state fairs, and hunting expos (Pepper, 2003). At these venues, conservation officers are available to interact with the public in a non-law enforcement setting, provide conservation-related information and to answer conservation-related questions from the public. Conservation officers may also conduct hunting and fishing clinics for youths (Mootz, 2006; Pepper, 2003; Shelley & Crow, 2009; Wagner, 2019). During these clinics, conservation officers teach participants about various species of game or fish, types of and the importance of regulations concerning hunting and fishing, and proper techniques for hunting and fishing. Fishing clinics generally have a hands-on portion where topics such as proper knot-tying, hook baiting, casting, retrieving, and methods to handle fish are taught. Similarly, hunting clinics may emphasize the proper handling of firearms and shooting techniques.

Landowner Assistance

A final type of outreach activity in which conservation officers participate is to provide technical assistance to landowners concerning wildlife and fisheries management on their property. Some of these visits are to inspect possible wildlife damage to crops or livestock (Calkins, 1970; Pledger & Hailey, 1981; Sherblom et al., 2002) and provide guidance on possible solutions to mitigate wildlife-related damage. Other types of landowner visits are to provide recommendations on how someone could make their property more attractive to wildlife (Pledger & Hailey, 1981). Some conservation officers have combined their participation in school-related clubs and landowner visits. McKinzie (1989) reported that some conservation officers have engaged the local high school chapter of the Future Farmers of America to participate in landowner visits regarding habitat improvement as well as nuisance animal activities.

Other Non-Law Enforcement Activities

Biological Surveys

Conservation officers also participate in non-law enforcement activities outside of public relations work and educational programming. Conservation officers routinely assist biologists with various wildlife and fisheries management projects, including prescribed burns, fish tagging, (Wagner, 2019) and biological surveys (Calkins, 1970, Lawson, 2003; NACLEC, 2021). By assisting biologists with management projects, conservation officers can establish rapport with their fellow employees, as well as provide extra help where it may be needed. When conservation officers participate in biological surveys, it allows for the surveys to be conducted on a broader basis than if only one biologist or team of biologists were conducting the survey. The officers may be assisting in surveys concerning different species of wildlife or fish, including deer, grouse, pheasants, beaver, Canada geese, antelope, ducks, aquatic insects, the number of farm ponds in an area, or the number of anglers on a particular stream or impoundment (Calkins, 1970).

Search and Rescue Operations

Another important non-law enforcement activity in which conservation officers participate is search, rescue, and recovery operations (Baxley, 2001; Carpenter & Rae, 1998; Connecticut Environmental Conservation Police Officers [EnCon] 2021; Jensen, 2019; LaCaze, 2017; NACLEC, 2021; Wagner, 2019). Conservation officers participate in a variety of different search, rescue, and recovery operations. Sometimes, the search, rescue, or recovery operation is a result of a disaster such as a flood, hurricane, or aircraft crash (EnCon, 2021; LaCaze, 2017; Wagner, 2019), but more commonly they are in response to lost hikers, snowmobilers, hunters, other outdoorsmen and women, or drownings (Baxley, 2001; Carpenter & Rae, 1998; EnCon, 2021; Jensen, 2019; LaCaze, 2017). Conservation officers are often integral parts of search, rescue, and recovery operations because they are generally knowledgeable about remote areas and the various water resources of their assigned jurisdictions (EnCon, 2021; LaCaze, 2017). Additionally, they often have specialized equipment that can assist in the operation such as four-wheel drive patrol vehicles, watercraft, all-terrain vehicles, snowmobiles, or aircraft (EnCon, 2021; Jensen, 2019). Conservation officer agencies also may have dive teams that specialize in search, rescue, and recovery or canine units that are specially trained on tracking that may also assist the operation (Baxley, 2001; Carpenter & Rae, 1998; EnCon, 2021). Even in departments that do not have specialized teams, conservation officers may receive specialized training in search and rescue techniques (Indiana Department of Natural Resources, 2021).

Hunting Accident Investigations

Conservation officers also investigate hunting-related accidents where someone is injured while hunting (NACLEC, 2021). While one may automatically associate a hunting-related accident with someone being shot by another hunter, that is not the most common hunting-related injury. The most common hunting-related incident is someone falling from a tree stand (Greninger, 2014). Other hunting-related incidents could be the result of drowning (Moncrief, 2020), accidental self-inflicted firearm injury (KCRG, 2018), heart attack (Fortin, 2008), or a hunter mistaking another hunter for game

(Lowerre, 2020; KCRG, 2018; Sanchez, 2019). Conservation officers investigate these incidents to determine what occurred and how (Sanchez, 2019). Sometimes these incidents are simply tragic accidents and are treated as such. In these situations, conservation officers may use these incidents to help to better inform the public on hunting safety. Other times, these incidents are investigated as criminal events and charges are filed (Coello, 2020).

Homeland Security Responsibilities

The chapter to this point has focused on mainly non-law enforcement duties in which conservation officers participate. However, there is another additional type of activity in which conservation officers participate that is not normally directly related to their enforcement of fish and game laws and that is homeland security responsibilities. These duties at times may coincide with their enforcement of fish and game laws and take place during the normal course of their duties, but they also may be separate from their traditional duties. Since 9/11, there has been an increased focus on homeland security preparedness at all levels of government (federal, state, and local). All levels of law enforcement have undergone some changes since the time of 9/11 to participate in the new homeland security enterprise and environment that emerged since that time, including a change from focusing only on crime to including a focus on potential threats (Carter & Gore, 2013). This includes conservation officers. Over the last couple decades, conservation officers have experienced an expansion of their role within the larger law enforcement community (Eliason, 2007; Falcone, 2004). A further expansion of this role also includes homeland security responsibilities.

The extent to which conservation officers participate in homeland security activities is not well known or established. Some agencies mention that their officers participate in homeland security, while other agencies do not. It appears that the most common homeland security role for conservation officers is patrolling and protecting waterways and shorelines (Carter & Gore, 2013) as evidenced by some agencies such as the Maryland Department of Natural Resources creating a specialized Homeland Security Unit that is responsible for maritime incidents that are not under the jurisdiction of the Federal Bureau of Investigation or the United States Coast Guard (Maryland DNR, 2020) or Lightfoot (2016) who discussed officers from the Texas Parks and Wildlife Department's responsibilities for patrolling the Texas coast for radiological and nuclear threats as well as other responsibilities such as port security.

While it seems that often the responsibilities of conservation officers in relation to homeland security revolve around protecting the waterways and coastlines from threats, they may also play a broader role in protecting against biological threats (Carter & Gore, 2013). Even though rural areas do not receive as much attention as urban areas with large population centers regarding homeland security preparedness, conservation officers can serve as effective members of the homeland security enterprise since they are already established in rural areas throughout the country and provide an infrastructure that homeland security professionals may utilize for threat detection. One way that this infrastructure may be utilized by homeland security professionals is by taking advantage of the community partnerships that many conservation officers already have established in their assigned districts. Through these community partnerships, conservation officers may be able to better educate citizens within their district about potential biological threats that may occur in rural areas, including the introduction of invasive species or crop and livestock disease or threats related to hazardous materials such as fertilizer (e.g., ammonium nitrate) or other chemicals (Carter & Gore, 2013). Ammonium nitrate is believed to have been used by Timothy McVeigh in the bombing of the Murrah Federal Building in Oklahoma City (Seidman, 2011).

In addition to these community partnerships, conservation officers become familiar with their patrol areas and may be able to determine if something is out of place. For example, conservation officers regularly patrol their assigned districts and become familiar with the landscape, flora, fauna, people, and vehicles that are commonly encountered. If they are patrolling and observe something that is different, it may alert them to a possible threat concerning invasive species, disease, or other type of threat. They could then create a Suspicious

Activity Report (SAR) and alert homeland security officials about what was observed (Carter & Gore, 2013).

CONCLUSION

While conservation officers are most well-known for the enforcement of fish and game laws, they also participate in a variety of other activities. They commonly participate in public relations activities (Hailey, 1988; Pledger & Hailey, 1981; Tobias, 1998), assist with educational activities (Falcone, 2004), interact with landowners concerning wildlife issues on their properties (Calkins, 1970; Pledger & Hailey, 1981; Sherblom et al., 2002), conduct public meetings (Lord & Cheng, 2006), assist biologists with various wildlife and fisheries management projects including prescribed burns, fish tagging (Wagner, 2019) and biological surveys (Calkins, 1970, Lawson, 2003; NACLEC, 2021), participate is search, rescue, and recovery operations (Baxley, 2001; Carpenter & Rae, 1998; Connecticut Environmental Conservation Police Officers [EnCon] 2021; Jensen, 2019; LaCaze, 2017; NACLEC, 2021; Wagner, 2019), investigate hunting-related accidents (NACLEC, 2021), and assist with homeland security responsibilities (Carter & Gore, 2013). Many of these other activities enhance the conservation officer's primary mission of enforcing fish and game laws. Their public relations activity and educational activities allow the conservation officer to educate the public about not only the various regulations, but also the purpose behind those regulations. This may increase the public's awareness and understanding of these regulations and thereby increase compliance (McGarrell et al., 2013). Interacting with landowners also benefits the conservation officer in the enforcement of fish and game laws. Through these interactions, conservation officers are not only benefitting the wildlife and fisheries they are sworn to protect but are also fostering relationships with local landowners that may increase compliance with game laws and potentially provide information about fish and game violations. Regardless of the type of activity in which conservation officers participate outside of the direct enforcement of fish and game laws, it is apparent that the role of conservation officers has expanded (Falcone, 2004) to one much broader than what is considered to be that of a traditional law enforcement officer.

DISCUSSION QUESTIONS

1. In addition to the more traditional law enforcement duties discussed in Chapter Seven, conservation officers participate in a wide variety of other types of activities. Do conservation officers have too many responsibilities? Should some of these other duties be performed by non-law enforcement personnel? Do these other duties detract from their main responsibility of enforcing law pertaining to natural resources? Do these duties enhance their ability to enforce laws pertaining to natural resources? Explain.

2. One of the more recent activities added to the conservation officer's role is homeland security responsibilities. Even though they have some responsibilities, larger municipal police agencies have received most of the attention relative to homeland security. What homeland security role will conservation officers have in the future? Will it be expanded? Reduced? In addition to the responsibilities discussed in the chapter, are there other areas of homeland security that would be important for conservation officers? Explain.

Key Terms

Community cooperation model: The third of Mastrofski's four non-crime models. By participating in non-crime matters, the police demonstrate to the community that they can help the community as well as enforce the laws through the use of coercion.

Crime prophylactic model: The first of Mastofski's four non-crime models. Police intervention in non-crime matters is to prevent non-crime incidents from becoming criminal incidents.

Legalistic style: One of Wilson's three styles of policing. It is a strict law enforcement function of the police.

Police knowledge model: The second of Mastrofski's four non-crime models. Police participate in non-crime matters to be exposed to a broader segment of the community and thereby gain knowledge of the larger community.

Service style: One of Wilson's three styles of policing. Police are responsive to the community's preferences for how they would like the police department to function. Officers are more likely to participate in public relations and educational opportunities, and to be more community-oriented.

Social work model: The fourth of Mastrofski's four non-crime models. Police have a role in steering people away from crime and helping them to internalize law abiding norms.

Watchman style: One of Wilson's three styles of policing. It emphasizes the maintaining of order over law enforcement and is closely aligned with the order maintenance function of police.

References

Baxley, T. (2001). Aquatic investigations and recovery. *Proceedings of the Southeastern Association of Fish and Wildlife Agencies, USA, 55*, 582–587.

Calkins, F. (1970). *Rocky mountain warden*. Alfred & Knopf Inc.

Carpenter, C. S., & Rae, G. A. (1998). The use of special response dive team in aquatic law enforcement. *Proceedings of the Southeastern Association of Fish and Wildlife Agencies, USA, 52*, 488–494.

Carpenter, T. M. (1984). Information and education programs and the youth resource. *Proceedings of the Southeastern Association of Fish and Wildlife Agencies, USA, 38*, 622–625.

Carter, J. G., & Gore, M. L. (2013). Conservation officers: A force multiplier for homeland security. *Journal of Applied Security Research, 8*, 285–307.

Coello, S. (2020, July 24). SC hunter charged with accidentally killing father and daughter, mistaking them for deer. *The Post and Courier.* https://www.postandcourier.com/news/sc-hunter-charged-with -accidentally-killing-father-and-daughter-mistaking-them-for-deer /article_3dc24c32-cdd1-11ea-92f4-4b257d340b5a.html

Connecticut Environmental Conservation Police Officers (EnCon). (2021). What we do. https://portal.ct.gov/DEEP/Environmental -Conservation-Police/Environmental-Conservation-Police-Officers

Cordner, G. W. (2015). Community policing: Elements and effects. In R. G. Dunham & G. P. Alpert (Eds.), *Critical Issues in Policing* (Vol. 7, pp. 481–498). Waveland Press.

Eliason, S. L. (2007). From wildlife specialist to police generalist? The scope of nonwildlife violations encountered by conservation officers. *Southwest Journal of Criminal Justice, 4*(2), 120–132.

Falcone, D. (2004). America's conservation police: Agencies in transition. *Policing: An International Journal of Police Strategies and Management, 27*(1), 56–66.

Forsyth, C. J. (1993). Chasing and catching the "bad guys": The game warden's prey. *Deviant Behavior, 14*, 209–226.

Forsyth, C. J. (2008). The game of wardens and poachers. *Journal of Rural Social Sciences, 23*(2), 43–53.

Fortin, J. (2008, October 24). Biggest danger for hunters? Heart attack, not stray bullet. CNN. https://www.cnn.com/2008/HEALTH/conditions/10/24/hm.hunter.hazards/index.html

Greninger, H. (2014, November 11). Falls from tree stands top hunting accidents: Half of hunters wear harnesses in stands. *Tribune-Star.* https://www.tribstar.com/news/local_news/falls-from-tree-stands-top-hunting-accidents/article_e7689704-616d-5724-b4e3-67202a465c55.html

Hailey, W. F. (1988). Getting the word out—Disseminating information utilizing the print media. *Proceedings of the Southeastern Association of Fish and Wildlife Agencies, USA, 42*, 540–545.

Hass, S. (17 September, 2021). Conservation agent shares insights of his job. *Daily Journal Online.* https://dailyjournalonline.com/outdoors/conservation-agent-shares-insights-of-his-job/article_33359faf-332e-5adc-a7f8-e7d3f3b0d335.html

Hawdon, J. (2008). Legitimacy, trust, social capital, and policing styles. *Police Quarterly, 11*(2), 182–201.

Hessler, K. (1997). Where do we draw the line between harassment and free speech? An analysis of hunter harassment law. *Animal Law, 3*, 129–161.

Indiana Department of Natural Resources. (2021). About us. https://www.in.gov/dnr/law-enforcement/about-us/

Jensen, J. (2019, October 29). DNR search-and-rescue aircraft save lives. *Duluth News Tribune.* https://www.duluthnewstribune.com/opinion/columns/4744213-Local-View-Column-DNR-search-and-rescue-aircraft-save-lives

Kalkomy. (2015). The difference between online hunter education and an in-person course. hunter-ed. https://www.hunter-ed.com/blog/difference-online-hunter-education-person-course/

KCRG-TV9. (2018). DNR investigating multiple hunting incidents. https://www.kcrg.com/content/news/DNR-investigating-multiple-hunting-incidents-502493822.html

Keefe, J. F. (1987). The first 50 years. Missouri Department of Conservation.

LaCaze, K. (2015). Resolving hunter conflict on a lease. *Louisiana Sportsman.* https://www.louisianasportsman.com/hunting/resolving-hunter-conflict-on-a-lease/

LaCaze, K. (2017). Search and rescue in the great outdoors. *Louisiana Sportsman.* https://www.louisianasportsman.com/fishing/search-and-rescue-in-the-great-outdoors/

Lawson, H. (2003). Controlling the wilderness: The work of wilderness officers. *Society & Animals, 11*(4), 329–351.

Lightfoot, S. (2016, March 15). Texas game wardens deploy new homeland security measures. Texasalloutdoors.com. https://tylerpaper.com/texas_all_outdoors/texas-game-wardens-deploy-new-homeland-security-measures/article_8543a220-462d-5326-9178-cc53239a9817.html

Lord, J. K., & Cheng, A. S. (2006). Public involvement in state fish and wildlife agencies in the U.S.: A thumbnail sketch of techniques and barriers. *Human Dimensions of Wildlife, 11,* 55–69.

Lowerre, V. (2020, September 6). Iowa DNR investigating fatal hunting incident. KWWL. https://kwwl.com/2020/09/06/iowa-dnr-investigating-fatal-hunting-incident/

Maryland Department of Natural Resources (DNR). (2020). Maryland DNR Homeland Security Unit. https://dnr.maryland.gov/nrp/Pages/homeland_security.aspx

Mastrofski, S. (1983). The police and noncrime services. In G. P. Whitaker & C. D. Phillips (Eds.), *Evaluating performance of criminal justice agencies* (pp. 33–62). Sage.

McGarrell, E. F., Suttmoeller, M., & Gibbs, C. (2013). Great lakes fisheries enforcement. In W. W. Taylor, A. J. Lynch, & N. J. Leonard (Eds.), *Great lakes fisheries policy and management* (2nd ed., pp. 455–472). Michigan State University Press.

McKinzie, B. (1989). Youth for wildlife. *Proceedings of the Southeastern Association of Fish and Wildlife Agencies, USA, 43,* 530–532.

Missouri Department of Conservation (MDC). (2020). Contact and engage. https://mdc.mo.gov/contact-engage

Moncrief, J. (2020, November 17). Conservation officers investigate death of a hunter in Graves County. WPSD Local 6. https://www.wpsdlocal6.com/news/conservation-officers-investigate-death-of-a-hunter-in-graves-county/article_e98fecee-2903-11eb-9a27-63ec34dc9130.html

Mootz, J. (2006). Conducting youth hunting workshops. *Proceedings of the Southeastern Association of Fish and Wildlife Agencies, USA, 60,* 241.

Muir, W. K. (1977). *Police: Streetcorner politicians.* The University of Chicago Press.

National Association of Conservation Law Enforcement Chiefs (NACLEC). (2021). What we do. https://www.naclec.org/about

Palmer, C. E., & Bryant, C. D. (1985). Keepers of the king's deer: Game wardens and the enforcement of fish and wildlife law. In C. D. Bryant, D. J. Shoemaker, J. K. Skipper, & W. E. Snizek (Eds.), *The rural workforce: Non-agricultural occupations in America* (pp. 111–137). Bergin & Garvey Publishers Inc.

Pepper, S. M. (2003). Law enforcement management of conservation outreach programs in Alabama. *Proceedings of the Southeastern Association of Fish and Wildlife Agencies, USA, 57,* 357–363.

Pledger, M., & Hailey, W. F. (1981). Methods of improving public relations. *Proceedings of the Southeastern Association of Fish and Wildlife Agencies, USA, 35,* 727–729.

Roznik, S. (2018, November 21). Hunters ask to track wounded deer onto private property, landowner says tough luck. *Fond du Lac Reporter.* https://www.fdlreporter.com/story/news/2018/11/21/fond-du-lac-county-hunter-trespassing-dispute/2077322002/

Sanchez, M. (2019, November 17). Missouri Department of Conservation confirms one person injured in hunting incident. KRCG. https://krcgtv.com/news/local/missouri-department-of-conservation-confirms-one-person-injured-in-hunting-incident

Seidman, A. (2011, August 2). Homeland security plans to regulate bomb fertilizer. *LA Times.* https://www.latimes.com/world/la-xpm-2011-aug-02-la-na-ammonium-nitrate-20110803-story.html

Shelley, T. O., & Crow, M. S. (2009). The nature and extent of conservation policing: Law enforcement generalists or conservation specialists? *American Journal of Criminal Justice, 34*, 9–27.

Sherblom, J. C., Keranen, L., & Withers, L. A. (2002). Tradition, tension, and transformation: A structuration analysis of a game warden service in transition. *Journal of Applied Communication Research, 30*(2), 143–162.

Sousa, W., & Kelling, G. (2014). Order maintenance policing. In G. Bruinsma & D. Weisburd (Eds.)., *Encyclopedia of criminology and criminal justice* (pp. 3349–3358). Springer.

Tobias, M. (1998). *Nature's keepers: On the front lines of the fight to save wildlife in America.* John Wiley & Sons Inc.

Viverette, C. B., Wilcox, T., & Garman, G. (2006). Virginia's waters, woods, and wildlife: A conservation education course for science teachers. *Proceedings of the Southeastern Association of Fish and Wildlife Agencies, USA, 60*, 237.

Wagner, G. (2019, July 17). A very cool job: Nebraska conservation officer. *Nebraskaland Magazine.* http://magazine.outdoornebraska.gov/2019/07/a-very-cool-job-nebraska-conservation-officer/

Walker, S., & Katz, C. M. (2013). *The police in America: An introduction.* McGraw Hill.

Weinstein, L. K. (2006). Strategies for aligning outdoor education programs to state learning standards. *Proceedings of the Southeastern Association of Fish and Wildlife Agencies, USA, 60*, 235.

Wilson, J. Q. (1968). *Varieties of police behavior: The management of law and order in eight communities.* Atheneum.

Nine

FUTURE DIRECTIONS AND CHALLENGES FOR CONSERVATION LAW ENFORCEMENT

Conservation law enforcement officers have existed in one form or another for many years. As discussed in Chapter Two, the role of conservation officers has changed throughout the years and will continue to evolve going into the future. The evolution of conservation officers and their role within society has been in response to various ecological and political issues and challenges that have presented themselves throughout the course of history. To this point, this book has focused on explaining where conservation law enforcement has been and where it is now. This chapter will focus on challenges facing conservation law enforcement heading into the future. Since no one has a crystal ball that can see the future, this is by no means an exhaustive list of possible challenges facing conservation law enforcement officers in the future but will identify and discuss some of what we the authors believe to be the important upcoming challenges.

FUTURE DIRECTIONS AND CHALLENGES

Citizens' Lack of Knowledge

One of the challenges facing conservation law enforcement officers is a general lack of knowledge about their role in society. A study completed by the National Association of Conservation Law Enforcement Chiefs (NACLEC), National Conservation Law Enforcement Education Foundation (NACLEEF), Responsive Management (RM), and the University of Wisconsin Stevens-Point (UWSP) (2021) found that 75% of the respondents to their survey knew very little or nothing at all about what conservation officers do or what their role was within their respective state. Less than half of those respondents could identify a particular duty or activity related to the enforcement of hunting or fishing laws in which conservation law enforcement officers would participate. Unsurprisingly, those that participate in the more traditional activities or activities that would be commonly associated with having interactions with conservation law enforcement officers such as hunting, angling, trapping, and boating reported having an increased knowledge of the role and function of conservation officers than did those that did not participate in those types of activities. Conversely, people of color, urban residents, and women reported lower levels of knowledge concerning the role and activities of conservation officers than did the overall sample of participants. It is not surprising that there was a disparity between those that participate in pursuits such as hunting, angling, and boating and urban residents and people of color because, according to the U.S. Fish and Wildlife Service's 2016 National Survey of Fishing, Hunting, and Wildlife-Associated Recreation, white males participate in outdoor pursuits such as hunting, fishing, and wildlife watching at higher rates than do females or people of color.

The fact that white males participate in outdoor pursuits such as hunting and angling at higher rates than other demographics is not a new development. Traditionally, hunting and fishing were white male-dominated pursuits. However, the demographics of America are changing, and this could pose other separate, but related future challenges for natural resources agencies and conservation law enforcement officers in the form of declining numbers of participants in outdoor pursuits such as hunting, but also decreased funding.

Changing Demographics

The overall population of the United States is increasing and similarly, the urban, elderly, minority, and immigrant populations are also increasing. As populations increase, there will be an increased need for housing, and urbanization will likely follow. An increase in urbanization due to the increased population will most likely result in a decrease in habitat for fish and wildlife and areas for people to pursue outdoor recreation (NACLEC et al., 2021). If there are fewer places for people to recreate in the outdoors, a decrease in participation is almost certain to follow. While the loss of habitat and opportunity will almost certainly impact the job of conservation officers, the change in population demographics of the residents of the United States will also likely impact natural resources agencies and subsequently conservation law enforcement officers. As the populations of urban, elderly, minority, and immigrant residents increase, there will also likely be fewer participants in outdoor wildlife and fisheries activities. Urban residents generally hunt and fish less frequently than their rural counterparts. Similarly, elderly residents participate in these activities less frequently than do younger people, and minorities and immigrants hunt and fish less than white Americans (Duda et al., 2010; NACLEC, 2021).

Changing Attitudes Toward Outdoor Recreation

Not only is there a demographic shift occurring in the United States, but attitudes toward outdoor recreation is also changing. Participation in hunting and fishing has been declining in the United States for decades. There was an increase in participation during the COVID-19 pandemic, but otherwise overall numbers have been declining. There was a slight increase in participation in fishing reported by the USFWS (2016), but generally speaking, participation in traditional activities such as hunting and fishing have been declining (NACLEC et al., 2021). However, a decline in traditional activities such as hunting and fishing does not necessarily mean that people are not enjoying wildlife-related pursuits. The number of people who participated in **non-consumptive outdoor pursuits** such as wildlife watching increased between the years 2011 and 2016 (USFWS, 2016). NACLEC et al. (2021) reported that the most popular outdoor pursuits identified in their survey were hiking (44%), wildlife viewing and photography (33%), camping (23%), fishing (15%), hunting (6%), and trapping (1%). This shift in the types of outdoor activities in which Americans are participating has a direct impact on natural resources agencies and therefore conservation law enforcement officers. Since natural resources agencies are mandated to provide hunting and fishing opportunities, there may be some disconnect between those the agencies are supposed to be serving and the agencies themselves. This disconnect could potentially result in a loss of legitimacy for the agency and a decrease in their funding (NACLEC et al., 2021).

Funding

One of the main ways that natural resources agencies are funded is through the sale of hunting and fishing licenses. Commonly, a significant portion of their budget is the result of hunting and fishing license sales (Blevins & Edwards, 2009; NACLEC et al., 2021). As fewer people engage in hunting, fishing, and trapping, natural resources agencies will sell fewer licenses, resulting in less revenue for agencies. Because license sales are such a significant portion of the revenue stream for natural resources agencies, if sales continue to decline, agencies may have to find alternative revenue streams that involve financial support from non-hunters and non-anglers (NACLEC, 2021).

Further complicating the matter is that a portion of a natural resources agency's revenue results from acts such as the Federal Aid in Wildlife Restoration Act (Pittman-Robertson Act) and the Dingell-Johnson Act (Sport Fish Restoration Act) (Bean, 1978; Dunlap, 1988; NACLEC, 2021; Trefethen, 1975; USFWS, 2013). These acts place an excise tax on hunting and fishing equipment that is redirected to state wildlife programs and fisheries conservation. So, simply stated, if people are hunting and fishing less, they will be spending less money on equipment and therefore agencies will receive less tax revenue. However, the revenue situation regarding these acts and in particular the Pittman-Robertson Act is not that simple.

The Pittman-Robertson Act is an excise tax on firearms and ammunition. When it was passed in 1937, most of the people who purchased firearms and ammunition were hunters, so those that were providing the tax revenue presumably were interested in the wildlife management efforts that resulted from these taxes. However, as participation in hunting has declined, a larger percentage of firearm and ammunition purchases are being made by those interested in target shooting and home protection. Certainly, there could be some hunters that are also interested in target shooting and home defense, but there is most likely a significant portion of target shooters and home defenders that is comprised of non-hunters and may not be interested in the wildlife management that results from their purchases (Duda et al., 2017; NACLEC, 2021; Southwick Associates, 2017). This could result in the goals and objectives of natural resources agencies becoming further disconnected from their funding sources.

Other forms of revenue also have implications for natural resources agencies. Some agencies, such as the Missouri Department of Conservation, are supported by a sales tax. This sales tax is different from an excise tax that is related to hunting or fishing gear in that it is enacted on every purchase made within the state. If states pursue a sales tax to replace lost revenue from license sales or excise taxes, even though these sales taxes are often very small (Missouri's is 1/8 of 1%) (Keefe, 1987), every person who purchases something in Missouri is paying that tax, and therefore may request input on how those tax monies are spent. If those constituents do not hunt or fish or are against hunting and fishing, it may create a disconnect between those that are funding an agency and that agency's mission and goals.

Lost revenues related to decreases in the sales of hunting and fishing licenses directly impact natural resources agencies and conservation law enforcement officers. Certainly, all revenues from hunting and fishing licenses do not directly fund conservation law enforcement officers within the larger parent agency. As discussed in Chapter Four, normally, there are many different divisions within a natural resources agency, with a law enforcement or protection division being just one of these divisions. If overall revenues for the larger natural resources agency decrease, then most likely the budget for the law enforcement or protection division will also be reduced. Budget reductions in the law enforcement division could lead to manpower reductions, older equipment that cannot be replaced, pay stagnation, or any number of different strategies that could be employed to reduce expenditures by the law enforcement division. While these budget cuts would be detrimental to the larger agency as well as the law enforcement division, eventually, the agency will devise a plan to replace the lost revenue. The strategies utilized to replace those lost revenues may have a larger and more permanent impact on the future of conservation law enforcement.

Traditional revenue sources for natural resources agencies, such as the sale of hunting, fishing, and trapping permits, have been decreasing for decades. Agencies have relied on these sources for many years and must find ways to replace this lost revenue. If those that have traditionally supported and financed fish and wildlife agencies are no longer supporting and financing those agencies, agencies must find someone else to do so. Possible alternatives to hunters, anglers, and trappers include non-consumptive resource users such as wildlife watchers, hikers, and campers and those that do not recreate in the outdoors (NACLEC, 2021). Regardless of which group is approached about funding the natural resources agency, they will most likely require some type of concessions for their support. It may be fairly benign, such as increased public areas dedicated to wildlife watching, more or improved hiking trails, or more or improved campground facilities. However, the possibility also exists that those who oppose certain types of outdoor recreation such as hunting, fishing, or trapping could demand concessions such as reduced or eliminated hunting or fishing opportunities for their financial support. This would create issues for natural resources agencies since generally these agencies are mandated to provide hunting and fishing opportunities (NACLEC, 2021). However, these mandates were created when hunting and fishing largely funded these organizations.

Similarly, those that are funding agencies through the Pittman-Robertson Act have also shifted from largely those participating in hunting to those that participate more in recreational shooting (NACLEC, 2021; Southwick Associates, 2017). It is possible that those participating in shooting sports, but who do not actively participate in hunting, would recognize the benefits associated with the wildlife management that is funded through the excise tax, but what would happen if this growing group of non-hunters that were funding wildlife management through the Pittman-Robertson Act decided they wanted that money to go elsewhere? Would they attempt to get Congress to change the act to direct the money elsewhere, or would they simply tell state-level agencies that they want more public target shooting opportunities? It is difficult to predict what could happen concerning the shift related to this excise tax. Getting a federal statute, especially one that has been in force since 1937, changed is no easy task, but it could be done if the target shooters were able to organize and successfully lobby Congress. What is not difficult to predict is that if this funding source were removed, natural resources agencies would be left in a precarious position, especially when coupled with the loss of revenues related to hunting and fishing licenses.

Obviously, a reduction in funding affects the larger natural resources agency and by default also affects the law enforcement or protection division. However, the impact on the law enforcement or protection division may go beyond traditional budget reductions such as equipment or manpower. If non-consumptive resource users become the main sources of revenue to natural resources agencies, it may not only cause a change in focus for these agencies from ensuring consumptive resources opportunities (hunting and fishing) and non-consumptive opportunities when possible to focusing on non-consumptive opportunities, it may also impact the role of conservation law enforcement officers. As described in multiple places in this book, the main role of conservation law enforcement officers is the enforcement of laws related to hunting and fishing (Forsyth, 1993, 2008; Palmer & Bryant, 1985). However, this could change if the focus of the larger natural resources agency changes.

Changing Role Due to Shift in Organizational Priorities

Minimally, if license revenues continue to decline, it will be more important for agencies to ensure that everyone that is participating in hunting, fishing, or trapping is properly licensed. Conservation officers already spend significant time on enforcing license requirements (Blevins & Lanham, 2012), but if revenues continue to decrease due to declining license sales, then enforcing the purchase of these licenses may receive increased focus. While this may be a shift in focus, it is not a dramatic shift, since the enforcement of licensing requirements is already one of the more common tasks associated with the conservation law enforcement officer role.

However, if providing hunting and fishing opportunities is no longer one of the primary functions of the natural resources agency, there may be less focus on the enforcement of laws pertaining to hunting and fishing. Certainly, the enforcement of laws regulating hunting and fishing will always need to occur, but if the focus of the agency changes, it may become less of a priority. Catering to a non-consumptive user base may require an increased focus on other aspects of the conservation officer's role. Areas such as educational programming and public relations may take on a much larger role. Conservation officers currently participate in these types of activities (Carpenter, 1984; Hailey, 1988; Lawson, 2003; NACLEC, 2021; Palmer & Bryant, 1985; Pledger & Hailey, 1981; Tobias, 1998), so these types of activities would not be completely new concepts for officers. However, the frequency with which they participate in these activities would most likely increase, while time spent on law enforcement may decrease.

Since conservation officers are often the most readily recognized representatives of their organization (McGarrell et al., 2013), it would make sense for agencies to modify their role to accommodate the overall change in focus of the larger agency. However, some departments of natural resources already contain education divisions, so some of these increased educational activities could potentially be subsumed within an already existing division within the agency. However, if the focus of the entire agency changes, then most likely the focus for conservation officers would also shift. To accommodate the increased educational focus, some agencies could potentially choose to create two types of conservation officers—one that has a law enforcement focus and one that has a more educational or programming focus. This would be similar to that of the National Park Service that has some park rangers that focus on law enforcement and some that have a more programmatic or interpretive focus (ParkRangerEDU.org, 2021). A final possibility that agencies could employ to accommodate this change in focus would be for the law enforcement or protection divisions to be removed from the natural resources agency and subsumed into a department of public safety. This would allow for the conservation law enforcement officers to maintain their focus on law enforcement. This arrangement would be similar to that already in place in Oregon, where conservation officers are part of the Oregon State Police (Oregon State Police, 2021). While this is a possible outcome, it is probably the least likely.

If this occurred, it would not be the first time that the role of conservation law enforcement officers evolved in response to external contingencies triggering changes to occur within their natural resources agency. Falcone (2004) reported that in response to the formation of departments of natural resources in the 1990s from the more traditional departments of fish and game or departments of conservation, the role of conservation officers was expanded to include not only more educational and programmatic responsibilities, but also expanded law enforcement responsibilities to include more traditional types of criminal enforcement, rather than simply the enforcement of laws pertaining to hunting and fishing. While not always a smooth transition to a more traditional law enforcement role, conservation officers have adapted and would most likely be able to adapt to this new set of circumstances as well. Regardless of the issues related to funding and changing demographics, the role of conservation officers is sure to evolve in the future. How and to what extent it changes will be dependent on those types of various factors such as changing revenue streams for natural resources agencies and changing demographics, but it is difficult to predict, and it may vary from agency to agency. Some areas of the country may not be as affected by these changes as other areas of the country, so changes to the conservation officer role may vary greatly from state to state. In addition to issues such as funding, other organizational issues such as the ability to recruit and retain quality conservation officers will also continue to be a challenge in the future.

Recruitment and Retention of Officers

Historically, recruiting enough qualified applicants for a career in policing was not a problem for law enforcement organizations. The lure of a stable, middle-class job with government benefits created an environment where police agencies could be selective from large applicant pools. Large-scale changes in both the priorities of the labor force, along with rapid changes in the economic outlook of the United States, created an unstable environment for the ability of police agencies to secure the proper personnel (Domash, 2002). During what has been termed the "dot-com bubble," many police agencies struggled to fill their ranks across the country for the first time in history. Following the 2008 economic crash as a result of the United States mortgage crisis, police agencies once again filled with highly desirable candidates, only to find the boon ephemeral, as the candidate pool once again dried up with a continuously growing US economy and record low unemployment (Domash, 2002; Johnson, 2009; SAPOA, 2018). Public opinion has also turned against police work, both in the institution of policing following high-profile incidents such as the murder of George Floyd (Main & Spielman, 2021; Mourtgos et al., 2021), as well as the nature of the job (Ernst, 2017).

Conservation law enforcement, which has often been viewed as a highly competitive occupation largely insulated from these pressures, has also begun to experience challenges in hiring qualified applicants in recent history. In addition to the challenging nature of conservation policing jobs that may be pushing potential candidates into simpler and more lucrative lines of work (Eliason, 2007, 2014; Forsyth & Forsyth, 2009), conservation policing also struggles with some additional recruiting challenges that are far less impactful on traditional police organizations. Namely, the proportion of Americans who recreationally fish and hunt is decreasing, those who do recreate outdoors are seeking pursuits that do not represent a direct pipeline to conservation policing, and conservation law enforcement organizations have failed to effectively recruit women and people of color (NACLEC et al., 2021). This is true even in comparison to traditional police organizations, which have also failed to effectively attract talent from these groups, which represent nearly 70 percent of the US population (Henderson, 2014; Rossler et al., 2019; Schuck, 2021). In fact, fewer than half of all conservation officers believe their agency is doing enough to recruit a diverse pool of candidates (NACLEC et al., 2021).

Entry into conservation policing not only requires an interest in a law enforcement career, but, for the most part, a background in hunting and fishing serve as a key gateway into this career path. Hunting and fishing have been on a historic downward trend since the 1980s, and despite some anomalies, such as a return to outdoor pursuits during COVID-19 lockdowns and limited indoor recreational opportunities, this has resulted in fewer potential applicants along this pathway (CAHSS, 2021). Organizations dependent upon hunting and fishing such as the US Fish & Wildlife Service, the Council to Advance Hunting and the Shooting Sports, and state resource organizations have instituted recruitment, retention, and reactivation ("R3") efforts to bolster conservation (CAHSS, 2021; USFWS, 2021a; Wisconsin Department of Natural Resources, 2021).

In addition to the general trend of reduced participation in outdoor pursuits, efforts to increase participation in hunting and fishing among women and people of color have not been highly successful, and these segments of the population still significantly trail participation by white men (USFWS, 2016). As a result of these realities, recruitment of conservation officers who fit a category other than white men has been rather abysmal. Rossler and Suttmoeller (2021) reported that only six percent of conservation officers in their sample were women, and only seven percent identified as people of color, which is about half of the national average for police officers (Reaves, 2015). The fact that about seventy percent of the US population is vastly underrepresented will make it much harder to continue to recruit at a level that maintains the current number of sworn officers.

A further complication of these recruitment setbacks is that it establishes a pattern that builds upon itself to prevent inclusion and belonging. Conservation officers are by and large the visible symbol of natural resources, fish and game, and conservation departments. When conservation agencies struggle to promote hunting and fishing through officer outreach to those who have little in the way of organic mentorship, it becomes a self-fulfilling prophecy that the outdoors remain a white male-dominated space and reduces the applicant pool for the new generation of female officers and officers of color. Conservation policing suffers from the lack of a "critical mass" of female officers and officers of color that would promote a sense of inclusion and belonging in the department, create beneficial organizational pressures, and may also have significant implications for retention of officers, which creates a similar feedback loop (Adams & Buck, 2010; Cordner & Cordner, 2011; Cooper & Ingram, 2004; Gachter et al., 2013).

With respect to retention of police officers, the general concerns are that the nature of police work, public hostility, compensation, the sense of fairness and internal procedural justice exhibited by command staff, and the treatment by officers of about the same rank have significant implications for whether officers remain in their careers or choose to leave (Adams & Buck, 2010; Gachter et al., 2013). While natural resources law enforcement occurs most often at the state level, and these organizations are typically better funded than many local agencies, conservation officers are usually more educated than traditional police officers, which may enhance their expectations for command staff, personal autonomy, and compensation (Paoline et al., 2015).

In a recent NACLEC et al. (2021) report, some glaring concerns for officer retention were evident given the more global models of what leads to officers leaving their agency or career path. Slightly over half of all conservation officers reported that their agency does a good job retaining officers. Among conservation officers, only about half were satisfied with their pay and less than half were satisfied with agency leadership. Unfortunately, the NACLEC report did not address interactions among officers of the same rank, and the degree to which discrimination internal to the organization may be a problem, given the lack of representation among women and racial and ethnic minority officers (NACLEC et al., 2021; Rossler & Suttmoeller, 2021). Additionally, while public hostility toward the policing profession as a whole, and conservation policing in particular, have not been addressed among conservation officers, perceptions of law enforcement and wildlife agencies both rank as high-level concerns among officers (NACLEC et al., 2021), which may be indicative of some significant concerns for officer retention.

Wildlife Crime, Trade, and Trafficking

Another challenge facing conservation law enforcement officers will be the continued prevalence of wildlife crime, the illegal wildlife trade, and the illegal trafficking of wildlife. The negative aspects of wildlife crime, the illegal wildlife trade, and trafficking of wildlife has been discussed multiple times in this book, but these issues will continue to be challenges that face conservation officers in the future. The illegal wildlife trade is a multi-billion-dollar business (USFWS, 2021b) and involves transnational criminal and terror groups (Moreto & Spires, 2018; Wyler & Shiekh, 2008, 2013). When a type of business is this lucrative, people are motivated to continue engaging in it regardless of what the potential consequences are for themselves or the world. This can be likened to the illegal drug trade. Agencies across the world have been combating the worldwide trade in narcotics for decades but have not successfully stopped it. As long as there is demand for wildlife and wildlife products, the illegal trade in wildlife is sure to continue (United States Agency for International Development, 2021). As identified in Chapter One, the illegal wildlife trade has severe ecological, economic, and human costs as well as public health and national security concerns (Moreto & Pires, 2018). Conservation officers will continue to be instrumental in working to eliminate the illegal trade in wildlife and other natural resources.

Of particular concern is the possibility of the transmission of zoonotic diseases from animals to humans. This has always been a concern associated with the illegal wildlife trade, with pathogens such as Severe Acute Respiratory Syndrome (SARS), Avian Influenza (H5N1) and Ebola being previously identified as types of diseases that could be passed from animals to humans (Moreto & Spires, 2018; Wyler & Shiekh, 2008). The COVID-19 pandemic has brought renewed attention to this aspect of the illegal wildlife trade. While at the time of this writing, officials are still unsure of the origins of COVID-19, one theory is that it originated in a market in China that sold wildlife and wildlife products. Some of these markets operate legally, but many operate illegally and specialize in products that are illegal (United Nations Office on Drugs and Crime, 2020). Even if COVID-19 is found to have originated somewhere other than a market in China, the threat of disease transmission from animals to humans is significant.

The participation in the illegal wildlife trade by transnational crime syndicates and terror groups is also an important area of concern for conservation officers looking into the future. These criminal syndicates and terror groups utilize the illegal trade in wildlife to finance their operations (Wyler & Shiekh, 2008; 2013), and in the case of terror groups, this is particularly concerning. Terror groups being able to fundraise using the illegal wildlife trade poses a threat to the United States' national security, but it is not the only conservation-related threat to national security. Invasive species also pose a threat to the country's national security.

Since 9/11, conservation officers have become increasingly involved in issues related to homeland security at all levels of government. Officers at the international and federal level would be more likely to encounter those involved in the illegal wildlife trade (Wyler & Shiekh, 2008), but officers at the state and local level may be the first to identify that an invasive species has emerged. Regardless of their position within the government hierarchy, national security issues are sure to be an important part of the conservation officer role moving into the future.

CONCLUSION

Conservation officers are sure to have an important role within the law enforcement community and larger natural resources community into the future. While their role may change, they will always be needed to protect natural resources and to ensure there are wildlife, forestry, and fisheries resources for future generations to enjoy. They have existed in one capacity or another for hundreds of years, and there is nothing to suggest that they will not exist for hundreds of years more.

DISCUSSION QUESTIONS

1. Due to the various factors outlined in this chapter, generally speaking, conservation law enforcement agencies have fewer minority and female officers than traditional police agencies. What are some strategies that they could employ to increase their ability to effectively recruit and retain minority and female officers?

2. Of the challenges discussed in this chapter, which is the most pressing? Which one poses the greatest challenge to conservation law enforcement officers and agencies? Is there a different issue that

is not discussed that would pose a significant challenge to conservation law enforcement heading into the future?

Key Terms

Consumptive use of resources: Outdoor activities that require the use of resources. Activities such as hunting and fishing would be consumptive uses of resources because animals are harvested and utilized.

Non-consumptive outdoor pursuits: Outdoor activities such as bird or wildlife watching that do not result in the actual use of the resource.

References

Adams, G. A., & Buck, J. (2010). Social stressors and strain among police officers: It's not just the bad guys. *Criminal Justice and Behavior, 37*(9), 1030–1040.

Bean, M. J. (1978). Federal wildlife law. In H. P. Brokaw (Ed.), *Wildlife and America: Contributions to an understanding of American wildlife and its conservation* (pp. 279–289). U.S. Government Printing Office.

Blevins, K. R., & Edwards, T. D. (2009). Wildlife crime. In J. M. Miller (Ed.), *21ˢᵗ century criminology: A reference handbook* (Vol. 1, pp. 557–563). Sage.

Blevins, K. R., & Lanham, C.M. (2012). *Occupational roles and practices of Kentucky conservation officers.* https://justicestudies.eku .edu/sites/justicestudies.eku.edu/files/files/Blevins%20SJRP %20Report%202012-2013.pdf

Carpenter, T. M. (1984). Information and education programs and the youth resource. *Proceedings of the Southeastern Association of Fish and Wildlife Agencies, USA, 38*, 622–625.

Cooper, C., & Ingram, S. (2004). *Retention of police officers: A study of resignations and transfers in ten forces.* Home Office.

Cordner, G., & Cordner, A. (2011). Stuck on a plateau: Obstacles to recruitment, selection, and retention of women police. *Police Quarterly, 14*(3), 207–226.

Council to Advance Hunting and the Shooting Sports (CAHSS). (2021). What is R3? CAHSS. https://cahss.org/what-is-r3/

Domash, S. F. (2002, May) Who wants this job? *Police, 26*(5), 34–39.

Duda, M. D., Beppler, T., & Organ, J. (2017). The growth of sport shooting participation: What does this mean for conservation revenue? *The Wildlife Professional, 11*(2), 38–41.

Duda, M. D., Jones, M. F., & Criscione, A. (2010). *The sportsman's voice: Hunting and fishing in America.* Venture Publishing.

Dunlap, T. R. (1988). *Saving America's wildlife.* Princeton University Press.

Eliason, S. L. (2007). From wildlife specialist to police generalist? The scope of nonwildlife violations encountered by conservation officers. *Southwest Journal of Criminal Justice, 42*(2), 120–132.

Eliason, S. L. (2014). Life as a game warden: The good, the bad, and the ugly. *International Journal of Police Science and Management, 16*(3), 196–204.

Ernst, D. (2017, December 12). Recruiting woes: Dallas PD rips "millennials who want all days off," be chief within "six months." *Washington Times.* https://www.washingtontimes.com/news/2017/dec/12/dallas-police-chief-rips-millennials-who-want-all-/

Falcone, D. (2004). America's conservation police: Agencies in transition. *Policing: An International Journal of Police Strategies and Management, 27*(1), 56–66.

Forsyth, C. J. (1993). Chasing and catching the "bad guys": The game warden's prey. *Deviant Behavior, 14,* 209–226.

Forsyth, C. J. (2008). The game of wardens and poachers. *Journal of Rural Social Sciences, 23*(2), 43–53.

Forsyth, C. J., & Forsyth, Y. A. (2009). Dire and sequestered meetings: The work of game wardens. *American Journal of Criminal Justice, 34,* 213–223.

Gachter, M., Savage, D. A., & Torgler, B. (2013). Retaining the thin blue line: What shapes workers' intentions not to quit the current work environment. *International Journal of Social Economics, 40*(5), 2013.

Hailey, W. F. (1988). Getting the word out—Disseminating information utilizing the print media. *Proceedings of the Southeastern Association of Fish and Wildlife Agencies, USA, 42,* 540–545.

Henderson, N. M. (2014, October 8). White men are 31 percent of the American population. They hold 65 percent of all elected offices.

Washington Post. https://www.washingtonpost.com/news/the-fix/wp/2014/10/08/65-percent-of-all-american-elected-officials-are-white-men/

Johnson, K. (2009, March 11). Police agencies buried in resumes. *USA Today.*

Keefe, J. F. (1987). *The first 50 years.* Missouri Department of Conservation.

Lawson, H. (2003). Controlling the wilderness: The work of wilderness officers. *Society & Animals, 11*(4), 329–351.

Main, F., & Spielman, F. (2021, January 15). Police retirements grow in Chicago, New York, Minneapolis amid anti-police backlash. *Chicago Sun Times.* https://chicago.suntimes.com/2021/1/15/22229584/police-retirements-backlash-chicago-new-york-minneapolis-john-catanzara-fop-michael-lappe

McGarrell, E. F., Suttmoeller, M., & Gibbs, C. (2013). Great lakes fisheries enforcement. In W. W. Taylor, A. J. Lynch, & N. J. Leonard (Eds.), *Great lakes fisheries policy and management* (2nd ed., pp. 455–472). Michigan State University Press.

Moreto, W. D., & Pires, S. F. (2018). *Wildlife crime: An environmental criminology and crime science perspective.* Carolina Academic Press.

Mourtgos, S. M., Adams, I. T., & Nix, J. (2021, July). Elevated police turnover following the summer of George Floyd protests: A synthetic control study. *Criminology & Public Policy.*

National Association of Conservation Law Enforcement Chiefs (NACLEC). (2021). What we do. https://www.naclec.org/about

National Association of Conservation Law Enforcement Chiefs (NACLEC), National Conservation Law Enforcement Education Foundation (NCLEEF), Responsive Management, & University of Wisconsin-Stevens Point. (2021, March 8). *Planning for the future of conservation law enforcement in the United States: National report.* https://www.naclec.org/press-pages/conservation-law-enforcement-usa-national-report

Oregon State Police. (2021). Fish and wildlife division. https://www.oregon.gov/osp/programs/fw/Pages/default.aspx

Palmer, C. E., & Bryant, C. D. (1985). Keepers of the king's deer: Game wardens and the enforcement of fish and wildlife law. In C. D. Bryant, D. J. Shoemaker, J. K. Skipper, & W. E. Snizek (Eds.), *The rural workforce: Non-agricultural occupations in America* (pp. 111–137). Bergin & Garvey Publishers Inc.

Paoline III, E. A., Terrill, W., & Rossler, M. T. (2015). Higher education, college degree major, and police occupational attitudes. *Journal of Criminal Justice Education, 26*(1), 49–73.

ParkRangerEDU.org. (2021). Career paths within the National Park Service. https://www.parkrangeredu.org/national-park -service-jobs/

Pledger, M., & Hailey, W. F. (1981). Methods of improving public relations. *Proceedings of the Southeastern Association of Fish and Wildlife Agencies, USA, 35,* 727–729.

Reaves, B. A. (2015). *Local police departments, 2013: Personnel, policies, and practices.* US Department of Justice, Bureau of Justice Statistics.

Rossler, M. T., Scheer, C., & Suttmoeller, M. J. (2019). Perceptions of barriers and patrol career interest among African-American criminal justice students. *Policing: An International Journal, 42*(2), 421–440.

Rossler, M. T., & Suttmoeller, M. J. (2021). Conservation officer perceptions of academy training: Resource specific and general policing tasks. *Policing: A Journal of Policy and Practice, 15*(2), 980–994.

San Antonio Police Officers Association (SAPOA). (2018, April 1). Consequences of police shortages. https://sapoa.org/san-antonio -police-department/consequences-police-shortages/

Schuck, A. (2021). Motivations for a career in policing: Social group differences and occupational satisfaction. *Police Practice & Research, 22*(5), 1507–1523.

Southwick Associates. (2017). *Proportions of excise taxes generated by hunting versus non-hunting activities.* https://www.southwick associates.com/proportions-of-excise-taxes-generated-by -hunting-versus-non-hunting-activities/

Tobias, M. (1998). *Nature's keepers: On the front lines of the fight to save wildlife in America.* John Wiley & Sons Inc.

Trefethen, J. B. (1975). *An American crusade for wildlife.* Winchester Press.

United Nations Office on Drugs and Crime (UNODC). (2020). *Preventing future pandemics of zoonotic origin by combating wildlife crime: Protecting global health, security and economy.* https://www.unodc.org/documents/Advocacy-Section/Wildlife _trafficking_COVID_19_GPWLFC_public.pdf

United States Agency for International Development (USAID). (2021). Combating wildlife trafficking. https://www.usaid.gov/biodiversity /wildlife-trafficking

United States Fish and Wildlife Service (USFWS). (2013). Federal Aid in Sport Fish Restoration Act. https://www.fws.gov/laws/lawsdigest /FASPORT.html

United States Fish and Wildlife Service (USFWS). (2016). *2016 national survey of fishing, hunting, and wildlife-associated recreation.* https://www.fws.gov/wsfrprograms/subpages/nationalsurvey /nat_survey2016.pdf

Unites States Fish and Wildlife Service (USFWS). (2021a). What is R3? Recruitment, retention and reactivation explained. https://www .fws.gov/midwest/news/WhatIsR3.html

United States Fish and Wildlife Service (USFWS). (2021b). Illegal wildlife trade. https://www.fws.gov/international/travel-and-trade /illegal-wildlife-trade.html

Wisconsin Department of Natural Resources. (2021). R3: Recruit, retain, and reactivate. https://dnr.wisconsin.gov/Education /OutdoorSkills/R3

Wyler, L. S., & Sheikh, P. A. (2008). *International illegal trade in wildlife: Threat and U.S. policy.* Congressional Research Service. https: //www.everycrsreport.com/files/20080519_RL34395_cde8c3750 ba147cce630ced60ed6a41b128b68e5.pdf

Wyler, L. S., & Sheikh, P.A. (2013). *International illegal trade in wildlife: Threat and U.S. policy.* Congressional Research Service. https: //fas.org/sgp/crs/misc/RL34395.pdf

GLOSSARY

ASEAN: An association of Southeast Asian nations that seeks to initiate economic growth, promote peace, share training and research resources, and maintain international cooperation.

Assize of Woodstock: Passed in 1184 and stated poaching offenses would be tried in ecclesiastical courts and mutilation would be no longer used as punishment for poaching.

Bona fide occupational qualifications: A quality or attribute that an employer may consider when making decisions on hiring an employee that could be considered discriminatory if it were not necessary to perform a particular job.

Bureaucratic structure: A formal organizational structure that creates a hierarchy or chain of command and is characterized by formal roles, rules, and regulations that coordinate the organization's activities.

Chief forester: The main type of gamekeeper in England until the 17th century.

CITES: The Convention on International Trade in Endangered Species of Wild Flora and Fauna (CITES) is a 1973 agreement between governments across the globe that seeks to ensure international trade in endangered animals and plants does not threaten their survival.

Clark R. Bavin National Fish and Wildlife Forensics Laboratory: Forensic crime lab operated by the USFWS that identifies animals and animal parts, determines animal cause of death, assist in determinations of illegal activities, and utilizes physical evidence to link suspects, victims, and crime scenes.

Commission: A group of people with administrative authority. Similar to a board of directors.

Community cooperation model: The third of Mastrofski's four non-crime models. By participating in non-crime matters, the police demonstrate to the community that they can help the community as well as enforce the laws through the use of coercion.

Community policing: An enforcement strategy that focuses on officer relationships with community stakeholders to solve crime and quality of life problems.

Conciliatory enforcement: An enforcement strategy characterized by encouraging area users to willingly comply with regulations and enjoy their time at the park or recreation area.

Conservation law enforcement: The segment of the law enforcement community that primarily consists of conservation officers, park rangers and other officers that specialize in the enforcement of laws that protect natural resources. It also may be known as wildlife law enforcement or natural resources law enforcement.

Conservation officer: Member of the law enforcement community primarily assigned to engage in the protection of natural resources. These officers may be known by other names such as park rangers, forest rangers, game wardens, conservation agents, fish and wildlife officers, environmental police or fish and game agent.

Consumptive use of resources: Outdoor activities that require the use of resources. Activities such as hunting and fishing would be consumptive uses of resources because animals are harvested and utilized.

Covert enforcement: An enforcement strategy that employs undercover work with no outward displays of traditional law enforcement symbols.

Crime prophylactic model: The first of Mastofski's four non-crime models. Police intervention in non-crime matters is to prevent non-crime incidents from becoming criminal incidents.

Damage Control Permits: Site-specific permits that allow landowners and designees to use lethal controls with the intention of limiting damage to property, often agricultural croplands.

Deer reeve: An early official appointed in Massachusetts that enforced closed season laws.

Endangered Species Act: The Endangered Species Act (ESA) is a 1973 law passed by the United States Congress that seeks to protect endangered and threatened flora and fauna, as well as the ecosystems they depend upon.

Forensic analysis: An enforcement technique utilizing scientific investigative methods to link evidence to suspects.

Forest Charter of Henry III: Death and mutilation were removed as punishments for poaching and were replaced with fines and imprisonment.

Formalization: A characteristic of a bureaucracy related to the number of rules and regulations present in the organization. An organization with a high degree of formalization will have many rules and regulations.

Game Act of 1671: Important piece of legislation that changed the property qualification for a someone to hunt to 100 pounds per year.

Germanic Codes: Early law from the 6th century to protect crops from damage due to hunting that had punitive sanctions such as being buried alive.

Hard enforcement: An enforcement strategy that more closely resembles a traditional policing strategy that utilizes more punitive sanctions such as arrests and citations to gain compliance.

Horizontal complexity: A characteristic of a bureaucracy that is related to how wide the organization is. Organizations will have various subunits at different levels of the organization. How many subunits occur at a particular level is related to its horizontal complexity.

Hot spots policing: An enforcement strategy that directs police resources to areas where crime is more likely to occur, rather than large scale preventative patrol.

IUU fishing: Fishing activity that violates the laws and regulations of a government entity, that is not reported to the relevant authorities, or that occurs in areas that are unregulated and are inconsistent with international law.

Kenya Wildlife Service (KWS): A state corporation operating with the goal to provide management and conservation of wildlife in Kenya.

Lacey Act: The Lacey Act, which was passed in 1900 by the US Congress, became the first federal law in the US seeking to protect wildlife. The law restricts trade in animals, their parts, or products produced from them, particularly when that trade involves the violation of US, Indian, or state laws.

Legalistic style: One of Wilson's three styles of policing. It is a strict law enforcement function of the police.

Lusaka Agreement Task Force: An inter-governmental organization focused on creating cooperation among member states to investigate illegal trade in flora and fauna.

Market hunters: A person who harvests wild animals with the intention of selling their meat, hides, plumage, or products derived from these items, and is primarily focused on these harvests to make or supplement their living. Market hunting has largely been outlawed in the United States.

Non-consumptive outdoor pursuits: Outdoor activities such as bird or wildlife watching that do not result in the actual use of the resource.

Non-enforcement: An enforcement strategy where the officer avoids potential law enforcement situations.

Open Fields Doctrine: Resulting from the SCOTUS case *Hester v. United States*, the court ruled that the Fourth Amendment did not require warrants or probable cause to search private property such as pastures, woods, water, or vacant lots. This has been the prevailing understanding following the decision.

Organic Act of 1897: Provided for the care and management of newly created federal forest reserves as well as the first forest rangers.

Organizational hierarchy: An organizational structure based on levels of authority. Those with more authority are located higher in the organization than those with less authority. It is directly related to a chain of command where supervisors are located above subordinates.

Park ranger: Person who is entrusted with the protection of the environment within a park, as well as outreach, education, programming, and mitigation of human-wildlife conflict within a park. These individuals may or may not be sworn officers with arrest authority.

Pittman-Robertson Act: Also known as the Federal Aid in Wildlife Restoration Act, this law created an eleven percent excise tax on firearms, ammunition, bows, and crossbows. In its current format, the law funds the acquisition, improvement, and access to habitat, as well as animal reintroductions and surveys. The funds may also be used for hunter safety.

Police knowledge model: The second of Mastrofski's four non-crime models. Police participate in non-crime matters to be exposed to a broader segment of the community and thereby gain knowledge of the larger community.

Problem-oriented policing: A versatile policing strategy that focuses on identifying, understanding, and then addressing the various reasons why citizens call the police for assistance.

Recreational hunters: People who participate in hunting as a form of recreation, rather than as an occupation such as market hunters.

Routine patrol: An enforcement strategy of a conservation officer patrolling their assigned district to demonstrate they are ever-present and create a deterrent effect. Also known as preventive patrol.

Service style: One of Wilson's three styles of policing. Police are responsive to the community's preferences for how they would like the police department to function. Officers are more likely to participate in public relations and educational opportunities, and to be more community-oriented.

Social work model: The fourth of Mastrofski's four non-crime models. Police have a role in steering people away from crime and helping them to internalize law abiding norms.

Soft enforcement: An enforcement strategy characterized by gaining compliance through informal methods of education, prevention, and community relations.

Spatial complexity: A characteristic of a bureaucracy related to how an organization is organized throughout a geographic area. The number of components of the organization that are spread out over a given area is related to its spatial complexity.

Standard minimum requirements: The minimum requirements that a prospective officer must meet before applying for a position as a conservation officer.

Technical assistance: Help provided to an organization that does not directly involve doing the labor of the organization. Examples might include policy briefs and analysis, needs assessments, outcome evaluations, training, or organizational development.

Terry **stop**: Established by the SCOTUS case of *Terry v. Ohio*, this type of detainment allows police officers to stop, question, and frisk citizens when the officer has reasonable suspicion to believe that a crime has been committed.

Threat enforcement: An enforcement strategy that uses the threat or promise of formal enforcement actions if someone does not correct their actions.

Vertical complexity: A characteristic of a bureaucracy that is related to how tall the organization is. An organizational hierarchy consists of levels of authority within an organization. The more levels that exist is related to its vertical complexity.

Watchman style: One of Wilson's three styles of policing. It emphasizes the maintaining of order over law enforcement and is closely aligned with the order maintenance function of police.

Wildlife crimes: Acts that are committed in violation of international treaties, national laws and regulations to protect natural resources to include the illegal wildlife market, illegal hunting, poaching for subsistence, hunting violations, illegal killing due to human and wildlife conflicts and politically driven poaching (Moreto & Spires, 2008).

Yellowstone Protection Act: Legislation that created the first national park—Yellowstone National Park.

INDEX